[13—0a]
American Elm
(Ulmus americana)

[13—0]
American Arborvitae
(Thuja occidentalis)

[13—0c]
Sargent's Weeping Hemlock
(Tsuga canadensis pendula)

[13—0b]
Hedge of Eastern American Hemlock
(Tsuga canadensis)

Tree Surgery: Treating Wound

[13–1]
Wound before treatment

[13–1a]
Paring edges of wound smooth

[13–1b]
Shaping base of wound

[13–1c]
Applying tree wound paint

NEW *ILLUSTRATED* ENCYCLOPEDIA OF GARDENING

UNABRIDGED

EDITED BY T. H. Everett

Assistant Director (Horticulture) and Curator of Education
The New York Botanical Garden

WITH CONTRIBUTIONS FROM

TWENTY HORTICULTURISTS AND AUTHORITIES IN THE UNITED STATES AND CANADA

Growers, Breeders, Exhibitors, Plantsmen, Writers, Lecturers, Professors, Editors and Superintendents of Famous Estates, who are Experts in all Fields of Horticulture, including Pests and Their Control.

VOLUME THIRTEEN—Ter-Wat

GREYSTONE PRESS/NEW YORK · TORONTO · LONDON

Copyright © MCMLXIV, MCMLXVII By The Greystone Press
100 Sixth Avenue
New York, New York 10013
Library of Congress Catalog Card Number 60-7000
MANUFACTURED IN THE UNITED STATES OF AMERICA

TERRARIUMS

Planting a fishbowl type of terrarium. Here the tools and plants are assembled.

Drainage material and gritty soil are packed into position and formed into pleasing contours.

A layer of sheet moss is then placed over the soil.

Plugs of soil may be removed with a special tool to make holes for the reception of the plants.

Small plants are removed from their pots and placed in position with a large pair of tweezers. The soil is then tamped around their roots.

After the planting is finished the terrarium is watered with a fine spray.

To plant a terrarium with soil mixture in the base, begin by placing a layer of either pebbles or broken bricks in the bottom to ensure drainage, and cover this with moss or dead leaves from trees to prevent the soil from washing through and clogging the drainage. On top of this place some soil (an open, porous, gritty mixture of topsoil, peat moss or humus and coarse sand or grit). Vary the depth of the soil in different places to give a pretty landscape effect but do not let it be so deep anywhere that it detracts from the decorative appearance of the finished terrarium. Small pieces of rock, pieces of cork bark, etc., may be introduced to suggest landscape features and, if desired, a "pool" made of a small mirror may be featured.

When the general contours of the miniature landscape are established, planting may begin. A few hours before planting is done, the plants to be used should be watered thoroughly. It is well to set the bigger plants first, then the smaller ones, and finally creepers, mosses and other ground covers.

Do not crowd the plants unduly; remember that if all goes well they will grow and need more space. After planting is completed, water gently with a fine spray and wash all leaves clean of soil and the glass clean of smears. Be careful, when watering, not to flood the terrarium, especially if it is one that does not have drainage holes.

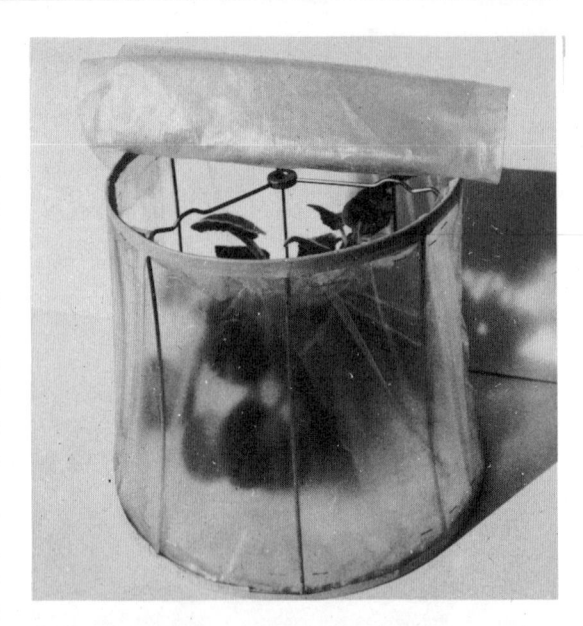

Propagating Units and Plant Hospitals. Be-

This terrarium, used as a temporary plant hospital, is made from an old lampshade frame which has been covered with polyethylene plastic. The roll of plastic shown on top of the shade is used as a cover.

cause humid atmospheric conditions can easily be maintained in terrariums they are excellent devices for sheltering leaf cuttings, stem cuttings and similar propagations when they are rooting. They are also especially useful to keep pots and flats of newly sown seeds in and to shelter young seedlings. This is especially true of Begonias, Gesnerias, African Violets and other kinds that need a moist atmosphere.

Plants that have become sickly through exposure to drafts or an excessively dry atmosphere or that have had their ability to absorb water from the soil reduced as a result of damage to their roots in the process of repotting or in other ways also benefit greatly from being given the protection of a terrarium.

Artificial Light. Where natural light is deficient the plants contained in a terrarium will make much better growth and will remain healthier if the terrarium is illuminated for 12-16 hours out of each 24 by artificial light. Fluorescent units give considerable light without generating much heat and should be depended upon as the chief source of illumination. The lights may be as close as 12 in. to the plants. Because fluorescent light is deficient in some light rays

A large terrarium such as this may be used as a plant hospital in which plants that become sickly are given an opportunity to recuperate. Additional light is supplied by fluorescent units above the terrarium.

that benefit plants, superior results may be had by supplementing it with a smaller amount of light from ordinary incandescent (Madza type) bulbs.

Bottle Gardens are arrangements of plants growing inside large bottles. They represent a special kind of terrarium and present special problems in planting because the plants used must be introduced through the bottle necks. See Bottle Gardens and Wardian Case.

TERRESTRIAL ORCHIDS. A term applied to those Orchids which derive their sustenance from the soil, in contrast with many other Orchids which grow wild on trees, and derive their nourishment chiefly from atmospheric moisture.

TESSELLATED. Marked with a checkered pattern.

TESTUDINARIA—*Elephant's-Foot, Hottentot's Bread* (Testudinar'ia). Testudinaria elephantipes is more curious than beautiful, and is usually grown only in botanical collections, for the curious structure of stems. The stems are quite unlike the trunk of ordinary trees, as they form hemispherical masses resting on the soil. These squat stems have a woody exterior, within which is contained a yellowish-white, soft-textured substance. These woody masses are sometimes called Hottentot's Bread, because the natives of South Africa used to cut out the fleshy parts, which they baked and ate like bread.

From the apex of the woody masses arise long, slender, vinelike stems, bearing small bright green leaves and inconspicuous yellowish flowers. Testudinaria is found wild in South Africa and belongs to the Yam family Dioscoreaceae. The name is derived from *testudo*, a tortoise, and alludes to the shape and conformation of the stem.

TETRACENTRON SINENSE (Tetracen'tron). A leaf-losing tree, 40-90 ft. high, with a trunk 6-7 ft. in girth, found wild in the forests of central and western China. It has grayish or sometimes brownish bark, ovate leaves with the margins finely toothed (see Leaf), and bears slender racemes, 3-6 in. long, of very small, yellowish flowers. It is a decorative tree throughout summer, although the flowers are not very conspicuous.

Propagation is by seeds, but branches may be layered when conveniently placed. Tetracentron belongs to the Magnoliaceae, the Magnolia family. The name is taken from the Greek *tetra*, four, and *kentron*, a spur, and refers to the four appendages of the fruit. The tree can be grown in light, loamy soil, and is hardy in the North.

TETRACLINIS ARTICULATA—*Arar Tree* (Tetraclin'is). An evergreen tree, 40-50 ft. high, a native of Algeria, Morocco and other parts of North Africa and Malta, which is only adaptable for outdoor cultivation in the warmer parts of the United States. It is distinguished by its flat, curiously jointed branches, and by its solitary, terminal, four-valved cones. It grows under hot and dry conditions, and is of slow growth.

The wood of this tree is hard, close-grained and handsomely marked. It is red or yellow in color and has a cedar-like odor. The wood is prized for turnery and cabinetwork. It is a wood that is said to have been in use by the ancient Romans, who paid very high prices for table tops made of it.

Sandarac Resin. A fragrant resin, known as Sandarac, or Sandarac resin, is obtained from the tree. It is used for high-class varnishes.

This curious tree is closely related to the Widdringtonia of South Africa and the Callitris of Australia. Tetraclinis belongs to the Cypress family, the Cupressaceae. The name is derived from *tetra*, four, and *cline*, a bed, and refers to the manner in which the leaves are arranged in four ranks.

Propagation is by seeds sown in light soil, or by short cuttings, 3-4 in. long, of semiripe wood in summer, inserted in a close frame.

TETRAGONIA. This is the botanical name of the vegetable commonly called New Zealand Spinach. Its cultivation is described under the heading of New Zealand Spinach, which see.

TETRAMICRA. Leptotes, which see.

TETRANEMA. Allophyton mexicanum, which see.

TETRAPANAX PAPYRIFERUM (Tetra'panax). An evergreen shrub or small tree that belongs to the Aralia or Ginseng family, the Araliaceae, and is a native of Formosa. Its name is derived from *tetra*, four, and the name

The tall shrub is Tetrapanax papyriferum, growing in a California garden.

of a nearly related group of plants, Panax. It refers to the fact that the parts of the flowers are in fours, rather than in fives, as in Panax.

This plant may be cultivated outdoors in mild regions and is occasionally grown in greenhouses, particularly where botanical collections of plants are cultivated, because of its interest as the source of rice paper, which is made of the pith of its stems.

Tetrapanax is a handsome shrub for garden decoration. It is of broad, spreading habit of growth and bears handsome, lobed leaves that measure up to 1 ft. across; they are green above and are furnished with a white, felty covering beneath. The variety variegatum has leaves beautifully marked with white and ivory.

Any fairly good soil that is not too dry suits this plant. It will grow in full sun but prefers light shade. Propagation may be effected by seeds, cuttings, root cuttings and air layering.

In gardens Tetrapanax papyriferum is sometimes known as Aralia papyrifera or Fatsia papyrifera.

TETRAPLOID. A genetical term for a plant that has four sets of chromosomes in its somatic (body) cells rather than two sets, as in the ordinary or diploid plant. Tetraploids are commonly larger and more vigorous than diploids of the same species and are often superior from a gardener's point of view. Tetraploids occur naturally and can also be induced to develop by plant breeders by using the drug colchicine.

TETRASTIGMA (Tetrastig'ma). Tender, climbing shrubs or vines belonging to the Grape family, the Vitaceae. The name is derived from *tetra,* four, and stigma, and alludes to the fact that the stigma is four-lobed. The Tetrastigmas are natives of the warmer parts of Asia.

In southern Florida T. Harmandii, a native

of the Philippines, is grown. It is an attractive, high-climbing vine which attaches itself to supports by means of tendrils. It produces large leaves and edible fruits. This plant grows well under a variety of conditions, and may be propagated by cuttings or seeds. For the plant sometimes named T. Voinierianum, see Vitis Voinieriana.

TETRATHECA (Tetrathe′ca). Tender, heathlike shrubs, which are grown for their ornamental flowers. These natives of Australia belong to the Tremandra family, Tremandraceae.

These shrubs grow from 12 in. to 2 ft. in height, and have numerous, upright, thin, wiry stems, which are clothed with narrow, heathlike, bright green leaves. In most cases the leaves are verticillate (in whorls of three of more). The flowers, which are rose, purple or pink, are rotate (wheel-shaped), and 1 in. in diameter; they are borne on slender pedicles (stalks) in spring or summer. The name Tetratheca is derived from *tetra,* four, and *theca,* a cell, and refers to the four-celled anthers.

Culture. Being natives of Australia, the shrubs are suited for growing outdoors in California and similar mild climates and are easily cultivated in a sunny greenhouse which is sufficiently heated to keep out the frost (minimum winter temperature, 40 degrees). Shading is only necessary when repotting has recently been carried out. Very little damping and syringing are necessary. Throughout the year they must have a sunny location and the ventilators should only be closed in frosty weather.

Repotting is done annually in March or April, and a sandy peaty soil is necessary. The shoots are first shortened by one half and encouraged to break into growth by syringing twice a day with water. The plants are then taken out of their pots and the ball of soil is lightly pricked over with a pointed stick to loosen the tightly packed roots. The plants are repotted in slightly larger pots and the compost is made firm.

The time after potting is a critical one for these plants, and watering must be done carefully. The best plan is to allow the soil to become moderately dry and then to saturate it thoroughly. This system must be followed throughout the year, as it is fatal to allow the soil to become very dry or excessively wet at any time.

The Chief Kinds. T. ericifolia, 12 in., pink, summer; T. hirsuta, 2 ft., pink, spring; and T. glandulosa, 2 ft., purple, summer.

TEUCRIUM—*Germander* (Teu′crium). Very few of the Teucriums are known in gardens, as most are not sufficiently decorative to merit cultivation. There are, however, numerous species, both hardy and tender. They are natives of many temperate and warm temperate regions, including North America.

The Teucriums, which belong to the Mint family, Labiatae, are mostly hardy herbaceous perennials; some few are shrubs or subshrubs. The name is an ancient Greek one.

Teucriums thrive in any moderately good well-drained soil. They may be increased by seeds sown in sandy soil in spring and by cuttings in summer. Herbaceous kinds can be propagated by division.

T. canadense, American Germander, is a 3-ft.-tall perennial that inhabits moist or wet soil throughout North America. It has cream- to purple-colored flowers and may be planted in wild gardens. T. Scorodonia is a 2-ft.-tall, hardy, herbaceous perennial that has yellow flowers and is a native of Europe; it is sparingly naturalized in eastern North America.

With Colored Leaves. T. Scorodonia variety variegata is sometimes cultivated for its variegated foliage. It grows 12 in. in height and is suitable for planting near the front of the herbaceous border. T. Marum (Cat Thyme) resembles the common Thyme in habit, has red or purple flowers in summer and grows 12 in. in height. Its white foliage is pleasantly scented. It is hardy only in mild regions and is usually grown in a well-drained position in a sunny rock garden. This kind is very attractive to cats, which like to roll in it and tear it to pieces.

T. Chamaedrys (Wall Germander) grows 6 in. in height and has reddish-purple flowers.

T. lucidum is similar to T. Chamaedrys and is often grown under that name. It differs from the true T. Chamaedrys in having stems that are much more erect; for this reason it is better adapted for forming very low hedges.

A Tender Kind. T. fruticans, a native of southern Europe, is a low, much-branched shrub with grayish foliage and comparatively large pale blue flowers. It is suitable for growing outdoors in mild, dry climates, such as that of southern California, and for cultivating in pots in cool greenhouses and window gardens. It thrives in full sun in any ordinary well-drained soil and is easily propagated from cuttings.

For Carpet Bedding. T. Polium, a dwarf, compact plant with whitish stems and leaves and small, pale yellow flowers, is occasionally used for edging summer flower beds. It is wintered in a greenhouse and increased by cuttings in spring.

TEXAS, GARDENING IN. See Regional Gardening.

TEXAS BLUE BONNET. Lupinus subcarnosus, which see.

THALIA (Tha'lia). Tender, herbaceous, perennial, aquatic flowering plants, which belong to the Maranta family, Marantaceae.

These are stemless herbs with canna-like leaves, 2-3 ft. in length. The leaves have long stalks and the leaf blades are dark green, smooth and shiny. The large, three-petaled blue flowers are produced in pairs on branching spikes 3-6 ft. in height, in summer. The name Thalia commemorates J. Thalius, a German naturalist of the sixteenth century.

Needs Warmth. T. geniculata, a native of the West Indies, may be grown in a greenhouse with a minimum winter temperature of 45 degrees. It requires a sandy, loamy soil. The plants are set in large pots or tubs and the soil is kept moist at all seasons of the year. The atmosphere must be kept moist and shade from bright sunlight afforded.

During the summer season the pots or tubs containing these plants may be submerged in an outdoor pool, but should be brought into the greenhouse before frost. In the deep South, where little or no frost is experienced, the plants may be grown in outdoor pools all the year around.

A Hardier Kind. T. dealbata, native from South Carolina to Florida and Texas, requires the same treatment as T. geniculata in the North, but in mild regions it may be grown out of doors the year around. It thrives best in a large tub or pot of light, rich loam, which is submerged in a tank or pool of water. Planting is done in April.

Propagation is by division of the rootstocks at planting time.

The chief kinds are T. geniculata, blue, 2 ft., summer; T. dealbata, 6 ft., blue, summer; T. divaricata, 10 ft., violet, summer.

THALICTRUM—*Meadow Rue* (Thalic'-trum). Hardy herbaceous perennials valued both for their graceful, ornamental leaves, and for their summer flowers. They are natives of various parts of Europe, as well as of North America and northern Asia. They belong to the Buttercup family, Ranunculaceae. The name is an old Greek one.

Beautiful Hardy Plants. These plants, which vary in height from a few inches to several feet, have deeply cut, somewhat fernlike leaves; the small flowers, borne in panicles, are chiefly purple, yellow and white. Most of them are suitable for planting in the herbaceous border; those of low growth are grown in the rock garden. They are easily cultivated in ordinary, well-tilled garden soil and may be planted in autumn or in spring.

Flower spray of the mauve-purple Thalictrum aquilegifolium purpureum.

Propagation is by division in fall or early spring and by seeds. Thalictrums may be raised from seeds sown in flats of sandy soil in a cold frame in spring. When the seedlings are 1-2 in. high, they are transplanted 2 in. apart in other flats filled with a mixture of loam, leaf mold, peat moss or humus and sand, and kept in a frame until well rooted. Then they are set

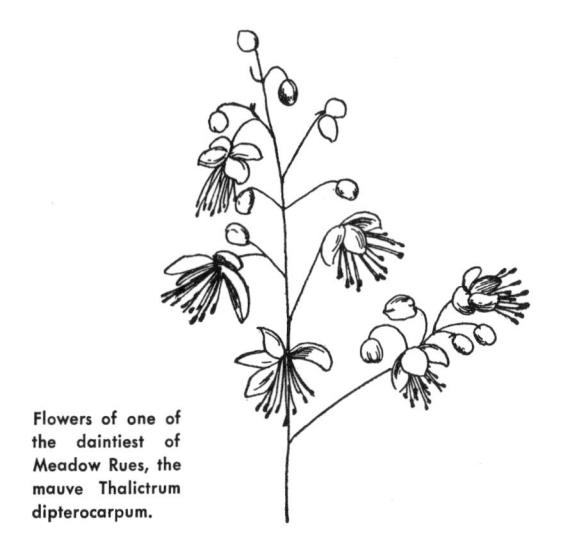

Flowers of one of the daintiest of Meadow Rues, the mauve Thalictrum dipterocarpum.

out in nursery beds, where they should remain until they are large enough to be planted permanently.

The finest of all for the herbaceous border is Thalictrum aquilegifolium. This reaches a height of 3 ft. and has cream-white flowers. There are several varieties, of which the best are album, white; purpureum, purple; and roseum, pale-rose.

Thalictrum dipterocarpum is a charming plant of slender growth which reaches a height of 3-4 ft., and bears large, loose panicles of small, mauve flowers; it is at its best in well-drained soil. There is an attractive double-flowered form called Hewitt's Double, and another variety has white flowers.

Other kinds suitable for the flower border are T. Delavayi, 2-3 ft., light purple flowers and stems tinged with purple; T. glaucum, 4 ft., yellow flowers and gray-green foliage; and T. flavum, 3 ft., light yellow flowers.

For Rock Gardens. Thalictrum minus (adiantifolium) is an attractive little plant, about 10 in. tall, with beautiful fernlike leaves which are most useful for cutting for decorative purposes indoors. This species is a good rock-garden plant. Thalictrum alpinum, 6 in., creamy white, is also suitable for the rock garden. Yet another dwarf Thalictrum and a first-rate rock-garden kind is T. kiusianum, a Japanese native which grows 3 in. tall and bears purple and white flowers.

THEA (The'a). A group of tender evergreen trees and shrubs from Asia, the most important of which is T. sinensis, the Tea plant. Thea belongs in the Tea family, the Theaceae. The name Thea is from the Dutch rendering of the Chinese dialect name for Thea sinensis. Thea is very closely related to Camellia and at one time the Tea plant was named Camellia Thea.

In the United States these trees and shrubs are grown for ornament in the South. They require the same care and culture as Camellia, which see.

The kinds most likely to be cultivated are T. cuspidata, a native of China which grows about 6 ft. tall and bears white flowers, and T. sinensis, the Tea plant, which may grow to a height of 30 ft. and has fragrant, white blooms. Several varieties of T. sinensis exist, including assamica, Bohea, cantoniensis and viridis. The plant is a native of China and India.

THECOSTELE (Thecoste'le). Orchids of little horticultural value. All are epiphytal (grow on trees), and have clustered pseudobulbs and evergreen leaves. They are found wild in Burma, Java and Malaya. The name Thecostele is from *theke,* a receptacle, and *stele,* a column, and refers to the shape of the upper part of the column.

The best-known kind is T. alata; its flowers, which are borne in drooping racemes in late summer, have narrow petals and sepals and a three-lobed lip, yellowish, spotted with red. The plant should be placed in a small pan, in a compost of two parts of osmunda fiber and two parts of sphagnum moss, the top of the compost being raised above the rim. In summer, a warm, moist atmosphere is necessary. In winter, the plants should be watered infrequently and kept in a temperature of about 60 degrees. Repotting is carried out in early spring.

THELESPERMA (Thelesper'ma). Shrubs, herbaceous perennials and annual flowering plants from Mexico, western America and southern South America, which belong to the Daisy family, Compositae. They are similar in appearance and closely related to Coreopsis. The kinds cultivated are annuals. The name Thelesperma is derived from *thele,* a nipple, and *sperma,* a seed, and refers to the appearance of the seeds.

T. trifidum, a native of the southwestern United States, grows 1-2 ft. in height, has slender stems and small, feathery leaves. The coreopsis-like flowers are about 1 in. in diameter, purple with yellow margins. T. Burridgeanum, from Texas, is brownish-purple and yellow, and 18 in. in height.

When to Sow. The seeds are sown out of doors in spring in the locations in which the plants are to flower. A sunny, open site is necessary and ordinary garden soil is suitable. When the seedlings are 2 in. in height, they are thinned out to 9 in. apart and, when coming into flower, are supported with twiggy sticks.

THELOCACTUS (Thelocac'tus). A group of medium-sized, globular or nearly globular Cacti from Mexico and Texas. They belong to the Cactus family, Cactaceae. Many of them were at one time included in the group called Echinocactus. The name Thelocactus is derived from *thele,* a nipple, and Cactus, and refers to the nipple-like protuberances on the ribs of the plants.

The cultivation of these plants is exactly the same as for Echinocactus. See Echinocactus and Cacti.

Many different kinds are likely to be grown by fanciers. Among them are T. bicolor, flowers purplish-pink; T. Ehrenbergii, flowers pink; T. hexaedrophorus, flowers purplish; T. leucacanthus, flowers yellow, tinged pink; T. Mandragora, flowers white with pink stripes; T. nidulans, flowers creamy white; T. Pottsii, flowers pale purple; T. Valdezianus, flowers violet-pink.

THELYMITRA — *Woman's Cap Orchid* (Thelymit'ra). Unfortunately, though having beautiful flowers, these terrestrial, deciduous (leaf-losing), tuberous-rooted Orchids are difficult to cultivate. They are found wild in Australia, New Zealand and Malaya. The leaves are usually narrow, and the erect stems terminate in a raceme of small flowers. The name is from *thelys,* a woman, and *mitra,* a cap, and refers to the shape of the column.

Those kinds from Malaya must have more warmth than the others. A suitable compost consists of fibrous loam with an addition of leaf mold and chopped sphagnum moss, with a scattering of sand. Shading is required in spring and summer, but exposure to light is necessary in autumn. In winter the tubers need to be kept dry in a temperature of 55-60 degrees.

No fewer than eleven kinds are known in which the flowers are more or less blue. The best is T. crinita, bright blue. T. ixioides and T. venosa have blue flowers; T. carnea is pink, and T. longifolia varies from blue to pink and lilac.

THENARDIA FLORIBUNDA (Thenard'ia). A climbing shrub or vine sometimes grown in California and other mild climates and valued for the fragrance of its pink or white-tinged-purple flowers. This vine belongs to the Dogbane family, the Apocynaceae. Its name honors the French biochemist, L. J. Thenard. In cultivation Thenardia requires the same conditions and care as Dipladenia, which see.

THEOBROMA — *Chocolate Tree, Cacao* (Theobro'ma). A small group of tropical trees, natives of Central and South America. Theobroma belongs to the Sterculia family, the Sterculiaceae, and the name is taken from the Greek *theos,* god, and *broma,* food, with reference to the food value of the seeds of T. Cacao.

The Chocolate Tree. T. Cacao is of outstanding importance because its seeds furnish the cocoa and chocolate of commerce. It grows 20-30 ft. high with a widely spreading head, and large, conspicuous leaves. The very small flowers are borne in profusion from small, cushion-like swellings on the older branches and trunks.

Comparatively few flowers set fruits. The fruits develop in the course of a few months, to a length of 6-8 or even 9 in. and a width of 3-4 in. They contain from 20-35 seeds, each of which may be an inch or more long.

Culture of the Chocolate Tree. T. Cacao needs a humid, tropical climate for its best development. It is sometimes grown in greenhouses, particularly in botanical gardens, as an item of interest. Plants grown in large pots or tubs or planted in a bed of soil inside a greenhouse, flower and sometimes fruit quite freely when only a few years old. They are attractive in foliage, especially when they are developing new leaves; these at first are a beautiful bronzy-pink

This Chocolate tree is blooming and fruiting. Note that the flowers and fruits are borne directly on the trunk of the tree and on the major branches.

color that contrasts splendidly with the bright green of the older foliage.

Theobroma Cacao thrives in any good potting soil. The receptacles or beds in which the trees are planted must be well drained. Repotting, as well as any pruning that is necessary, should be done in late winter. The plants should be watered freely from March to November, less frequently at other times. Established specimens benefit greatly from regular feeding with applications of dilute liquid fertilizers.

Good light is necessary but light shade from strong summer sunshine must be provided for plants grown indoors. Propagation is by seeds, cuttings, air layering.

THERMOMETER. No garden is complete without a set of thermometers for recording temperatures in the greenhouse and elsewhere. The temperature is indicated by the expansion or contraction of a column and small reservoir of alcohol or mercury enclosed in a hermetically sealed glass tube on which a graduated scale is marked. The figuring on the scales varies according to the type of thermometer. That which is in general use in gardens is marked in degrees Fahrenheit, in which the freezing point of water is indicated at 32 degrees and the boiling point 212 degrees. Centigrade thermometers register freezing point at 0 degrees (zero) and the boiling point at 100 degrees.

The Minimum and Maximum Thermometer. This is the most useful type, as it indicates the minimum and the maximum temperature during any desired period. These thermometers have two columns of mercury, each of which supports a small movable needle. The needles have to be set by drawing them down with a magnet, so that they touch the columns of mercury. The readings are taken from the bases of the needles. Each greenhouse should be furnished with a thermometer with a small label attached, on which the mimimum night temperature is written.

Outdoor thermometers are fixed on a pole, 4 ft. from the ground, in a screened box shaded from the sun.

A plunging thermometer is used to ascertain the temperature of hotbeds, Mushroom beds, etc. This thermometer is narrow and cylindrical in shape and has a pointed metal base so that it is easily pushed into manure, soil, sand and similar materials.

THERMOPSIS (Thermop'sis). A group of hardy and tender herbaceous perennial plants which are found wild chiefly in North America but are represented also in northern and eastern Asia. They belong to the Pea family, Leguminosae. The name is derived from *thermos*, Lupine, and *opsis*, like, and refers to the resemblance of Thermopsis to Lupine.

These are not at all common in gardens, though one or two of them are worth cultivation in any collection of hardy plants. They vary in height from 1-3 ft., have trifoliate (consisting of 3 leaflets) leaves, and bear pealike flowers of various colors (those of the commonly cultivated kinds, yellow) in summer. They thrive in ordinary, well-cultivated garden soil,

The yellow, Lupine-like flowers of Thermopsis montana.

need a sunny position, and should be left undisturbed as long as possible, for, like most other members of the Pea family, they do not flourish if transplanted frequently. If the plants are moved, the long taproots are liable to be broken or damaged and, as a result, the plants suffer a severe check.

Raising Seedlings. If an increased stock of

Thermopsis caroliniana is the hardiest kind. It has yellow flowers.

plants is needed it is better to raise them from seeds than to disturb the old plants. The seeds are sown in a flat of sandy soil placed in a greenhouse in late winter or outdoors in early spring. If raised out of doors, the seedlings should be planted in their permanent places as soon as possible; those raised under glass should be potted in 3-in. pots; when well rooted in these, they are transplanted to the border where they are to remain.

Comparatively few kinds are in general cultivation. These are the best: T. caroliniana, 3 ft., yellow; T. fabacea, 2-3 ft., yellow; T. lanceolata, 2 ft., yellow; and T. montana, 2 ft., yellow. They bloom in June and July.

THESPESIA POPULNEA — *Portia Tree* (Thespes′ia). This native tree of Asia, Africa and the Pacific islands attains a height of 30-60 ft. It is hardy only in the far South, and there it is popular for planting near the sea. It has naturalized itself in Florida.

The Portia Tree, also called the Bendy Tree and the Seaside Mahoe, provides dense shade and thrives well in sandy soil. Its showy, bell-shaped flowers are yellow, changing to a purple hue as they age. In the South they appear in spring or early summer. The tree is propagated by seeds and also from cuttings of well-ripened shoots.

Thespesia populnea belongs in the Mallow family, Malvaceae. Its name is derived from *thespesios,* divine, and was given in recognition of the fact that T. populnea is often planted near temples in some parts of the tropics.

THEVETIA NEREIFOLIA—*Yellow Oleander* (Thevet′ia). An evergreen shrub or tree that attains a maximum height of about 30 ft. It is a native of tropical America and is suitable for planting outdoors in the far South only. It is sometimes cultivated in greenhouses. Thevetia is a member of the Dogbane family, the Apocynaceae. It was named in honor of a French monk, André Thévet, who traveled in Brazil and other parts of tropical South America. By some botanists this plant is named T. peruviana.

Thevetia nereifolia has handsome, saffron-yellow flowers which are delightfully fragrant. It thrives well in fertile sandy soil. It will withstand a few degrees of frost, but young plants should be protected from this by hilling sand, soil or peat moss around their bases. Propagation is easily effected by means of cuttings.

When grown in greenhouses, Thevetia needs a minimum temperature of 55 degrees and exposure to full sunlight. The atmosphere must be fairly moist. Well-drained pots and a porous, fertile soil are essential. Repotting, and whatever pruning is necessary to shape the plants suitably, should be done in late winter. During summer the plants benefit from being plunged (sunk) to the rims of their pots in a bed of sand or ashes in a sunny place outdoors.

THIMBLEBERRY. Another name for the Blackcap Raspberry, Rubus occidentalis, which see. See also Raspberries.

THIMBLE CACTUS. Mammillaria fragilis, which see.

THINNING. This is a detail of considerable importance in the management of trees, shrubs and plants. When pruning is practiced, it is often necessary to thin out the branches, that is, to remove the superfluous ones, to prevent overcrowding; this is, in fact, one of the most important details of pruning. Many vigorous herbaceous perennials—for example, Delphinium, Helenium and Michaelmas Daisy—produce numerous fresh shoots in spring and, if all were left, the plants would become overcrowded with growth and the flowers would be poor. It is advisable to thin out the weakest

Thinning surplus plants from a hill of Cucumber seedlings.

Thinning a row of Beet seedlings.

of the shoots to allow the remainder sufficient room for development.

Thinning of fruits often has to be practiced in the orchard and fruit garden; when the fruits are small, those which are unshapely, ill-developed, or damaged should be removed; it may be necessary also to take off a number of sound fruits, if the crop is unusually heavy, to allow the remainder sufficient space. If a tree is allowed to bear a very heavy crop one year, it is probable that the following year it will bear few fruits or none.

Seedlings must be thinned before they become crowded, to prevent them from getting drawn and weakly. See Propagation: Seed Sowing.

THISTLE. See Carduus and Cnicus.

THISTLE, BLESSED. See Cnicus benedictus and Silybum Marianum.

THISTLE, COTTON. See Onopordum.

THISTLE, FISHBONE. See Cirsium Diacantha.

THISTLE, GLOBE. See Echinops.

THISTLE, HOLY. Silybum Marianum, which see.

THISTLE, MILK. Silybum Marianum, which see.

THISTLE, SAFFRON. See Carthamus.

THISTLE, SCOTCH. Onopordum Acanthium, which see.

THLADIANTHA DUBIA. (Thladianth'a). An uncommon tender, climbing, perennial flowering plant from northern China. This plant somewhat resembles a Squash, and belongs to the same family, the Gourd family, the Cucurbitaceae. It has slender, hairy stems, large, ovate, cordate (heart-shaped at the base) leaves and large yellow dioecious (male and female organs in separate flowers) blooms. It climbs by

Pruning Gooseberries by thinning out old branches.

means of its twining tendrils and has tuberous roots. The name Thladiantha is derived from *Thladius,* eunuch, and *anthos,* flower, because anthers were missing on some of the original botanical specimens.

For Covering a Trellis. The plants may be raised in a greenhouse and planted out of doors when the weather is warm and settled. They are set in a sunny position in deep, rich soil, and the shoots are trained to wires or a trellis.

New plants may be raised each year or the tuberous roots can be lifted and stored in a box of dry soil in a frostproof place for the winter and planted out the following spring.

THLASPI — *Penny Cress, Bastard Cress* (Thlas'pi). A large genus of hardy, annual and perennial herbaceous plants, many of which are common in gardens as weeds. They are widely distributed in temperate regions and belong to the Mustard family, Cruciferae. The name Thlaspi is derived from *thlaein,* to crush, and refers to the flattened seeds. Only one kind, T. rotundifolium, is much grown, although a few others may be found in rock gardens where large collections of plants are grown.

A Dainty Rock-Garden Plant. T. rotundifolia is a little rock-garden plant which forms a compact tuft a few inches high. It has small roundish or oval leaves and dense, short-stemmed clusters of fragrant rosy-lilac, four-petaled flowers in summer. It requires a sunny location and well-drained, sandy compost. New plants are easily obtained by dividing the old plants at planting time in spring, or they may be raised from seeds.

The seeds are sown in a well-drained pan of sandy soil in March or April. The seedlings are transplanted to other seed pans or flats of light soil, hardened off when established, and planted out in their permanent quarters the following spring.

THOMASIA PURPUREA (Thomas'ia). A low evergreen shrub, suitable for planting as a ground cover in southern California and similar mild climates. It is a native of western Australia and belongs in the Sterculia family, the Sterculiaceae. The name commemorates Abraham and Peter Thomas, who collected plants in Switzerland.

This plant is not very commonly grown. It thrives in sandy, peaty soil and is propagated by cuttings.

THONG. A name sometimes given to the pieces of root, or root cuttings, used in the propagation of Seakale and Horseradish.

THORN. A sharp-pointed, woody outgrowth from a stem; a spine.

THORN. Crataegus, which see.

THORN APPLE. See Datura Stramonium.

THORN, CHRIST'S. See Paliurus Spina-Christi.

THORN, COCKSPUR. Crataegus Crus-galli, which see.

THORN, GLASTONBURY. See Crataegus monogyna biflora.

THORN, HEDGE. Carissa Arduina, which see.

THORN, JERUSALEM. Paliurus Spina-Christi, which see.

THORN, WASHINGTON. Crataegus Phaenopyrum, which see.

THOROUGHWORT. Eupatorium, which see.

THRIFT. See Armeria.

THRIFT, PRICKLY. Acantholimon, which see.

THRINAX — *Peaberry Palms* (Thri'nax). Palms from the West Indies, Central America and southern Florida. They grow 3-30 ft. in height, have slender, ringed trunks and terminal clusters of large, rounded leaves, which are deeply lacerated all around the margins. They belong to the Palm family, Palmaceae. The name Thrinax is derived from *thrinax,* a fan, and refers to the shape of the leaves.

These slow-growing, elegant Palms are suitable for planting outdoors in frost-free climates and for cultivating in a warm greenhouse or conservatory—minimum temperature 55 degrees—or they may be used as house plants. They require well-drained pots and a porous soil consisting of 1 part loam, 1 part peat moss or leaf mold and ½ part sand. When small, they are repotted in slightly larger-sized pots each year in spring. Larger plants in big pots or tubs do not need repotting for several years, as they can be kept growing vigorously by top-dressing with fresh compost in spring.

Peaberry Palms should be shaded from strong sunlight and the atmosphere kept moist by damping and syringing. They require copious supplies of water at the roots in summer, but during the winter the soil is only moistened when it becomes nearly dry.

Propagation Is by Seeds. Seeds are soaked in tepid water for a few hours to soften the seed coats. They are then sown, 1 in. deep, in deep, well-drained pans of sandy soil. They are placed in a propagating case with a bottom heat of 70 degrees and the compost is kept evenly moist. The seedlings are potted singly in 3-in. pots and returned to the case until established. They are then set on the greenhouse benches and repotted as becomes necessary.

The Chief Kinds. T. excelsa, 20 ft. or more, Jamaica; T. microcarpa, 30 ft. or more, West Indies, Bahamas and southern Florida; T. Morrisii, 3-4 ft., Anguilla and Anegada Islands; T. parviflora, 25 ft., Bahamas, Cuba, Jamaica, Haiti, Florida Keys and probably Yucatan and Honduras.

THRIPS. See Pests and Diseases.

THRIXSPERMUM. (Thrix'spermum). A small group of epiphytal Orchids now included by some botanists in the genus Sarcochilus, which see.

THROAT. This term is used by gardeners and botanists for the orifice or opening at the top of the calyx tube and corolla tube in flowers which have the sepals or petals joined together, at least in their lower parts, to form a distinct tube or bell-shaped portion.

THROATWORT. Trachelium, which see.

THRYALLIS GLAUCA. (Thryal'lis). An evergreen, flowering shrub which is a native of Mexico and Central America and is suitable for planting outdoors in the far South and for growing in greenhouses. It is sometimes known as Galphimia glauca and is also, wrongly, sometimes called T. brasiliensis, a name which correctly belongs to a distinct species, probably not cultivated. This attractive shrub belongs to the Malpighia family, the Malpighiaceae. Its name is the old Greek one for an entirely different plant, Verbascum.

Thryallis glauca is a handsome shrub that blooms over a very long period. Its flowers are clear yellow and are borne in panicles or clusters. It thrives in a peaty, sandy soil and appreciates sunshine. It is propagated by cuttings inserted in a warm propagating frame in a greenhouse.

When this shrub is grown in a greenhouse, a minimum temperature of 55-60 degrees is satisfactory. A humid atmosphere should be main-

The handsome Thryallis glauca bears a profusion of bright yellow flowers over an extended period.

tained. Watering should be done freely from March to November, more sparingly during the winter. Repotting and any necessary pruning should receive attention in late winter. When the plants have filled their containers with healthy roots, a program of regular feeding with dilute liquid fertilizer is of great benefit. During the summer the plants may be plunged (buried) to the rims of their pots in a bed of sand or ashes in a sunny place outdoors.

THUJA—*Arborvitae* (Thu'ja). Evergreen trees of imposing dimensions, found wild in North America, China, Korea and Japan. The several kinds are among the most decorative evergreens and, as they are hardy, they can be used in most parts of North America where suitable soil conditions prevail and the atmosphere is moderately free from impurities. The leaves are very small, and almost scalelike, and they closely overlap on the shoots, giving a frondlike arrangement.

In general appearance these trees resemble Chamaecyparis, but the cones are different in shape and the seeds in several instances have larger wings. Although there are not many species or wild kinds, there are a very great number of horticultural varieties of some of these species.

When bruised, the branches of some kinds, particularly T. plicata and T. occidentalis, emit a characteristic odor rather like a mixture of Tansy and Turpentine. Thuja belongs to the Pine family, Pinaceae. Although the spelling Thuya was widely used until a few years ago, and still is in many places, research has decided that the correct rendering is Thuja, which is a variation of *Thuia,* a name used by the Greek scholar Theophrastus.

Propagation by Seed. Seeds should be used for propagation purposes whenever possible. When large numbers of trees are required, the seeds may be sown in late spring in prepared beds of light soil out of doors as are Pine seeds. They should have only a slight covering of soil, for the seeds are very light, and sowing should take place on a calm day.

An informal group of Arborvitaes. The one at the left is Thuja orientalis, the others are Thuja occidentalis.

Small quantities of seed may be sown in pots or flats of light soil placed in a greenhouse or frame early in February. The young plants should be planted in a nursery bed in May or, if that cannot be done, they should be potted singly in small pots and be plunged (buried to the rims of their pots) in a cold frame.

Inserting Cuttings. The numerous varieties of the different kinds can be increased by cuttings of young shoots inserted in a bed of sand or sand and peat moss in a warm greenhouse in September or October, or in a similar bed in a cold frame, during August, and left undisturbed until well rooted. They can also be increased by grafting them, in a warm greenhouse in winter, on stocks of their respective types which have been previously established in pots. As a rule, trees raised from cuttings are found more satisfactory than those which have been grafted.

Although these trees are not very satisfactory when planted on very limy soils, they thrive where a limestone subsoil is covered with a moderately deep layer of nonlimy (noncalcareous) soil. Otherwise, they succeed in somewhat acid soils, sandy soils, and those of a peaty nature, where the climatic conditions are rather moist. They should be planted in permanent places when moderately small, though when properly lifted, with the roots balled and burlaped (see Ball), specimens 8-10 ft. high and even higher can be moved without much danger of loss or serious harm. The more vigorous kinds grow rapidly once they are established, and very soon form sufficient growth to screen out unsightly objects when used for that purpose. Planting may be done in mild weather in early fall or spring.

As Hedge Plants. Some of the Thujas form good hedge plants and screens. When they are grown as decorative trees very little pruning is necessary other than restricting them to a single leader and removing any lower branches that may deteriorate as the trees age. When grown as hedges they may be sheared once or twice a year but care should be taken not to cut back into wood more than one year old.

There are numerous varieties of Thujas of dwarf habit of growth which are excellent for rock gardens and foundation plantings. They

Thujas or Arborvitaes may be planted to form handsome and durable evergreen hedges.

grow slowly and keep compact. Several of these are referred to under their respective types below.

Thuja Wood Is Durable. Thuja wood is used for construction, cabinet work and cooperage; it is favored for purposes where great durability is required when wood must be exposed to weather changes. So resistant to decay is the timber of this tree, that instances have been known of trees falling in the forest, seedlings appearing on the fallen trunks, rooting into the ground, and growing into specimens showing 300 to 400 annual rings and eventually being cut for timber; the original logs remained sound and were cut up and used for shingles.

T. occidentalis, the American Arborvitae, is a native of eastern North America, where it is a widely distributed tree, often growing on wet ground. In a natural state it grows 60-70 ft. high, with a trunk of moderate size or sometimes up to 5 ft. in diameter. The frondlike branchlets are compact and clothed with tiny scalelike leaves, each one carrying a globeshaped oil gland on the back. When the leaves are crushed, a strong tansy-like odor is given off. The cones are small and brown; as a rule, fertile seeds are found at the base of two of the scales. There are many varieties. The typical T. occidentalis and some of its varieties turn an unattractive yellowish color in winter.

Golden-leaved Varieties. Notable are aurea, Douglasii aurea, lutea, lutescens, semperaurea, and Vervaeneana, all with yellowish or golden foliage; the last-named turns to a bronze tint in winter. Several varieties are distinguished by their stiff, pyramidal outline—Buchananii, compacta, conica, fastigata, filicoides (in this the branchlets are divided into fine sprays), Riversii, robusta, Rosenthalii and viridis.

Dwarf kinds are Boothii, dumosa, globosa, Hoveyi, nana, pumila (Little Gem), pygmaea, recurva nana and umbraculifera. Varieties with abnormal or curious branch systems are filiformis, Ohlendorfii and pendula. In Ellwangeriana and ericoides the juvenile foliage is maintained throughout life.

T. orientalis, Oriental Arborvitae. At one time this was placed in the separate genus Biota, by reason of its differing from other kinds in its fleshy cone scales and large seeds. Under natural conditions it may grow 50-60 ft. high with spreading branches. In cultivation it is usually seen as a compact, shapely tree, with numerous erect branches, up to 20 or more feet high. When planted in exposed places there is a definite tendency for the branches of old trees to be separated by wind, and it may be necessary to tie them together for security.

The tree is very variable in character, but the typical form and many varieties can be recognized by the way the secondary branches stand out at right angles, or edge on, to the main branches. The leaves are small, scalelike, and

Dwarf varieties of Arborvitae growing vigorously in a nursery. These kinds are propagated by cuttings

[13–2a]
Yellow Plum Tomatoes

[13–2]
Tomatoes

[13–2c]
Cattail
(Typha latifolia)

[13–2b]
Spanish Moss
(Tillandsia usneoides)

[13—3]
Tulip Border

bright green in summer but they may turn to a brown or bronze shade in autumn and retain that shade until spring, when they regain their original green coloring. It is not a very fast-growing tree and is useful where space is limited. There are many varieties, some of them being notable for their rich golden color.

Useful varieties are aurea, a compact shrub of globelike outline with golden foliage; semperaurescens, a low, slow-growing bush with golden leaves; bonita, a slow-growing bush of conelike outline; elegantissima, a pyramidal variety with golden leaves in the spring but the color may deteriorate later in the year; Hillieri, a compact, slow-growing bush with yellowish leaves in summer, turning green in autumn; minima glauca, a very dwarf form with blue-green leaves, suitable for the rock garden; Rosedalis, a dwarf form with the juvenile type of leaf prominent; flagelliformis, with long, slender, abnormal branchlets; meldensis, an erect, narrow, compact shrub with bluish-green leaves which are often of the juvenile type; and stricta, a tall plant of narrow, stiff, erect habit.

T. plicata, the Giant Arborvitae, is a very handsome tree, native to western North America, where it sometimes grows 200 ft. high with a trunk of considerable size. It grows rapidly and its rich green foliage is very attractive. When bruised, the leaves emit a characteristic tansy-like odor. In addition to its value as a decorative tree, it is also planted under forest conditions. The timber known as Western Red Cedar is the wood of this tree.

A number of varieties of T. plicata have been given distinctive names. Good ones are atrovirens, with dark green leaves; aurea or zebrina, with golden and green leaves intermixed; fastigiata, of columnar form; Hillieri, a slow-growing, densely branched form; and pendula, with slender, abnormal, pendulous branches. T. plicata has also been known as T. gigantea and T. Lobbii.

T. Standishii, the Japanese Arborvitae, is sometimes called T. japonica. In Japan it grows up to 50 ft. high. It is a handsome tree and well worth planting.

T. koraiensis is the most recently introduced kind. A native of Korea, it first became known about 1918. It may form a low spreading bush, or grow into a small tree, 20-25 ft. high. In a young state it tends to spread widely at the expense of height. The leaves are dark green above and silvery beneath.

THUJOPSIS DOLABRATA—*Hiba Arborvitae, False Arborvitae* (Thujop′sis). One species of evergreen tree resembling Thuja and at one time included in that genus. It is a member of the Pine family, Pinaceae. The name is derived from Thuja and *opsis,* resembling.

Thujopsis dolabrata is a native of Japan, where it is called Hiba. The usual type grows to a maximum height of 50 ft. and is a very handsome tree, clothed with branches from the ground up. The frondlike arrangement of the branches is very attractive and the leaves are a dark, glossy green.

The Hiba Arborvitae is hardy in the central states and as far north as southern New England, provided it is in a sheltered location. It requires the same general conditions and care as Thuja, which see. For its satisfactory growth it must have adequate summer moisture; it does not stand summer dryness and oppressive heat well.

Varieties are T. dolabrata Hondai, taller than the type (reaching a maximum height of about 100 ft.) and with smaller leaves; T. dolabrata nana, which grows very slowly into a spreading bush, 1-2 ft. high; T. dolabrata variegata, a variegated form in which some of the branches have cream-colored or yellowish leaves (it is no improvement on the type). When selecting trees of T. dolabrata, preference should be given to those with clean, free-growing leading shoots.

THUMB POT. A term sometimes used, but now rarely, to describe a very tiny flowerpot.

THUNBERGIA—*Clock Vine* (Thunberg′ia). Mostly tender climbing plants of beauty. They are found wild in tropical Africa, tropical Asia, India and South Africa, and belong to the Acanthus family, Acanthaceae. The name Thunbergia was given in honor of Professor Karl Thunberg, of Upsala, Sweden, who died in the early part of the nineteenth century.

These plants are all actually perennials but some are treated in gardens as annuals. The

Thunbergia alata, sometimes known as Black-eyed Susan, is often grown as an annual. Its dark-centered flowers are orange, yellow or cream color.

The beautiful orange-flowered Thunbergia Gibsonii, from tropical Africa.

stems are slender, mostly four-angled and hairy, and the leaves are triangular, as in T. alata, or ovate, as in T. grandiflora. The flowers are mostly solitary (produced singly) in the axils of the leaves, as in T. alata, or in small clusters, as in T. grandiflora. They are funnel-shaped, spreading out broadly at the tips, and vary from 1-3 in. in diameter. The colors vary from violet to blue, scarlet, yellow and white.

Treatment of Greenhouse Kinds. These require a minimum winter temperature of 50-55 degrees. They may be grown in large, well-drained pots or tubs, but the best results are obtained by planting them in a bed of soil in the greenhouse. The soil is taken out to a depth of 2 ft., then 6 in. of broken crocks, broken bricks, stones or coarse gravel is placed in the bottom for drainage and is covered with rough leaves or similar material to prevent the soil from washing down, and the remainder of the space is filled with a mixture of two parts of good topsoil, one part of peat moss or leaf mold and well decayed manure and a scattering of sand.

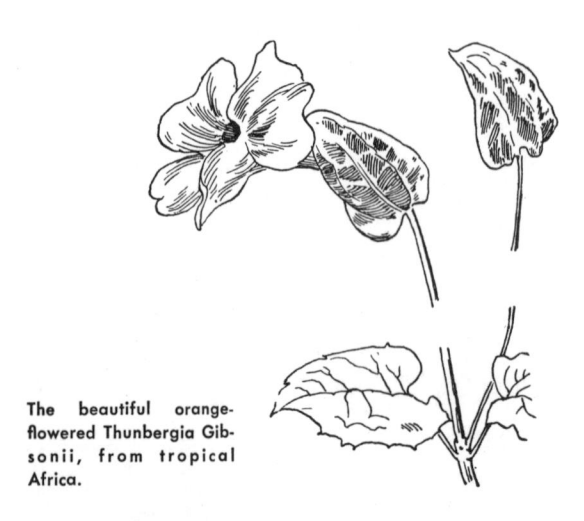

Planting is done in March and the soil is made firm. The soil is not watered until it becomes moderately dry; it is then thoroughly saturated, and during the summer months it is kept moderately moist. Less water is given as the autumn approaches, and during midwinter the soil is kept fairly dry. Dilute liquid fertilizer is applied to the soil when the plants are growing vigorously in midsummer. A moist atmosphere is necessary in summer. It is also beneficial to syringe the foliage frequently (except when the plants are in flower and on cold days in winter).

Pruning, which is done in spring, should be rather severe, especially in small greenhouses, as these plants make rampant growth. All shoots are cut back and so regulated as to fill the allotted space; the main branches are trained to wires or a trellis fixed to the greenhouse wall or roof.

Propagation. The seeds are sown in a deep, well-drained pot or seed pan filled with light, finely sifted soil. The seeds are sown thinly on the surface, and covered with a light layer of soil and a pane of glass.

As soon as the seedlings have germinated, they are exposed to the light, and, when 2 in. in height, are potted singly in 3-in. pots. As they become ready they are potted in larger pots, and when well rooted in 5-in. pots they are planted in the prepared bed of soil.

Cuttings, which are obtained from the young side shoots when they are about 3 in. in length in spring, are inserted in a bed of sand, sand and peat moss or vermiculite in a propagating case in a warm greenhouse and, when they have rooted, are potted individually in small pots and treated as advised for the seedlings.

Thunbergia alata, Black-eyed Susan. Although

a perennial, this popular kind is generally treated as an annual. When grown in a greenhouse, it requires a minimum temperature of 50 degrees, and is raised from seeds in the manner already described. The seedlings should be inserted in 7-in. pots, and the shoots trained to stakes arranged in the form of a tripod in the pot. This plant is also suitable for planting out of doors in summer for covering a low trellis or other support.

Plants raised from seeds are planted out from 3-in. pots as soon as the weather is warm and settled, or seeds may be sown directly outdoors where the growing season is a long one. A semi-shaded position and light rich soil are required. During summer and autumn the slender twining shoots bear attractive orange, yellow, or cream-colored flowers, each with a dark purple center.

The Chief Kinds. T. grandiflora, 20 ft., blue, and the variety alba, white; T. coccinea, 6 ft., scarlet; T. erecta, 5 ft., blue, and the variety alba, white; and T. alata, 6 ft., orange and yellow. T. erecta, unlike other kinds, is a shrub rather than a vine. It is popular in Florida and other warm climates.

THUNIA (Thun'ia). Botanically these Orchids are sometimes classed with Phaius, but from the gardener's point of view they are distinct. They are epiphytal (grow on trees) or occasionally terrestrial, with tall, stemlike leafy pseudobulbs, 2-4 ft. high, which shrivel as the new stems develop and mature. The inflorescences are very handsome, bearing several rather large flowers. All are found wild in Burma and northern India, and generally flower in early summer. The name Thunia commemorates Count Von Thun Hohenstein of Bohemia.

Orchids for a Warm Greenhouse. Thunias require rather different management from Phaius. They need repotting annually, in February or early March. A suitable potting compost consists of cut osmunda fiber, Tree Fern fiber, or Fir bark or Redwood bark. For some time after potting, care in watering is essential, but when the roots have permeated the compost, water may be given abundantly. The plants must be grown in a warm moist greenhouse; shading is required from strong summer sun.

As the plants approach the flowering stage, weak liquid fertilizer may be given and continued after the flowers are faded.

After flowering, the plants must still be kept in a warm greenhouse and watered liberally until the foliage begins to turn yellow; the supply of water is then decreased. When they are in full growth, the plants may be syringed freely, but water must not touch the flowers or they will become spotted.

After the leaves have fallen, the plants are placed in a temperature of 50-55 degrees, and kept quite dry. When the young growths are seen, the plants should be repotted, keeping the old stems attached to the young growths. The old stems may, if firm, be cut into lengths of about 3 in. and placed on sand, in a warm propagating case, and young shoots will appear; new plants are obtained in this way.

T. Bensoniae has flowers of deep amethyst-purple; T. alba is white with purplish keel; T. alba variety Marshalliana has white flowers, the center of the lip orange-yellow; T. venosa is white, the lip veined with purple; T. pulchra has flowers which are white with crests of brown and yellow on their lips.

THYME. The Common Thyme, Thymus vulgaris, is a hardy perennial subshrub. The leaves are used for flavoring foods, and an oil extracted from them is employed in perfumery and medicines.

Although classed as hardy, Common Thyme is likely to suffer from winterkilling where severe winters are the rule and where the soil is heavy or tends to be wet. In such locations plants may be carried through the winter by protecting them with burlap coverings, evergreen branches or similar devices; or by lifting them carefully in the fall and planting them in well-protected cold frames over winter and then resetting them in the garden in spring. In cold regions Thyme may be treated as an annual, the seeds being sown each year where the plants are to grow, in early spring. They do not make very large plants when grown this way, but a usable crop is obtained.

For its satisfactory growth Thyme needs a sunny location and a well-drained, sandy soil that is not too fertile. Generous amounts of nitrogenous fertilizer make for good growth but relatively poor development of the aromatic qualities for which this plant is generally known and valued.

The seeds may be sown in early spring, directly out of doors. The young plants may be thinned or transplanted so that, the first year, they stand 4-6 in. apart. The rows may be 12-15 in. apart.

Thyme Trees. The Common Thyme forms an interesting plant when it is grown as a standard (in the form of a miniature tree). This is accomplished by starting a young plant in a pot and through its early stages restricting it to a single stem. To do this all laterals or side shoots that it produces are pinched out as soon as they appear. The stem is kept neatly tied to a central vertical stake. Its tip is pinched out when it reaches a height of 18-24 in. and then a few branches are allowed to develop from just beneath the point where it is pinched. These branches are in turn pinched when they are 2-3 in. long and the branches that develop from them are pinched in the same manner. This treatment is continued until a dense, rounded head has developed. During the time taken for the head to form the supporting stem thickens and an attractive Thyme tree results.

For drying, Thyme should be cut in high summer just before it begins to flower. The stems should be cut early in the morning of a warm, dry day, bundled and suspended upside down in a dry, cool, airy room or shed. See also Thymus.

THYME, LEMON. Thymus Serpyllum variety vulgaris, which see.

THYMOPHYLLA TENUILOBA—*Dahlberg Daisy, Golden Fleece* (Thymophyl'la). An attractive annual of considerable value for planting as an edging to beds and borders and in rock gardens. It blooms over a very long period and may be had in flower 3-4 months after the seeds are sown. This plant is a native of Mexico and Texas. It belongs to the Daisy family, the Compositae. Its name is derived from *thymos,* Thyme, and *phylla,* a leaf, and refers to the supposed thymelike appearance of the foliage.

The Dahlberg Daisy grows well where summers are warm. It thrives in any reasonably fertile, well-drained soil in full sun. It may be raised from seeds sown directly outdoors where the plants are to bloom, the young plants being thinned out as growth makes necessary; or the seeds may be started early indoors, the young plants transplanted to flats, and later set outdoors.

In fertile ground this plant may attain a height of 1 ft. but usually it is lower, and in poor soils it forms a neat plant only 3-4 in. tall. The daisy-like flower heads are about ½ in. in diameter and are bright yellow. They are profusely borne.

THYMUS—*Thyme* (Thy'mus). A group of mostly hardy subshrubs and herbaceous plants, natives of northern temperate regions, and most abundant in the Mediterranean region. In the Alps they are found at as great an elevation as 6,000 and 7,000 ft. Thymus belongs to the Mint family, Labiateae. The name Thymus is the old Greek name used by Theophrastus for this plant or some closely allied sort.

The Thymes are delightful and most useful plants in the garden. For the rock and the wall garden they give us several enchanting, minute, flowering shrubs; the creeping kinds form the basis of the alpine lawn (which see), and they are also invaluable for planting in the crevices of paved paths.

The common Thyme, T. vulgaris, is a bushy plant with lavender-colored flowers. It should be in every herb garden so that it may be used fresh, as required, for flavoring in cooking. Bunches should be gathered and hung to dry in an airy place for winter use. See Thyme.

Thymus membranaceus, from Spain, is a dwarf, neat bush, 6-9 in. high, with heads of pure white flowers. It is an ornamental plant for a sunny position in light, well-drained soil in the rock garden. It is hardy, and may be increased by cuttings rooted in sand in a cold frame in early summer.

Creeping Thyme or Mother-of-Thyme. Thymus Serpyllum is the Creeping Thyme of Europe, Asia and northern Africa and is naturalized in North America. It is a fragrant, creeping plant with small, dark green leaves and, in June, heads of mauve or heather-purple flowers. The wild type is one of the most charming and useful of all rock-garden plants, clothing any sunny slope with a close evergreen carpet. It is one of the best of all ground covers for choice bulbs, is neat and brilliant when used in

Thymus membranaceus, from Spain, forms compact cushions smothered with heads of white flowers.

the crevices of paved walks, and it forms the essential groundwork of the alpine lawn (which see). It may be raised from seeds sown in a pan of sandy loam in a cold frame in spring; cuttings can be rooted in sand in a cold frame in early summer, or it may be increased by division of the roots at almost any time of year.

There are several distinct and beautiful varieties, all of which are increased by cuttings or division in the same way as the type, but they cannot be relied upon to come true from seeds. The best varieties are: albus, with white flowers, a most valuable acquisition; Annie Hall, flesh-pink; aureus, of which the leaves are green during summer, but in autumn turn a brilliant gold color, and so remain all the winter; coccineus, a magnificent plant, with dark green foliage and crimson flowers; and coccineus superbus, having larger flower heads of the same splendid color, is larger in leaf, somewhat

Mother-of-Thyme, Thymus Serpyllum, is a low creeping kind that bears a profusion of white, pink or lavender flowers in summer.

Thymus Serpyllum is suitable for planting in crevices between paving stones.

looser in habit, and does not creep so widely nor in such a definitely prostrate manner as others.

A Silvery-Gray Thyme. T. Serpyllum variety pseudolanuginosus (probably the correct name of the plant grown in gardens under the name of T. lanuginosus) is a most distinct and attractive kind, with leaves densely clothed in silky gray hairs which give the whole plant a silvery-gray appearance. It does not flower very freely and the flowers are a pale, somewhat insignificant lilac color, but it is an extremely attractive carpeter and first-rate for the alpine lawn and as ground cover for choice bulbs. It will form beautiful silver-gray cushions if planted at the top of a dry wall, where it can hang down freely and without restraint.

T. Serpyllum minus is a valuable dwarf form, in effect an exact counterpart of the common Creeping Thyme, but only half the size of the latter. It is particularly valuable for small alpine lawns where little space is available.

The Lemon Thyme, Thymus Serpyllum variety vulgaris, is often misnamed T. citriodorus. A native of the Mediterranean region; it is a dwarf, subshrubby plant, 6-9 in. tall, the leaves of which smell of lemon. There are several varieties in cultivation. The plant known in gardens as T. citriodorus aureus, with golden-colored leaves, makes a neat edging, and clumps of it are attractive in the rock garden. It should be planted in rather light, poor soil and a sunny position to maintain its golden color. In too-rich soil it tends to revert to green. It is increased by division in spring, or by cuttings of small twigs inserted in a pan of sand in a cold frame.

Silver-leaved Lemon Thyme. T. Serpyllum vulgaris argenteus has small leaves margined with silver. It is a pretty plant for the rock or the wall garden, and makes a good edging. It is easily increased by small branches, removed in early summer and inserted in sandy soil in the cold frame.

The Seedcake Thyme. Thymus Herbabarona, the Seedcake Thyme, is a prostrate creeping plant, not unlike T. Serpyllum in habit and general appearance, though the leaves are rather larger, thicker, and more fleshy. The flowers, borne in heads, are pale lilac in color. The plant is distinguished by its strong aroma of caraway, to which it owes its name Seedcake Thyme.

Thymus Herbabarona is a native of the mountains of Corsica, where it was collected on the Vizzatona Pass in 1909, and introduced to cultivators in England. It is an attractive plant for the rock garden, dry wall garden, and for the crevices of paved paths. It is propagated by division of the roots, or small shoots may be rooted as cuttings in sand in the cold frame in early summer.

Thymus hirsutus, planted in a sunny cranny in a rock garden.

Two Other Good Thymes. T. pectinatus, sometimes called T. odoratissimus, is a low kind, notable for its very fragrant foliage. Its lavender or pale purple flowers are borne in distinct heads or clusters. T. hirsutus is a low, spreading plant which has hairy grayish foliage and erect flowering stems with heads of lavender or lavender-pink flowers. Both T. pectinatus and T. odoratissimus are good rock-garden plants.

Beautiful Bush Thymes. Thymus nitidus is perhaps the most beautiful of all the bush Thymes. It forms a small twiggy shrub about 18 in. high, clothed with small gray-green leaves, and is covered in June and July with small rosy-lilac flowers.

This delightful plant is probably closely related to the Mediterranean T. vulgaris, but is altogether superior, and invaluable in the rock

The pale purple, very fragrant Russian Thyme, Thymus pectinatus (odoratissimus).

garden, where it should be given a fully sunny position, in the dry wall garden and in the front of the flower border. The foliage has the same aromatic smell as T. vulgaris.

This plant may be increased from seed sown in a pan of light loam and sand in the cold frame in spring, or from cuttings of small branches taken in early summer and inserted in a pan of sand in the cold frame. This kind is not very hardy in the North.

Thymus caespititius (micans) makes neat rounded bushes about 6 in. high, of close heathlike foliage. It is a shrubby plant, and most attractive in a sunny position in the rock garden, where its evergreen domes of slightly golden-green, aromatic foliage give a very good effect. It is also useful for the dry wall garden. The flowers are pale lilac, almost white, but are of no account in comparison with the characteristic habit of the plant. It is increased most easily by division, and cuttings may be rooted in the ordinary way. It is a native of Spain, Portugal, the Azores and Madeira and is not very hardy in the North.

Thymus carnosus is an attractive small bush or shrub of erect growth, 12-18 in. high. The rigid stems are thickly clothed with dark green, heathlike leaves, and in summer it bears clusters of small white flowers. The whole plant is pleasantly aromatic. This Thyme is most valuable in the rock garden, not so much for the sake of its flowers, but because of the striking character of its rigid growth, suggesting a clump of minute Irish Yew. It is increased by cuttings taken in summer.

THYRSACANTHUS. Odontonema, which see.

THYSANOTUS—*Fringe Lily* (Thysano'tus). A small group of perennial plants, suitable for cultivation in a cool greenhouse, which are found wild in Australia. They belong to the Lily family, Liliaceae. The name is derived from *thysanotos,* fringed, and refers to the form of the segments of the perianth.

These plants are rarely met with in cultivation. They may be grown outdoors in California or in a greenhouse in which a minimum winter temperature of 45 degrees is maintained. The most suitable potting compost consists of loam mixed with a little leaf mold and sand. Little watering is necessary during winter. Repotting should be done in spring.

These plants have narrow leaves, and in summer bear flattish bunches of small flowers.

The chief kinds are T. dichotomus, 18 in.; T. junceus, 18 in.; and T. tuberosus, 12-15 in. All bear purple flowers in summer.

TIARELLA—Foam Flower, False Mitrewort (Tiarel'la). A small group of hardy herbaceous plants, belonging to the Saxifrage family, Saxifragaceae. Only some five kinds are known; one is a native of Bhutan and Nepal and the others are natives of North America. The name Tiarella is from *tiara,* a Greek word for a little turban, and alludes to the shape of the seed capsules.

The Favorite Kind. Tiarella cordifolia, a native of eastern North America, the Foam Flower or False Mitrewort, is a very pretty plant for cool situations in the rock garden, in shrubberies and in the woodland garden. It is of tufted habit, 6-12 in. high, with rough, green, heart-shaped leaves, acutely lobed and toothed, and in spring bears numerous erect spikes of fluffy, creamy white flowers on 6-9-in. stems, resembling a small Astilbe. It is very easy to grow, and spreads rapidly by means of runners or stolons which root themselves, thus affording an easy means of propagation. The plant may be divided at almost any time of year but, preferably, in spring or early fall. There is a dark-leaved form of T. cordifolia called purpurea, with pinkish flowers.

Tiarella unifoliata is a larger plant, 12-18 in. high, with splendid spikes of cream-colored flowers. It forms dense clumps and does not run like T. cordifolia, but may be increased by division in spring or early summer. Its flowering season continues longer than that of T. cordifolia. T. unifoliata is somewhat rare in cultivation, but is perfectly easy to grow and a most desirable plant. It occurs as a native from California to Alaska.

T. polyphylla, from Bhutan and Nepal, is a smaller plant than T. cordifolia, and not so robust, though otherwise not unlike it.

T. cordifolia has been crossed with Heuchera to produce the hybrid called Heucherella tiarellioides, which see.

TIBOUCHINA — *Brazilian Spiderflower, Glory Bush* (Tibouch'ina). Tender, evergreen, shrubby, free-flowering plants of great beauty. They are found wild in Brazil and belong to the Melastoma family, Melastomaceae. They are also known in gardens as Lasiandra and Pleroma, but Tibouchina is the correct name.

The Foam Flower, Tiarella cordifolia, a dainty plant for cool, semishady locations.

One of the most brilliant of tropical flowering shrubs is Tibouchina semidecandra, a native of Brazil.

The chief kind, T. semidecandra, has woody stems and ovate or oblong-ovate, stemless, opposite, dark green leaves, with conspicuous longitudinal veins. It bears large, purple, roundish flowers, 3-4 in. in diameter, which have conspicuous yellow anthers. The filaments of the stamens are long and slender and resemble spiders' legs, hence the common name. The name Tibouchina is the original native name.

Culture. In frostless or nearly frostless climates, as in the far South, Tibouchinas may be planted permanently outdoors. They can also be successfully cultivated in a greenhouse with a minimum winter temperature of 55 degrees. In the North they may be put outdoors during the warm summer months and brought into a greenhouse before frost. The plants may either be grown in a bush form in pots or planted in a bed of soil and the shoots trained, more or less as a vine, to cover the greenhouse wall or roof. The best compost for potting or planting consists of two parts of loam, one part of peat and a liberal quantity of sand, together with a small amount of crushed charcoal.

Treatment as Pot Plants. The plants are raised in spring from cuttings, which should consist of short, firm shoots. After being trimmed, by removing their lower leaves and cutting them cleanly across beneath a joint, these are inserted in a bed of sand, or sand and peat moss, in a propagating frame in a greenhouse and, when well rooted, are potted separately in 3-in. pots. As soon as they are established in these, the tips of the shoots are removed to cause them to produce side branches. When these are 1 in. long, the plants are repotted in 5-in. pots and the same system of pinching is practiced with the side branches. No more pinching is required until after the plants have flowered for the first time, which they will do the following summer.

After the plants have flowered, they may be pruned back again in the following spring, and repotted in larger pots, or they may be planted in a bed of soil, similar to that recommended above for potting, and trained as climbing plants.

As Greenhouse Climbing Plants. The site should be prepared by digging a hole 2 ft. deep and 2 ft. wide, and placing a 12-in. layer of broken bricks or stones in the bottom for drainage. These are covered with rough leaves or grass sods and the remainder of the space is filled with the prepared compost. After the soil has settled, planting should be done and the compost made as firm as possible. The shoots, as they develop, are then tied to wires fixed to the wall or roof of the greenhouse.

Pruning. The leading shoots should not be pruned until they have reached their full height, when they are stopped (pinched); all laterals or side shoots are pruned back to a few buds in February or March. During the summer months, the plants are shaded from the fiercest rays of the sun, and the greenhouse is ventilated freely on warm days.

After potting or planting, very little water is required until the plants are established, when the soil is kept moist throughout the summer; throughout the winter months the soil is only moistened when it becomes quite dry. Very little damping or syringing is required.

The chief kind is T. semidecandra, 15-20 ft., purple, summer. Other kinds are T. Benthamiana, 6 ft., violet, August; T. elegans, 6 ft., purple, June; T. heteromalla, 5 ft., blue, July; and T. laxa, 7-8 ft., violet or violet-purple, summer.

TICKSEED. See Coreopsis.
TICK TREFOIL. See Desmodium.
TIDYTIPS. Layia elegans, which see.
TIGER-FLOWER. See Tigridia.
TIGER IRIS. Tigridia, which see.
TIGER LILY. See Lilium tigrinum.
TIGER'S-JAW. See Faucaria.
TIGER'S-MOUTH. See Faucaria tigrina.

TIGRIDIA — *Tiger-Flower* (Tigrid'ia; Ti'gridia). Tender, bulbous plants with large, conspicuously blotched flowers. They are found wild from Mexico to Chile and belong to the Iris family, Iridaceae. The name Tigridia means tiger-like, from *tigris*, and refers to the peculiarly blotched flowers.

These beautiful bulb plants grow 12 in. to 2½ ft. in height, have long, narrow, wrinkled leaves, and bear large flowers at the tips of long slender stems in summer.

In some kinds the flowers are 5-6 in. across, and last but one day, but they open in quick succession, so that a display is maintained for several weeks. They have six petals, which are scarlet, rose, yellow or white, and are heavily

The Tiger Flower, Tigridia Pavonia, a showy summer-flowering plant for a sunny well-drained location.

blotched with purple, carmine, rose, or yellow.

The bulbs may either be grown in pans in a cold frame or greenhouse, or planted out of doors in early summer. The treatment out of doors is similar to that of Gladiolus. The sunniest spot is chosen, where the soil is light and well drained, and where there is shelter from cold winds. If the soil is clayey it should be removed to a depth of 18-24 in. and a layer of broken bricks placed in the bottom for drainage. The hole is then filled with loam, leaf mold and sand. Alternatively, the clayey soil can be lightened and made porous by mixing with it liberal amounts of coarse sand or gritty coal cinder and, in addition, peat moss, leaf mold or compost.

When to Plant. In spring, after danger of frost has passed, the bulbs are planted 3 in. deep and 6 in. apart. During dry weather the soil is kept moist by mulching and watering and, when the foliage has died down in autumn, the bulbs are lifted, dried off, and stored in a frostproof place for the winter.

Cultivation in Pots. Tigridias make excellent pot plants for the cool greenhouse. The bulbs may be potted singly in small pots, or several placed in larger pots or deep pans. They are potted in March, in a compost of sandy loam and peat, and are set 1 in. deep. The potted bulbs are placed in a cold frame and covered with peat moss or sifted ashes until the roots are well developed, when they are taken into the greenhouse. Until growth becomes active they are watered very moderately; then the soil is kept moist and applications of liquid fertilizer are given when the flower spikes are forming. After the flowers have faded, less water is given, and when the foliage has turned brown the soil is kept dry until repotting time in March.

Methods of Propagation. The principal method of propagation is by removing the small offsets at potting or planting time and growing them in the way advised for the older bulbs until flowering size is reached.

Seeds may also be sown, although these do not all come true to type. They are sown in a deep, well-drained pot of sandy soil in April and set in a warm greenhouse to germinate. When 1 in. in height, the seedlings are pricked off into a deep seed pan or flat, hardened off when established, and placed in a cold frame for the summer. They are dried off in the autumn, and the small bulbs replanted in a flat of soil in the following spring or in nursery rows in the garden, where they are kept until flowering size is reached.

The chief kind is T. Pavonia, 1½-2 ft., with large, showy flowers, the margins of which are scarlet and the centers orange-yellow spotted with red. Of this kind there are several varieties, of which alba has white flowers heavily spotted with carmine; conchiflora is yellow; rosea, pink and yellow; and speciosa, orange-red. T. Pringlei is scarlet and orange with scarlet blotches.

TILIA—*Linden, Basswood, Lime* (Til'ia). Leaf-losing trees, often of large size, natives of Europe, some of the central regions of Asia (particularly parts of China), Japan and of North America southward to Mexico. Many are hardy in the North. The leaves are in most instances more or less heart-shaped or rounded and sometimes of considerable size, and they have long, slender stalks. The flowers, usually cream-colored and fragrant, are produced in summer, several together in stalked clusters, each cluster having attached near its base a thin, strap-shaped bract which may be 2-3 in. long. Some kinds are quite popular for planting as specimen shade trees and as avenue trees. Tilia gives its name to the family Tiliaceae, and the name is the ancient Latin name for the Linden.

Propagation may be effected by means of seeds, layers and grafts. In the case of species or

The Crimean Linden, Tilea euchlora, becomes a splendid specimen when given plenty of space in which to develop. It has rich glossy green foliage.

distinct wild kinds, seeds should be used whenever possible. They should be sown as soon as ripe, the more common kinds out of doors, in light, well-drained soil. Rarer kinds may be sown in pots or flats of light soil and stood out of doors plunged (buried to the rims of the containers) in ashes for the winter. They should be taken into a warm greenhouse in February, and germination will soon follow. If the seeds are stored for a few months before sowing, germination may be delayed for several months.

Layering. When it is not possible to procure a good supply of seeds, layering affords a means of propagation. This method is especially popular in Europe. For this form of propagation trees are planted specially for the purpose. They are cut down to the ground when well established, and from the cut stumps vigorous young shoots appear. These may grow 3-4 ft. long in a season. The following spring as many as possible of the shoots are layered, care being taken to keep the points of the shoots erect. The layers are usually well enough rooted for removal by the first autumn, and quickly grow to a size suitable for permanent planting.

Grafting is usually practiced in propagating varieties that cannot be raised true from seed and that cannot very well be layered. Stocks of the same species to which the varieties belong should be used; grafting may be carried out in greenhouses on stocks established in pots, or it may be practiced on outdoor trees in early spring. Lindens may also be propagated by budding in summer.

Soils—Transplanting. The various kinds of Tilia thrive in a great variety of soils, including light and heavy loam, and clay soil provided it has been drained, but they do not withstand dry conditions or drought. It is fatal to plant them in ground subject to waterlogging; heavy ground should be drained and gritty material added before trees are planted. They succeed in places where lime is prevalent in the soil.

Transplanting may be carried out at any time in mild weather in spring or fall. Linden trees can be transplanted when of large size if a considerable mass of soil around the roots is moved with them.

Disadvantages of the Common Linden. Some kinds are excellent for planting to form specimen trees, but the common Linden, Tilia europaea (vulgaris), is not well suited for this purpose, for in summer a good deal of honeydew is secreted by insects feeding on the tree, and this not only dirties the leaves but falls down onto whatever is beneath.

Although it is sometimes planted along roads and streets, the common Linden is actually less suitable for the purpose than several other

The Silver Linden, Tilia tomentosa, is so called because of the whitish undersurfaces of its leaves. It forms a broad-spreading tree with distinctly upright branches.

kinds, for after a dry summer the leaves often begin to fall early in August and continue falling until late autumn.

For Avenues and Pleached Walks. Linden trees have always been popular for planting to form avenues. Not only have the avenues often been made too narrow, but the trees have been put too close together, so that at maturity the space between the rows of trees is dark and does not dry quickly after wet weather. These are quick-growing trees and, when planted in good soil, vigorous young trees make rapid growth.

Linden trees have for a very long period been used, especially in Europe, as screens, first for forming the popular "pleached walks" (see Pleaching) of many generations ago, and later, to block out unsightly objects. They are very useful for the purpose, for they respond very well to pruning, and are not harmed if the shoots are cut back annually. Moreover, crossed branches often unite by natural grafting and strengthen the screen.

Pollarding. In Europe, Linden trees are pollarded at 8 or 10 ft. from the ground, and are allowed to form several main, erect branches from that point. (See Pollarding.) Such trees are not so strong as those in which a central trunk is carried well up into the head, and steps may have to be taken to secure the several branches together to prevent their being broken.

Pruning of large trees may be carried out during summer or autumn. The annual pruning of pleached trees should be done in late autumn or winter. One form of common Linden (T. europaea) is very liable to form masses of twiggy branches from the base and lower part of the trunk. These should be removed annually, for if allowed to remain, they become very dirty and full of dead and dying branchlets.

The Tilias are long-lived trees, but the wood is soft and easily decays; therefore, old trees are often badly decayed and the trunks weakened. In all cases where branches are broken off, the broken ends should be sawed close to the trunk and the wounds dressed with tree-wound paint. At the same time, any decayed places that may be noticed in the trunk should be cleaned out and painted. Dead branches should also be removed from the tree, the wounds being protected with tree-wound paint.

Old trees can be assisted by loosening the ground beneath the branches and applying a generous surface dressing of well-decayed farmyard manure, manure and leaves, or of compost, together with an application of a complete fertilizer. As there are many roots near the surface of the ground, a quick response may be expected from such a dressing.

The flowers have a medicinal value by reason of their tonic and stimulative properties. In some countries they are collected and dried, and afterwards made into tea for use in cases of headache. The flowers are also rich in honey and are widely worked by bees. Honey from the flowers is usually dark-colored and may be almost black when the leaves are badly affected by honeydew, for the bees appear to work the sweet secretion on the leaves as well as the flowers. It should be noted that the flowers of T. petiolaris and of T. tomentosa are poisonous to bees.

The Common European Linden, T. europaea, forms a large tree up to 100 or 120 ft. high, of fairly erect habit, with weeping branchlets. The flowers are very fragrant. It is regarded as being a natural hybrid between T. cordata and T. platyphyllos, and is increased by layers and grafting.

The Large-leaved Linden, T. platyphyllos, is a large tree, a native of Europe. Under cultivation it may grow 100-120 ft. high. It has generally larger leaves than T. europaea, dark-green above and densely hairy beneath. The shoots are also downy. The flowers are yellowish-white and open in June. It is actually a better tree than T. europaea, for it is less likely to form masses of adventitious growths on the trunk, and is less liable to disfigurement by honeydew.

Linden Trees with Ornamental Leaves. A number of distinct varieties of the Large-leaved Linden are in cultivation. Prominent among them is T. platyphyllos variety rubra, the so-called Red-twigged Linden, which is an excellent kind for decorative planting. T. platyphyllos variety laciniata, also called asplenifolia, the Fern-leaved Linden, is distinct because the leaves are divided into numerous deep segments. T. platyphyllos variety aurea is distinct by its yellowish branchlets; T. platyphyllos variety pyramidalis by its stiff, erect branches; and T. platyphyllos variety vitifolia by the leaf margins, which are coarsely toothed or lobed.

Two very abnormal varieties are T. platyphyllos variety tortuosa, with curiously contorted branches and T. platyphyllos variety asplenifolia in which the leaves are smaller than those of the normal type and are deeply cut or divided into fine segments of irregular form.

The Small-leaved Linden, T. cordata, is distinct by reason of its small, rounded leaves. As a rule it is of shapely habit. It is a native tree in Europe.

A Good Lawn Tree. T. euchlora, the Crimean Linden, is presumed to be a natural hybrid between T. cordata and T. petiolaris. It has been known since 1860 and is popular by reason of its large, deep and glossy green leaves, the down on the undersurface being confined to tufts in the axils of the veins. The yellowish flowers open in July and they are very fragrant. This tree is one of the best of the Lindens and maintains a fresh appearance until late autumn. It is an excellent kind of plant to form a lawn specimen. It is sometimes confused with T. dasystyla, which it somewhat resembles. T. dasystyla is a very much rarer tree from the Caucasus and western Asia.

A Weeping Linden. T. petiolaris, the Weeping White Linden, is a very handsome tree. It keeps its foliage well into autumn and flowers late, usually during July. It is thought to be a native of southeastern Europe and western Asia but there is some doubt as to its true origin. It may grow 60-90 ft. high and has a rounded but graceful habit, the branchlets being pendent. The rounded leaves, produced on long stalks, are 2-4½ in. long and almost as wide, dark green above and silvery beneath. The flowers are poisonous to bees. This tree is usually increased by grafting.

The White or Silver Linden. T. tomentosa, the White Linden or Silver Linden, sometimes called T. argentea, is closely related to T. petiolaris. It is a tree 60-100 ft. high, of rather stiff, erect habit, with the young shoots covered by felty hairs. The rounded or heart-shaped leaves are 2-5 in. long and almost as wide, dark green above and covered with silvery felt beneath. A native of southeastern Europe and Asia Minor, it was introduced to northern European gardens in 1767. It is distinct from any other Linden by its habit and the silvery underside of the leaves. Its flowers are poisonous to bees.

T. Moltkei is a hybrid, the suggested parentage of which is T. americana and T. petiolaris. It appears to have been raised as a chance seedling in a German nursery. It is chiefly remarkable for its large leaves, which are up to 7 in. long and 5 in. wide.

The American Linden, T. americana (glabra), is the principal North American kind. It forms a tree 100-120 ft. high, and occurs naturally from New Brunswick to Missouri and eastern Texas, favoring moist, fertile soils. The leaves are coarsely toothed, 5-6 in. long and 3-6 in. wide, light green above, with tufts of hairs in the lower vein axils beneath. T. americana variety dentata has leaves that are coarsely and irregularly toothed. T. americana variety macrophylla has larger leaves.

Other American Lindens. T. heterophylla is a large tree, native to rich woods from New York to Ohio, Indiana and Missouri and southward to Florida and Arkansas; it has reddish or yellowish-brown branchlets and large, ovate leaves, glossy green above and covered with white, downy hairs beneath. T. monticola grows naturally in forests from Virginia and West Virginia to Georgia and forms a large tree with leaves equivalent in size to those of T. americana. T. neglecta, which chiefly differs from T. americana in having its leaves finely hairy (pubescent) on their undersides, attains a height of 100 ft. and occurs naturally from Canada to North Carolina and westward to Minnesota.

Asiatic Lindens. T. Henryana is one of the newer Lindens from central China. It grows 40-50 ft. high, and bears more or less heart-shaped leaves, up to 5 in. long and 3 in. wide, with rather large clusters of almost white flowers. It was introduced to cultivation in 1901.

T. Oliveri is another of the more recently introduced kinds. It was received from central China in 1900. This tree grows 40-50 ft. high, and is recognized by its tapering leaves with a heart-shaped base, which are 3-4 in. long and 2-3 in. wide, dark green above, white beneath. This is a distinct tree, naturally suited for a prominent place as a specimen on a lawn.

The Manchurian Linden, T. mandschurica, is a native of northeastern Asia. It attains a height of about 60 ft. and has leaves that are gray or grayish-white on their undersides.

The Japanese Linden, T. japonica, grows about 60 ft. tall. Its leaves are about 3 in. long, sharply toothed but not lobed, and bluish-green when young.

Other Japanese kinds are T. Maximowicziana, which in its native country grows to a height of about 100 ft. and has leaves green above and grayish beneath, and the kind called T. Miqueliana, which has glossy green leaves which are retained later than those of most other Lindens. T. Miqueliana attains a height of about 50 ft., and is known only as a cultivated tree; it has not been found growing wild.

The Mongolian Linden, T. mongolica, is a small tree 25-30 ft. high, with reddish branchlets and distinct, rather small-lobed leaves, which are 1½-3 in. long. It is a native of northern China and Mongolia, and was introduced to France in 1880.

T. Tuan, a western Chinese Linden, was introduced to cultivation in 1888. It is a tree 40-50 ft. high in its native country. Two other little-known Lindens are T. insularis, a native of Korea, and T. intonsa, a native of western Szechuan, China.

TILLAGE. This word refers to loosening or stirring the soil with the object of improving its productivity for farming and gardening. It includes all operations, such as digging, plowing, rototilling, harrowing, forking, raking and hoeing, that are commonly grouped under the heading of soil cultivation. The chief purposes of tillage are to improve the mechanical condition of the soil, to make it more friable or crumbly, to render it more permeable to water and to air, and—not least important—to incorporate with the soil such conditioners as manures, compost, fertilizers and lime.

The roots of plants penetrate hard, unloosened ground only with difficulty. On the other hand, they permeate well-tilled soil much more easily. In such soil the plants develop more extensive root systems and are able to draw the moisture and nutrients they need from a greater volume of soil; as a result they grow more luxuriantly.

For deep tillage in gardens, spading fork, spade and mechanical rotary tiller are used.

Many of the disappointments that amateur gardeners experience can be traced to planting in ground that is insufficiently tilled. Adequate soil preparation is especially important before planting trees, shrubs and perennials that are to remain undisturbed for a number of years. (See Digging: the Basis of Good Garden Cultivation.)

TILLANDSIA (Tilland'sia). Tender, evergreen plants with, usually, attractive flowers and large, beautifully colored bracts. They are closely allied to Billbergia and Vriesia, and belong to the Bromelia or Pineapple family, Bromeliaceae. The leaves, which are usually smooth, rigid and leathery, rise straight up from the base of the plant, except in the case of T. usneoides, the Spanish Moss. They are mostly sword-shaped, prickly-edged and concave, and overlap to form a cylindrical cavity at their bases. The flowers are on slender spikes which appear in the centers of the tubes of leaves; they are yellow, violet or blue.

Each flower is formed in the axil of a large, conspicuous, yellowish-green, silvery-green, violet, carmine or rose-colored bract. The various kinds bloom at different times of the year, in spring, summer and autumn. The name Tillandsia commemorates Professor Elias Tillands, of Sweden.

Greenhouse Plants. As most Tillandsias are natives of tropical forests of the Americas, a greenhouse in which a minimum winter temperature of 55 degrees is maintained is required for their cultivation, except in the very warmest parts of the United States, such as Florida, and in other warm countries. A moist atmosphere is also necessary. These plants are epiphytic (growing wild on trees but without taking nourishment, as parasitic plants do, from the trees on which they grow) and, in consequence, when they are grown in pots, they must have free drainage and a compost which will absorb plenty of moisture and not become waterlogged.

Deep pans, or orchid pots, are the most suitable containers. They should be filled to one third their depth with crocks. A good potting compost consists of 1 part of turfy topsoil, 1 part of peat moss, 1 part of leaf mold, 1 part of coarse sand and 1 part of crushed brick, all well mixed together.

Because these plants thrive best when they are somewhat pot-bound, repotting is not necessary every year, but it should be done whenever the compost becomes decayed and sour and whenever the roots are very crowded. Spring is the best season to repot.

Propagation is most commonly effected by suckers, which develop at the bases of the old plants. The suckers are taken off in spring and potted in the same compost as advised for the mature plants. Tillandsias may also be raised from seeds sown in a mixture of peat moss and sand.

The Spanish Moss. Tillandsia usneoides bears no superficial resemblance to the other kinds of Tillandsia. It consists simply of long grayish filaments several feet in length, which hang from trees in great masses. This peculiar plant occurs naturally from Virginia to Florida and Texas and southward to Argentina and Chile. It is sometimes cultivated in greenhouses as a curiosity. It is fastened to a block of wood with a little sphagnum moss and is suspended from the roof. All that is necessary to keep it alive is to moisten the moss as soon as it approaches dryness and to syringe the Spanish Moss with water daily.

The Chief Kinds. T. circinata, silvery leaves, flowers lavender; T. fasciculata, gray-green foliage, flowers blue, bracts red-tinged; T. Lindeniana, leaves green, often with narrow, brownish

Tillandsia Lindeniana is remarkable for its spikes of large blue-purple flowers.

stripes, flowers large, blue-purple, very handsome, bracts carmine-red; T. usneoides (Spanish Moss), foliage gray, flowers insignificant, yellow.

TILTH. This term is used by gardeners to describe the condition of surface soil which has been broken down into fine particles by digging, hoeing and raking to render it crumbly or friable and thus suitable for sowing or planting.

TINCTORIUS. A botanical specific term applied to some plants that have been used as sources of dyes.

TI PLANT. Cordyline terminalis, which see.

TIPULARIA DISCOLOR—*Crane-Fly Orchis* (Tipular'ia). A terrestrial Orchid belonging to the Orchid family, Orchidaceae, which occurs as a native from Massachusetts to Florida, Texas and Indiana. The name is derived from the Latin *tipula,* the crane fly, which the flower is supposed to resemble in form.

Tipularia discolor is a native of rich, damp woods and should be afforded a similar environment when an attempt is made to cultivate it in wild gardens and rock gardens. The flowers, which are green and purple, are borne on stems 1 ft. or less tall in summer.

TITANOPSIS (Titanop'sis). A group of small, South African succulent plants that formerly were included in Mesembryanthemum and which require the same general culture as that group. See Mesembryanthemum. They belong to the Carpet Weed family, the Aizoaceae. The name is from *titan,* sun, and *opsis,* like, and was bestowed because of the resemblance of the flower to a miniature sun.

The thick fleshy leaves of Titanopsis calcarea are covered with white tubercles.

These plants often resemble small pebbles or stones. They are choice plants for the fancier of succulents.

The following kinds are likely to be found in specialists' collections: T. calcarea, flowers yellow; T. Hugo-Schlechteri, flowers yellow; T. Schwantesii, flowers yellow; T. setifera, flowers orange-pink.

TITHONIA (Titho'nia). This group of plants consists of a few annuals, herbaceous perennials and tender shrubs with large sunflower-like heads of yellow or orange-colored blooms in

A pan of seedlings of Titanopsis calcarea.

Tithonia rotundifolia, sometimes known as the Golden Flower of the Incas, is an excellent summer- and fall-blooming annual.

summer and early autumn. They are found wild in Mexico, Central America and the West Indies and belong to the Daisy family, Compositae. The name is derived from the mythological Tithonus.

Tithonia rotundifolia (speciosa) is cultivated as an annual, and modern, early-flowering strains flower well even in northern gardens. They are extremely valuable for providing summer and fall blooms for decorating flower borders, and also are excellent as cut flowers. This plant is sometimes known by the name of Golden Flower of the Incas.

Seeds may be sown directly outdoors as soon as the ground is fairly warm and the weather is settled (about the time it is safe to plant the first Corn); of an early start may be gained by sowing the seeds indoors 6-7 weeks before it is safe to set the plants out in the garden; then transplant the seedlings to flats or individually to small pots and set them in their permanent locations outdoors when it is safe to plant Tomatoes outside. The plants should be given ample space; a distance of 2-3 ft. between individuals is not too much.

The chief kinds are T. diversifolia, a shrub to 30 ft. tall; T. rotundifolia (T. speciosa), a shrub to 6 ft. high; and T. tagetifolia, a herbaceous perennial to 8 ft. high.

TOADFLAX. See Linaria.

TOADFLOWER. Stapelia, which see.

TOAD LILY. Tricyrtis, which see.

TOADSTOOL. The term Toadstool is generally used for certain fleshy fungi which have gills; it is applied especially to kinds which are not edible or are suspected of being inedible because of their color, odor, surface appearance and other characteristics. Sometimes the term is used to include all the gilled fungi, but more frequently the edible kinds are called Mushrooms, although this name may be further restricted to include only the cultivated kind. See Mushroom.

In one sense, an individual Toadstool is rather like the fruit on an Apple tree, in that it is only the fruiting body of the fungus plant. The plant body upon which the Toadstool develops consists of a more or less extensive mat of microscopic threads hidden within the material upon which it grows. The ordinary Toadstool is more or less umbrella-shaped, with the top rather like a coolie cap, supported on a central column or stalk. On the undersurface of the cap, radiating from the stalk to the outer edge of the cap, hang a number of flat plates (gills) which are thickly, though microscopically, covered by the spore-bearing structures and their spores. Each Toadstool sheds millions of spores which are scattered about by the wind for long distances, each one germinating, under proper conditions, to produce a new plant body.

Toadstools grow on wood, leaves, manure and other decaying organic matter and in soil. They are important in the balance of Nature because they destroy dead plant and animal tissues. For example, the plant body of a wood-destroying Toadstool gains its nutrients by secreting enzymes which dissolve cells of the dead wood and then it absorbs the solution which results. Besides the large numbers of such wood-inhabiting fungi, there are many more which play a part in converting into rich humus the dead leaves that fall each autumn.

For a long time it has been recognized that certain kinds of Toadstools are always found under the same species of tree. This observation has an easy explanation in a curious relationship that exists between the tree and the fungus. The thinnest roots of most plants are extremely small, hairlike threads called root hairs. These absorb water for the life activities of the plant. With at least some species of trees, the tips of the underground mat of the Toadstool plant body come in contact with the root hairs of the tree, and the roots are either penetrated or enveloped by the fungus threads. This is not simple parasitism, because there is a nicely adjusted balance between the fungus and the tree, and both derive advantages from the relationship. The combination of tree roots and fungus is called a mycorrhiza. Mycorrhizae are sometimes important in horticulture because certain trees, especially conifers, are not able to grow unless their associated fungus is present in the soil.

Many Toadstools are edible and delicious when properly cooked. However, the danger of collecting for food one of the poisonous kinds should not be dismissed lightly. Although there are only a few poisonous kinds, they include species which produce violent illness and death, as well as others which, although disagreeable, bring about a mild reaction only.

About 90 per cent of all deaths caused by eating Toadstools result from the consumption of one particular kind, often called the Destroying Angel or Death Cup. Not only is the poison of this Toadstool extremely virulent but, because the fungus occurs commonly in North America, the possibility of collecting one when gathering edible mushrooms indiscriminately for food is rather high.

About six to ten hours after eating the Destroying Angel vomiting and diarrhea begin. By then the poison of the Toadstool is already well distributed through the body. Death does not usually occur, except with children, until after about seven days. During the interval the patient is in extreme pain.

The only reliable assurance for safe Toadstool and Mushroom collecting and eating is to know how to recognize the different kinds with certainty. The rule-of-thumb methods sometimes recommended for differentiating between edible and poisonous kinds are completely unreliable.

TOBACCO. The Tobacco, Nicotiana Tabacum, was among the most noted seventeenth century introductions from America to Europe. The earliest account of it is to be found in Nicolas Monardes' book, *Dos libros el veno que trata de todas las cosas que traen de nuestras Indias Occidentales* (1569), and the first illustration of the plant in John Frampton's translation of the above book, published in 1597, with the title *Joyfull newes out of the newe founde Worlde*.

Nicolas Monardes (a Spanish doctor living in Seville) gives a lengthy account of Tobacco, and states that it was a herb of great antiquity among the Indians, who taught the medicinal uses of it to the Spaniards. The natives called it Picielt, the name Tobacco being given by the Spaniards either from the island Tobago, or from a native word connected with the use of the dried leaves for smoking.

Tobacco was introduced into Spain, he says, as a garden plant, but was soon valued for its medicinal virtues and regarded as an all-heal. In the city of Seville, "they know not what other to do, having cut or hurt themselves but to run to the Tabaco as to a most ready remedy. It doth marvellous worke without any need of other surgery but this only herb." Monardes states further that the name Nicotiana was bestowed on the plant in honor of his friend Nicot, who introduced the herb into France. See Nicotiana.

TODEA. See Leptopteris.

TOES. A name sometimes given to swollen pieces of root that are produced by certain

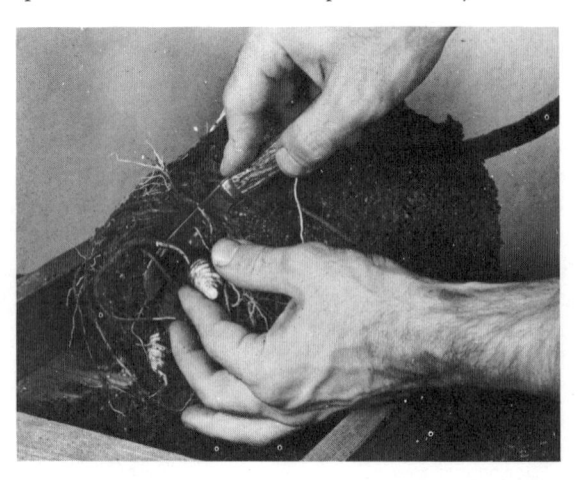

Toes to be used for propagation are removed from a plant of Cordyline terminalis.

plants, such as Cordyline terminalis, and which may be removed and planted separately to give rise to new individual plants.

TOFIELDIA (Tofield'ia). A group of plants of comparatively small horticultural importance that are natives of the North Temperate and Arctic Zones and the Andes of South America. Tofieldia was named in honor of an English botanist, Thomas Tofield. It belongs to the Lily family, the Liliaceae.

Tofieldias are mostly hardy and thrive in a light, moist, acid soil in full sun. They are propagated by seeds and division. Kinds that may be occasionally cultivated in wild gardens are: T. glabra, White Featherling, 2 ft., flowers white, a native from North Carolina to Georgia; T. intermedia, 1 ft., flowers yellow, a native from California to Alaska; T. occidentalis, 20 in., flowers yellow, a native from California and Idaho to British Columbia; T. racemosa, 2 ft., flowers whitish, a native from New Jersey to Florida and Alabama.

TOLMIEA MENZIESII—*Pickaback Plant* (Tol'miea). This hardy herbaceous plant belongs to the Saxifrage family, Saxifragaceae, and is closely related to Tiarella, Heuchera and Mitella. It is the only kind. The name Tolmiea was given by Torrey and Gray in honor of Mr. Tolmie, surgeon to the Hudson's Bay Company at Puget Sound. The plant is native from Alaska to California, and was formerly known as Heuchera Menziesii and Tiarella Menziesii.

Tolmiea Menziesii has leaves much like those of Mitella, and sprays of greenish flowers 12-18 in. high, in spring. It is a useful plant for the woodland and shady places, though not a particularly showy one. It can be used successfully as a low ground cover.

Tolmiea has the peculiarity of producing buds at the base of each leaf blade (that is, at the top of the petiole or leafstalk) which give rise to young plantlets even while the leaves are yet attached to the parent plant. It is because the older leaves have young plants growing out of them that the common name of Pickaback Plant was given to Tolmiea Menziesii. Sometimes the common name appears as Piggyback Plant.

In Tolmiea's native habitat and in gardens, when the older leaves bend down and come in contact with the earth the plantlets root and establish themselves as separate individuals. As a practical method of propagation the leaves bearing plantlets may be cut off and planted in moist sand, peat moss and sand, or vermiculite, in a shaded propagating case, cold frame or under a bell jar, and there left to root. After rooting, they are potted individually in a loose soil that contains a generous proportion of peat moss, leaf mold or humus or are planted in a shaded place outdoors. Tolmiea Menziesii may also be increased by division, which operation is best done in spring or early fall.

A Good House Plant. In addition to its usefulness as an outdoor plant Tolmiea Menziesii is a splendid foliage house plant. It thrives where light is poor and grows without trouble, provided it is given a well-drained pot and a soil that is rich with peat moss, leaf mold, humus or some other organic matter, and that is kept always moist. It is an excellent subject for growing indoors under fluorescent light.

This plant thrives in a wide variation of temperatures, from those of a very cool room to those of the more usual living-room range. An atmosphere that is excessively dry is detrimental. Specimens that have filled their pots with healthy roots benefit greatly from being given a weekly application of dilute liquid fertilizer.

Pickaback plants that need repotting should receive this attention in spring or early summer. Young specimens are likely to benefit from repotting again in August or September.

TOLPIS—*Yellow Hawkweed* (Tol'pis). Uncommon annuals which are natives of southern Europe. They belong to the Daisy family, Compositae, and closely resemble Crepis (Hawkweed), with which they are sometimes classified. T. barbata, the chief kind, is an upright, branched annual 2 ft. in height. It has lanceolate leaves with toothed margins, and bears attractive heads of yellow flowers in summer. The origin of the name is not known.

For a Sunny Border. The seeds are sown out of doors in early spring where the plants are to flower. A sunny position and light, well-drained soil are required. A fine, crumbly surface is obtained by digging and raking, and the seeds, after being scattered thinly on the surface, are raked in.

When the seedlings are 2 in. high, they are thinned out to 9 in. apart, after which little further attention is required beyond the regular routine tasks of watering and weeding.

TOMATILLO. Physalis ixocarpa, which see.

The Pickaback Plant, Tolmiea Menziesii.

TOMATO: A FAVORITE GARDEN CROP
How to Grow Good Tomatoes in the Garden and Greenhouse

The Tomato is highly esteemed as a delicious food when cooked or eaten raw, and as a source of juice. It is known to be a source of health-protective vitamins and because of the ease with which it can be cultivated it is one of the most popular of home vegetable-garden crops as well as a commercial crop of vast importance.

With comparatively little care the Tomato yields well and produces, over a long season, a succession of delicious fruits. It exists in many different varieties, some having fruits not much larger than a currant, others having fruits that weigh a pound or more each. The fruits are usually red, but varieties with yellow fruits and with pink and white fruits are also grown. In height the plants vary considerably according to variety.

Characteristically, the Tomato is a lover of sunshine and warm weather. It is grown as a tender annual and is one of the first plants to be damaged by fall frosts; even slight frost harms the tender foliage.

The parent species or wild progenitors of the garden varieties of Tomato are two tender perennials that are natives of western South America, Lycopersicon esculentum and L. pimpinellifolium. When cultivated, as they sometimes are in botanical gardens and similar places, they are treated as annuals. The Tomato was introduced into gardens in Europe during the early part of the sixteenth century, but for a long time its value as a food was not appreciated, perhaps because it belongs in the Nightshade family, the Solonaceae, and so shows a resemblance to many well-known plants that have poisonous characteristics. Before it was accepted as a food the Tomato was cultivated as a curiosity and as an ornamental.

Tomatoes were grown in Virginia by Thomas Jefferson in 1781, but according to report they were almost totally unknown in America as an edible vegetable until after 1834, and it appears that another ten years passed before they began to attain any real popularity. The popular name of the Tomato for a long time was Love Apple, and sometimes it was known as Gold Apple.

Raising Plants. Although the Tomato is usually raised from seeds, it is very easily increased by means of cuttings. Side shoots removed from plants early in the season and planted in sand in a cold frame root readily and may be used to give successive plants that will yield well late in the season.

In the South the seeds may be sown directly out of doors in carefully prepared seedbeds and the young plants lifted from the beds and set directly in the garden. In the North, and wherever earlier plants are needed than can be obtained by sowing outdoors, the seeds are sown in a greenhouse 8-10 weeks before it is expected to transplant the young plants outdoors. Certified seed (seeds certified by governmental authorities as having been collected from plants free of seed-borne disease) only should be sown.

Tomatoes are one of the easiest of vegetable garden crops to grow.

Rather than scatter them broadcast, some growers prefer to sow their Tomato seeds in shallow parallel rows in flats. When this is done, seeds may stand closer together than if broadcast.

When the young Tomato plants have developed their second pair of leaves, they are dug up carefully to avoid excessive breaking of the roots and are transplanted to other flats or individually into small pots.

When sowing indoors, prepare pots, pans or flats (according to the quantity of seeds to be sown) by placing drainage material in their bottoms and filling them with a sifted, rather sandy soil mixture (loam, sand and leaf mold, humus or peat moss in about equal proportions make a good mixture). Water the soil thoroughly with a fine spray and sow the seeds, spacing them about half an inch apart and covering them with soil to about a quarter of an inch.

Keep the newly sown seeds in a temperature of 60-70 degrees; shade them at first, but, as soon as the seedlings emerge from the soil, expose them to full sunshine. Maintain the soil in an evenly moist but not a constantly saturated condition and keep the plants growing in a greenhouse having a night temperature of 60-65 degrees and a daytime temperature about 5-10 degrees higher.

When the young plants have developed their second pair of leaves (the first pair of regular tomato-leaf shape), transplant them to flats, spacing them 2-3 in. apart, or plant them individually in small pots. At this time use a soil consisting of equal parts of loam (topsoil), sand, and leaf mold, humus or peat moss, with bone meal added at the rate of one pound to each bushel of the mixture. Keep the plants growing under the same conditions as before and, about two weeks before they are to be planted in the garden, gradually harden them and accustom them to outdoor conditions.

If set in flats, the young Tomato plants are spaced 2-3 in. apart in fertile, porous soil.

Immediately after they are transplanted, the young Tomato plants are watered with a fine spray and are placed in a warm greenhouse.

This sturdy young Tomato plant was grown in a small pot. It has a healthy root system and is now ready for planting outdoors.

Soil and Location. Tomatoes thrive in any reasonably good garden soil that is well drained. It should be deeply spaded or plowed well before the Tomatoes are planted and, if deficient in humus, it should be enriched by adding compost, leaf mold, peat moss or commercial humus. Manure should be used, if at all, with caution, because excessive nitrogen tends to make the plants produce an overabundance of foliage at the expense of flowers and fruit. A dressing of a fertilizer that analyzes high in phosphate and potash and low in nitrogen may be beneficial; if the soil is fairly rich the addition of organic matter together with a dressing of superphosphate is likely to prove sufficient.

Tomatoes need full sunshine. The earliest crops are likely to be produced on south-facing slopes or in locations that are shaded by a wall or building. Later crops may be had from flat or sloping ground without difficulty.

Planting. Plants for setting out should be sturdy and short-jointed (the leaves comparatively close together on the stems). Tall, weak plants with undersized, yellowish leaves, widely spaced on the stems, are not satisfactory. Wait until the weather is warm and settled before planting; nothing is gained if, after the plants are set out, the weather turns cold and the plants assume a blue or purplish coloring and cease to grow.

The space between plants should vary according to methods of training and cultivation and

Two or three hours before young Tomato plants are removed from their flats to be set outside, the soil in which the plants are growing should be soaked with water.

Near the base of the stake up which the plant is to be trained, a hole is dug with a trowel to accommodate the root ball.

After the plant is set in position the soil is made firm about the roots.

Young, healthy Tomatoes making sturdy growth in the garden.

according to the variety (the more vigorous varieties need more room than others).

If the plants are to sprawl on the ground without staking, and mechanical cultivators are to be used to keep down weeds, as is the practice with commercial growers, the rows should be about 6 ft. apart, and 4 ft. should be allowed between the plants in the rows.

Amateur gardeners who raise only a few Tomato plants will find that it pays to support them off the ground rather than to let them grow without training. If this is done, the proportion of clean, undamaged fruit harvested is higher. The plants may be tied to individual stakes or to a trellis. In the former case a spacing of 2½-3½ ft. between rows and 2-2½ ft. between plants in the rows is sufficient; the closer spacings are adopted if the plants are to be pruned to one stem each, more space being given if each plant is to develop 2-3 stems. Rows of trellis may be spaced 4-6 ft. apart and the plants grown against the trellis about 2½-3 ft. apart. Stakes for Tomatoes should be of good, sound wood at least 2 in. square and long enough to project from the ground 5 or 6 ft. when they are driven in sufficiently far to fasten them securely. Trellises are usually made 4 or 5 ft. high.

When planting, the holes should be made large enough to accommodate the roots without crowding and the plants set deeper than they previously were (because Tomato plants root freely from the portions of the stems buried beneath the soil, they may be planted down to the

As the young plants grow they must be carefully tied to their stakes.

These Tomato plants, each staked individually, are beginning to bear fruits.

In this garden a framework of metal pipes and wires supports the stakes on which Tomatoes are trained. The stakes lean inwards.

first leaf). After they are planted, each plant should be well watered.

Freedom from weeds is important in the cultivation of Tomatoes. The ground in which they are planted either should be mulched, or should be kept stirred to a depth of about 1 in. with a hoe or cultivator. Keeping the ground free of weeds with a hoe or cultivator in the early stages of growth and applying a mulch after the plants are well established and at the beginning of really hot, summer weather is the best practice.

Tying and Pruning. Plants that are grown on stakes and trellises will need attention in the matter of tying at regular intervals throughout the summer. Do not tie stems so tightly that they are likely to be strangled by the ties as the stems grow and thicken. Use soft string or strips of old sheeting or other soft material for tying.

Pruning, or the removal of unwanted shoots, is an important task with Tomatoes trained to supports. Shoots that are to be removed should be taken off when they are quite small and, as Tomatoes grow fast during favorable weather, this work should receive attention at least once a week. Once the number of main shoots that are to be allowed to grow has been decided upon, no others should be allowed to develop, and all laterals or side shoots should be pinched out as soon as they are big enough to be taken hold of easily between the finger and thumb.

When the main shoots reach the tops of their supports, which should be when the summer is well advanced, and any further fruit set will not have time to develop and ripen (or even reach while still green a size of use for making chutney or other conserves), pinch out or cut off the tops of the main shoots; this tends to concentrate the energies of the plant in plumping up and ripening the fruits already set on the vines. When the lower fruits begin to ripen some growers cut away a portion of each of the lower leaves to make for better air circulation and to admit more sun to hasten ripening. This should be done with caution, however, for if too much foliage is removed the fruits will not attain their largest size and the growth of the plants may be checked.

Watering Is Important. For the best results, Tomato plants should never suffer from lack of moisture at any time. Excessive dryness is very likely to cause a physiological disturbance called blossom-end rot, which shows as large blackened areas surrounding that end of the ripe fruit which is not attached to the stock. Cracking of the fruits is caused by the availability of ample supplies of moisture following a very dry period. The best way of avoiding this trouble is to make sure that the plants never suffer from dryness.

Unwanted lateral or side shoots should be pinched out while they are yet small.

Harvesting. When the fruits are ripe they should be picked promptly and stored in a cool, dark place; under these conditions they keep better than if left on the vines. In hot, damp weather the fruits will be firmer if they are picked slightly before they are fully ripe and are then allowed to ripen at room temperature indoors.

At the end of the season all green fruits should be picked before hard frost. The greenest may be used for making conserves. Those approaching ripeness may be stored in shallow boxes or trays in a cool but frostproof shed, cellar, attic or garage, where they will ripen gradually and provide usable fruits over a period of many weeks. Fruits ripened in this way lack the flavor and quality of those that are vine-ripened, but, even so, are likely to be superior to Tomatoes shipped from long distances and sold in stores at that season. An alternative method is to pull up the entire vines just before hard frost and suspend them from the ceiling of the storage place; the fruits then ripen on the vines and are, perhaps, of a little better quality than those picked green and ripened in trays or boxes.

Greenhouse Culture. A greenhouse in which a night temperature of 55-60 degrees is maintained, where the day temperature is a few degrees higher, and where there is full sunshine makes it possible to have fresh Tomatoes from November until the fruits from outdoor plants are available the following summer. The Tomato plants may be grown in large pots or in soil beds. Each plant should be restricted to a single stem by pinching out all side shoots when they are quite small. If grown in beds or benches, the plants may be spaced 12-15 in. apart; if the plants are potted, pots measuring 9-10 in. in diameter will be large enough for the final potting. The plants should be neatly tied to stakes or to wires or strings stretched tightly between supports.

For greenhouse culture it is usually wisest to select a variety especially recommended for that purpose. Such kinds, sometimes called forcing varieties, are offered in seedsmen's catalogues. The sowing of the seed and general care of the young plants are the same as previously described for raising plants for outdoor planting.

To secure fall and early winter crops the seeds should be sown in July; to have plants that will crop in late winter and spring the seeds should be sown in September or October.

In order to ensure a setting of fruit in greenhouses it is necessary to pollinate the flowers or to treat them with one of the special hormone sprays which are sold for the purpose of causing Tomatoes to set fruit. Pollination is effected by gently shaking the plants during the middle of each warm, dry day at a time when the air in the greenhouse is fairly dry. An alternative method is to take a soft camel's-hair brush and gently stroke it across each open flower each warm, bright day.

Varieties. There are a large number of varieties of Tomatoes offered by seedsmen, and new ones are introduced yearly. Some are more suited for one section of North America than others, some are more adaptable for a particular purpose than others. The best commercial varieties are not necessarily the best for the home gardener, who does not have to consider problems connected with shipping and marketing. Certain varieties, indicated in catalogues, are resistant to wilt disease; only these should be attempted if the soil has grown wilt-infected Tomatoes previously.

Tomato varieties are divided into two chief groups, earlies and maincrops. The former are

Tomato variety Yellow Pear produces small fruits that are both decorative and edible.

the only kinds suitable for planting outdoors in most of Canada and in the northernmost parts of the United States; these are used also to provide early crops elsewhere. Maincrop varieties come into bearing a little later than earlies and continue to produce well until frost.

Among early varieties the following are recommended: Earliana, Fordhook Hybrid, John Baer, Manalee, Pritchard, Valiant and Victor. Good maincrop varieties include: Burpee Bigboy, Burpee Hybrid, Homestead, Kopiah, Manalucie, Marglobe, Queens, Rutgers and Stokesdale. Among yellow-fruited varieties Jubilee and Sunray are highly rated. Oxheart and Ponderosa are pink-fruited varieties that bear very large fruits. Small-fruited varieties that yield fruits suitable for garnishing as well as eating are Red Cherry, Red Pear, Yellow Pear and Yellow Plum.

TOMATO, TREE. Cyphomandra betacea, which see.

TOMENTOSE. A term used in describing leaves whose surface is covered with matted, feltlike hairs.

TOOLS. It is said that a good workman never criticizes his tools, but it is certain that good tools lighten the labor of gardening. Those of the greatest importance are the spade, fork, hoe, rake, shovel, handfork, trowel, wheelbarrow, roller, mowing machine, broom and shears. If they are left in the open, exposed to all weathers, garden tools soon deteriorate. After use, they should be cleaned, metal parts should be rubbed down with an oily rag, and then the tools should be stored under cover. Implements with moving parts, such as lawn mowers, should be oiled regularly. Tools with cutting blades such as hoes and shears should be kept sharp.

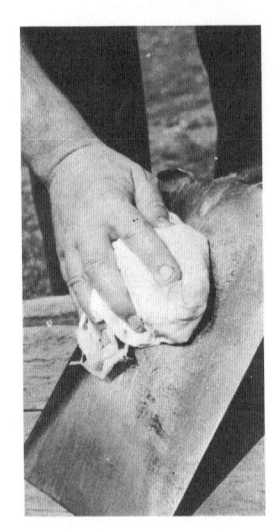

Dirty tools like this spade should be wiped clean. A piece of burlap is handy for this purpose. The tool will last longer if, before it is put away, all metal parts are wiped over with a slightly oily rag.

A collection of tools like these—together with such accessories as wheelbarrow, hose, sprayer and sprinkler—is needed in larger gardens.

To keep mower blades clean and sharp, rub them with a swab dipped in oil after each use of the machine.

Implements such as lawn mowers, lawn sweepers and wheelbarrows should be kept oiled to reduce friction.

Edge tools such as this scuffle hoe are easier to use if their blades are kept sharp.

TOOTHACHE TREE. Zanthoxylum Clava-Herculis, which see.

TOOTHWORT. Dentaria, which see.

TOPATO. A name applied to a plant produced by grafting a Tomato on a Potato or a Potato on a Tomato. The name Potomato is also used for the same combinations.

TOP-DRESSING. This is a term used by gardeners to describe the application, to the soil surface, of any material, the chief purpose of which is to supply nutrients or to improve the physical condition of the soil. It differs from mulching in that the chief purpose of the latter is to conserve moisture or to protect the plants from cold, drying or other adverse conditions. Nevertheless, the two procedures do overlap somewhat; mulching is often done with a material (such as compost and littery manure) which provides nutrients as well as protects, and top-dressing is often done with materials which serve to conserve moisture and to protect the plants from harmful environmental conditions as well as provide nutrients.

Top-dressing may be applied both to plants growing outdoors and to those cultivated in pots, tubs and benches in greenhouses and to house plants as well.

Lawns greatly benefit from annual top-dressing.

Lawns and rock gardens should be top-dressed each spring with an application of sifted soil or humus with which a suitable fertilizer has been thoroughly mixed. Pot plants which are not to be repotted at the beginning of their growing season usually benefit from a top-dressing of a rich soil mixture. As much of the old topsoil as can be loosened from the surface without damaging the roots should be removed before the top-dressing is applied.

TOPIARY WORK. This is the term used to describe the art of training shrubs and small trees, by repeated pruning and shearing, to assume odd and fanciful forms. In a sense topiary work is sculpture. Sometimes shrubs are cut in the forms of animals, birds and human beings; more often geometrical forms such as cubes, spheres, pyramids and columns are favored by topiarists.

Topiary work is an art of very ancient origin. According to Pliny it was invented by one Chaeus Martius, and even in Pliny's day the art was so advanced that ships, hunting scenes, etc., were shown in clipped evergreens. During the Dark Ages the art was probably carried on by the monks, but there is no definite proof of this.

The illustrations of medieval topiary work are interesting, particularly the miniature topiary work practiced on dwarfed shrubs growing in pots. There is an excellent illustration of miniature topiary work in the fifteenth-century manuscript of the Romance of Renaud de Montauban. In Elizabethan and Stuart times topiary work was very popular. Bacon, in his essay "Of Gardens," condemned the art as childish, but he added that he liked "pretty pyramids" and "fair columns."

Yew, Rosemary, and Privet were the shrubs commonly clipped into different shapes. Parkinson, in his *Paradisus* (1629), states that Privet was "cut, led and drawn into what forme one will either of beasts, birds, or men, armed or otherwise." Barnaby Googe, in his *Four Bookes of Husbandry* (1577), says Rosemary was cut by women into "the fashion of a cat, peacock, or such things as they fancy."

William Lawson, in his *New Orchard and Garden* (1618), depicts topiary work in the

Boxwood used as topiary work in a Virginia garden.

Two good examples of topiary formed of Yew.

form of a man with a drawn sword and a prancing horse. "Your Gardener," he says, "can frame your lesser wood to the shape of men armed in the field ready to give battle; of swift-running grey-hounds or of well-scented and true-running Hounds to chase the Deer or hunt the Hare. This kind of hunting shall not waste your Corn nor much your Coin." In the late seventeenth century the art was carried to excess and gardens were overcrowded with specimens of topiary work.

A most famous topiary work is at Levens Hall in England, where the garden was made in the seventeenth century when the place was owned by Colonel James Grahame, Keeper of the Privy Purse to James II. He retired there on the accession of William III, and the garden was laid out by Beaumont, a Frenchman, who had worked under the great landscape architect Le Notre.

In the early years of the eighteenth century the famous English writers Pope and Addison poured ridicule on the excessive display of topiary work. Pope's witty catalogue of topiary work (*The Guardian,* No. 173) is well known. Addison, in his essay "The Pleasures of a Garden," in *The Spectator,* June 25, 1712, wrote: "Our British gardeners, instead of humoring nature, love to deviate from it as much as possible. Our Trees rise in Cones, Globes and Pyramids. We see the mark of the scissors upon every Plant and Bush. I do not know whether I am singular in my Opinion but, for my own part, I would rather look upon a tree in all its Luxuriancy and Diffusion of Boughs and Branches, than when it is thus cut and trimmed into a Mathematical Figure."

In spite of the contempt of the landscape school, topiary work persisted in many small gardens and it is in such gardens in Great Britain that some of the finest specimens of the art may still be seen.

Topiary finds little place in contemporary American gardens, but gardeners sometimes exercise their fancy by clipping Privets, Yews and other plants into globes, pyramids and occasionally more elaborate shapes.

TOP-WORK. A synonymous term for topgraft. See Grafting.

TORCH LILY. See Kniphofia.

TORENIA—*Wishbone Flower* (Tore′nia). These beautiful plants include both annuals and perennials, but in gardens are ordinarily grown as annuals. They belong to the Figwort family, Scrophulariaceae, and are found wild in tropical Asia and Africa. The name commemorates Olaf Toren, who discovered one of the kinds in China. Of the several kinds introduced into cultivation, only two have become popular. These are T. Fournieri and T. flava (Baillonii).

Beautiful Flowering Plant. The Torenias grow about 12 in. in height and have slender, four-angled, light green, herbaceous stems,

The flowers of Torenia Fournieri are a striking violet and pale mauve.

clothed with opposite oval leaves, 1 in. in length. By regular stopping (pinching), plants cultivated in pots are made to produce numerous upright stems which bear large, two-lipped flowers in great profusion. Plants grown in outdoor flower beds do not require stopping. The flowers of T. Fournieri are violet, blue and pale mauve, T. Fournieri variety alba has white flowers each with a yellow blotch, and those of T. flava are yellow with purple throats.

When to Sow Seeds. To produce plants for use in the outdoor garden, seeds are sown in March or April, in a greenhouse having a temperature of 50 or 55 degrees. Well-drained seed pans or flats are filled with a finely sifted soil mixture of equal parts of peat, loam, leaf mold and sand. This is moistened and allowed to drain before the seeds are scattered on the surface, and covered with a slight layer of soil. A pane of glass is laid over the pan, whch is set in a greenhouse, minimum temperature 55 degrees. To have plants for winter flowering in the greenhouse the same procedure is followed, but the seeds are sown in August or September.

When two pairs of leaves have formed, the seedlings are potted singly in small pots or are set 2 in. apart in a flat of light, rich soil. When the plants are to be grown throughout in pots the former method gives better results. From the small pots they are transferred to 4-in. pots and later on to 5- or 6-in. pots, in which they produce their flowers. When the plants are established in the small pots, the tips of the shoots are removed and the side shoots are similarly treated later on.

To prevent the plants from becoming "drawn" or leggy, they are exposed to good light; shade is needed from the fiercest rays of the sun only. As they make progress, they are gradually given cooler treatment and, when coming into flower, they are set in a cool greenhouse or conservatory. At this stage a weekly application of dilute liquid fertilizer is beneficial. When in flower, they provide an attractive display for many weeks.

For Hanging Baskets. These plants can also be grown in wire hanging baskets. The baskets are lined with moss and filled with rich soil. Small plants from seed flats are inserted around the sides of the basket and a few are planted on the top. The soil is then well watered and the planted baskets are hung in a shaded position and are syringed regularly until the plants become established; subsequent treatment is the same as that given to plants that are grown in pots.

Torenia Fournieri is attractive when grown as a pot plant.

For Planting Outdoors. Torenias are especially valuable because they are among the few annuals that bloom well in part shade. They stand heat well and in the deep South are used with great success as a substitute for Pansies. They flower for a very long season.

In the South these plants may be raised from seeds sown directly out of doors, in a finely prepared soil, in early spring, or they may be sown early indoors in the way described above and the young plants later set in the open garden. In the North the latter plan is preferred because plants raised from seeds sown directly outdoors do not bloom until late in the season.

Torenias thrive best in a rich soil that is well supplied with organic matter and that is never allowed to become excessively dry. The plants should be spaced 8-9 in. apart.

TORREYA—*California Nutmeg, Stinking Cedar* (Torre′ya; Torr′eya). Evergreen trees and shrubs, natives of North America and eastern Asia. T. nucifera is the hardiest kind; it survives in sheltered places in New England. The other kinds are suitable for the South and other mild localities only.

In appearance, Torreyas most closely resemble the Cephalotaxus, and have rather similar fruits, which in outward appearance resemble acorns. The leaves may be aromatic or pungent; they are 2-3 in. long, sharp-pointed, and dark green in color.

Male and female flowers may be borne on different branches of the same tree, but are usually on separate trees. Torreya belongs to the Yew family, Taxaceae, and the name commemorates John Torrey, an American botanist of the last century.

Propagation by Seeds. The Torreyas are most satisfactory when raised from seeds, which should be sown singly in small pots of sandy soil in a greenhouse in spring. When large enough to handle, the seedlings are placed in a cold frame and eventually planted in a nursery bed until a permanent place is found for them. They should be planted finally in moist, but well-drained, loamy soil, where the atmospheric conditions are rather moist. No regular pruning is necessary.

The Chief Kinds. T. nucifera, a Japanese tree up to 75 ft. high in Japan, forms a large bush or small tree in the North but grows larger in milder climates. Its lance-shaped leaves, an inch or so long, are sharp-pointed. The seeds are wholesome and are eaten in Japan. T. californica, the California Nutmeg, may grow 90 ft. high in California, with a trunk 9 ft. in girth. In less favored climates it may develop as a large bush. Its leaves are 1¼-3 in. long. It is one of the most attractive kinds.

T. taxifolia, the Stinking Cedar, is a tree up to 40 ft. high in Florida, where it grows on limestone soils and in swamps. Its leaves are malodorous when crushed. T. grandis, a Chinese tree, 60-80 ft. high, is rare in cultivation.

TOUCH-ME-NOT. Impatiens, which see.

TOWNSENDIA (Townsen′dia). A small group of hardy herbaceous plants belonging to the Daisy family, Compositae, and native to western North America. The name honors David Townsend, a Pennsylvania botanist.

These plants are dwarf in habit, and extremely ornamental in the rock garden, where they should be given light, well-drained gritty loam or scree, and a fully sunny position. They may be increased by seeds sown in spring in a pan of light loam, sand and leaf mold kept in the cold frame, or by division of the roots in early summer.

Townsendia exscapa, also known as T. sericea and T. Wilcoxiana, forms a compact tuft of narrow, rather silky, gray leaves with almost stemless flowers like large Asters; they are white, pink or mauve, in June. The whole plant is only about 1 in. high.

Townsendia grandiflora, from South Dakota to New Mexico, grows 2-6 in. tall, with rosettes of long, narrow leaves broadening at their ends, and in June bears numerous, fine, violet, daisy-like flowers, of large size for so small a plant.

TRACE ELEMENTS. In addition to the chief nutrient elements that plants take from the soil in appreciable quantities, such as nitrogen, phosphorus and potassium, it is now well established that they need, for their well-being and successful growth, a number of others in exceedingly minute quantities. In most soils these so-called trace elements are present in sufficient amounts, but this is not always the case and, should one or more be missing, the harmful effect on the quality of the plants can be serious (see Physiological Diseases under Pests and Diseases). Examples of necessary trace elements are boron, copper, zinc, manganese and magnesium.

State Agricultural Experiment Stations are glad to advise gardeners, upon request, whether any trace elements are likely to be missing from their soils.

TRACHELIUM CAERULEUM—*Throatwort* (Trache′lium). This tender herbaceous perennial is valuable for cultivation in pots for blooming in summer. It produces large, cloudlike heads of tiny mauve flowers. There is also a white variety album, but the mauve form is more popular.

Trachelium belongs to the Campanula family, Campanulaceae. The name is derived from *trachelos,* a neck, and refers to the plant's supposed value in treating diseases of the throat; hence also the common name Throatwort.

Sowing Seeds in Spring. Trachelium caeruleum can be propagated by cuttings, but this method is rarely adopted. Seeds germinate very readily and the seedlings quickly develop into flowering plants. Seeds may be sown in February or March to yield plants that will bloom in late summer, or they may be sown in July to flower the following summer. A greenhouse having a temperature of 50-55 degrees is required for early sowings.

Trachelium caeruleum raised in pots and planted out for summer display in a garden. This plant has numerous small flowers arranged in large heads.

The seeds are sown in well-drained flowerpots or seed pans filled with a sandy soil. The soil is moistened by standing the seed pan or pot in water until moisture rises from below to the soil surface. Glass is then laid over the pot or shallow pan, which is placed in a warm greenhouse. When the seedlings are 2 in. high, they are set, 2 in. apart, in flats of light soil and, when growing freely, are potted separately in 3-in. pots.

When well rooted, the seedlings are transferred to 5-in. pots; extra-vigorous plants may be repotted in 7-in. pots, in which they produce their flowers. No stopping (pinching) is required, as the plants produce larger heads of flowers when grown on single stems. They must be grown in a cool, airy atmosphere and fully exposed to the light to keep them sturdy. They require watering generously. The best compost for these later pottings consists of two parts of loam and one part of leaf mold and well-decayed manure, and a generous sprinkling of sand in addition.

Sowing Seeds in Summer. When treated as biennials (by sowing seeds in July–August), the seedlings are potted in 5-in pots, in which they remain until the following March. They are then potted in 7-in. and finally 10-in. pots, and so form much larger specimens than those raised in spring. Plants treated as biennials may also be established out of doors in summer, either in the flower beds or in the perennial border. A sunny position and light, well-drained soil are required.

In very mild localities Trachelium may be grown entirely out of doors.

The chief kind is T. caeruleum, mauve, 2 ft.; T. caeruleum album has white flowers.

TRACHELOSPERMUM (Trachelosper′mum). Attractive free-flowering, evergreen, tender climbing plants which belong to the Dogbane family, Apocynaceae. T. jasminoides (Rhynchospermum jasminoides), the Star Jasmine or Confederate Jasmine, which was introduced into cultivation from China in 1846, is the principal kind in cultivation. It is a favorite outdoor vine in the far South. A woody climber, it grows about 15 ft. high and has ovate-lanceolate, smooth, evergreen leaves. In summer it bears loose terminal trusses (clusters) of white flowers.

[13–4a]
Water Lily Tulip
(Tulipa Kauffmaniana)

[13–4]
Late Double Tulips

[13–4c]
Darwin Tulips

[13–4b]
Tulipa Fosteriana hybrid,
Red Emperor

[13—5]
Torenia Fournieri alba

[13—5a]
Spiderwort
(Tradescantia virginiana)

[13—5b]
Speedwell
(Veronica maritima subsessilis)

[13—5c]
Speedwell
(Veronica spicata nana)

The flowers are salver-shaped, with slender tubes at the base and five twisted petals. The name Trachelospermum is derived from *trachelos*, a neck, and *sperma*, a seed, and refers to the shape of the seeds.

A Climbing Plant for the Greenhouse. T. jasminoides is a very ornamental plant for a greenhouse with a minimum winter temperature of 45 degrees. It should be grown in a large pot or tub, the shoots being trained to wires fixed to the greenhouse roof. The pots must be well drained and filled with a compost of equal parts of peat, loam and leaf mold and a liberal quantity of coarse sand. Planting or potting is done in March.

Very little pruning is required, extra-vigorous shoots being slightly shortened, if necessary, after the flowers have faded. Shade from strong sunlight is necessary. The floor and benches should be wetted down to maintain a moist atmosphere and the foliage syringed daily except when the plants are in flower.

How to Take Cuttings. Young plants are easily grown from cuttings. Short side shoots are taken off in spring or summer, and are inserted in a propagating case with a bottom heat of 70-75 degrees. When well rooted, they are potted separately in 3-in. pots and then in 5-in. pots, and finally planted in large pots or tubs, as mentioned earlier.

The principal kind is T. jasminoides (Rhynchospermum jasminoides), 15 ft., white, fragrant, summer. T. asiaticum, a native of Japan and Korea, has yellowish flowers and broader leaves than T. jasminoides. T. fragrans, from India, is a tall climber with white flowers. T. jasminoides variety variegatum has its leaves handsomely variegated with creamy-white.

TRACHYCARPUS (Trachycar'pus). Palms from Japan, China and the Himalayas. T. Fortunei, the Windmill Palm, is the hardiest. In its native habitat it grows up to 50 ft. in height, but it is slow growing. The stem is upright, round, and clothed with coarse brown fibers formed from the decaying leafstalks. At the apex there is a large cluster of fan-shaped, evergreen leaves, each 2-4 ft. in width. The long, slender leafstalks are prickly-edged and, from the axils of those near the tip of the stem, large panicles of yellow flowers are produced in summer. The flowers are unisexual (male and female in different flowers). The female flowers are less ornamental than the male, and are followed by blue-black berries. The name Trachycarpus is derived from *trachys*, rough, and *carpa*, a fruit, and refers to the seed coats.

Trachelospermum jasminoides, a fragrant-flowered vine suitable for subtropical climates and for greenhouse culture.

A Hardy Palm. This Palm withstands many degrees of frost and succeeds outdoors as far north as North Carolina along the East Coast and to Oregon on the West Coast. Loamy soil suits it best, but is not absolutely necessary. A poorer soil can be made suitable by adding peat moss, compost or decayed manure.

Planting should be done in spring and the soil kept moist afterwards. Near the northern limits of their range of cultivation, for the first few winters these plants should be protected by being wrapped in burlap or other suitable material, but once they are well established no protection is needed. Established plants need little attention beyond an occasional soaking of the soil with water in dry weather.

Cultivation in Pots. These Palms are too large for cultivation in ordinary greenhouses, but in large conservatories they make very imposing specimens. They are set in large pots or wooden tubs. A compost of two parts of loam, with one part of leaf mold or peat moss and a liberal sprinkling of sand is used for potting. Very little damping, syringing, or shading is required. The soil should be watered freely during summer, moderately in the winter. Propagation is effected by detaching the suckers and potting them in spring, or by planting seeds.

The principal kind is T. Fortunei (Chamaerops excelsa). This, the Windmill Palm, is often misnamed T. excelsus in gardens. Another is T. Martianus, a native of the Himalayas and adjacent territory, which is more tender and is suitable for planting outdoors only where little frost is experienced. It grows about 9 ft. high and is similar to T. Fortunei.

TRACHYMENE CAERULEA—*Blue Laceflower* (Trachym'ene; Trachyme'ne). T. caerulea, the only kind worth cultivating, is a pretty annual. It is suitable for growing in pots for decorating the greenhouse and in beds and benches in greenhouses to produce cut flowers, or it may be planted out of doors in summer. It grows 2 ft. in height, has hairy stems and finely divided leaves. Each stem is terminated by an umbel (which see), 2-3 in. in diameter, of small, blue flowers.

Trachymene is a native of Australia and belongs to the Parsley or Carrot family, Umbelliferae. The name is derived from *trachys,* rough, and *hymen,* a membrane, and refers to the rough seed coats.

Treatment as an Outdoor Annual. The seeds are sown in a well-drained pot or pan of light soil in March, in a greenhouse, temperature 50 degrees. When large enough to handle, the seedlings are set 1½ in. apart in another pan or flat of light soil. When established, they are gradually hardened off and planted out of doors in May. A sunny position and light, well-drained soil are necessary. The seedlings are kept moist until well rooted and the stems are supported with twiggy sticks.

When well grown, the plants produce a succession of flowers and make a bright display for the remainder of the summer in regions that are not subject to very torrid weather. Where summers are very warm, however, the plants are likely to fail when really hot weather arrives.

An alternative method is to sow the seeds directly outdoors in spring and then thin out the seedlings to 6-8 in. apart.

As a Greenhouse Plant. The seeds are sown in a well-drained pot of light, finely sifted soil. When the seedlings have formed their first pair of seed leaves, they are set, 1½ in. apart, in a pan of light soil, and watered and shaded until established. They are then potted separately in 3-in. pots, or three plants are set in a 4-in. pot. When established in these pots, they are repotted in 5- or 6-in. pots, in which they produce their flowers.

Instead of being kept in pots, the young plants may be set out 6-8 in. apart in solid soil beds or in soil benches in the greenhouse.

When grown in a greenhouse, Trachymene requires an abundance of fresh air at all times and should be given full sunshine. The plants require careful watering until well rooted in their final pots, when the soil must be kept moist. After flowering they are discarded.

The chief kind is T. caerulea, 2 ft., blue. This plant is also known as Didiscus caeruleus.

TRACHYSTEMON ORIENTALE (Trachyste'mon). A hardy herbaceous plant, closely related to the common Borage, and belonging to the Borage family, Boraginaceae. It has been incorrectly called Italian Borage, and different botanists have at various times given the plant the generic names of Borago, Nordmannia and Psilostemon. The name is from *trachys,* rough, and *stemon,* stamen.

Trachystemon is an attractive spring-flowering, herbaceous plant; it is wild in Asia Minor. It grows 1-2 ft. high.

Trachystemon orientale (Nordmannia cordifolia), the only kind, is one of the earliest herbaceous flowers. It has hairy stems and leaves; the first ones are cordate and the larger, later leaves are ovate-lanceolate. In March and April it sends up elegant panicles of purplish-blue flowers, the segments of which recurve at the tips, showing a conical tuft of white stamens.

This plant thrives in ordinary garden ground; while the soil may, with advantage, be dug deeply, it should not be heavily fertilized, as this usually results in very coarse leaf growth.

Propagation is by division of the roots in fall, which is also the best time to lift and transplant the roots. Seeds are sometimes procurable, and if these are sown in a sheltered place outdoors in April the resulting plants will

The large-leaved Trachystemon orientale is a handsome hardy herbaceous plant. It produces panicles of purple-blue, borage-like flowers in early spring.

flower satisfactorily in eleven or twelve months.

Because of its rather coarse leaves and early flowering, Trachystemon is not suitable for a prominent position in the flower border, but it is a most useful early-flowering subject for the shrub border, the half-shady border, the wild garden and the waterside.

TRADESCANTIA—*Spiderwort* (Tradescant'-ia). Hardy and tender perennial flowering and ornamental foliage plants. The hardy kinds are natives of the United States and the tender kinds grow wild chiefly in Mexico, Peru and Guatemala. The name commemorates John Tradescant, who was gardener to King Charles I of England. Tradescantia belongs to the Spiderwort family, Commelinaceae.

The Hardy Kinds. The hardy kinds cultivated in gardens are varieties and hybrids of T. virginiana, the Common Spiderwort, which is native from Maine to South Dakota and Arkansas. This species, as it grows naturally, is 2-3 ft. tall and has blue or purple flowers. Improved

The hardy perennial Common Spiderwort, Tradescantia virginiana.

have larger flowers in a wider color range. Among the most popular of these varieties are Osprey, white; Iris Pritchard, white, tinged violet; James Stratton, deep blue; James C. Weguelin, porcelain-blue; Pauline, orchid-mauve; Purple Dome, brilliant purple.

These Spiderworts are well suited for planting in perennial beds and borders and in clumps in wild gardens. They are extremely easy to grow. A soil that is fertile and fairly moist suits them best and they appreciate a little light shade from the strongest sunshine. Division, in spring or early fall, is the means of propagation.

Flowers of the Common Spiderwort, Tradescantia virginiana.

When in full bloom the hardy Spiderworts are very beautiful. The individual flowers are short-lived but a succession is kept up over a long period. One fault is that, after flowering, the stems and foliage die down and give to the plants an untidy appearance.

A number of native species other than T. virginiana may occasionally be brought into cultivation and have some value as subjects for planting in wild gardens. Chief among these are T. bracteata, 1 ft., blue or reddish (or rose-pink in the variety rosea); T. humilis, pale blue or pink; T. micrantha, a prostrate creeper, rose-purple; T. occidentalis, 2½ ft., blue or reddish; T. subaspera (pilosa), 3 ft., blue or white.

The Wandering Jew. The most popular tender Spiderwort is the one called Wandering Jew (T. fluminensis). This is cultivated as a house plant and in greenhouses and outdoors in the far South, where it is naturalized. It is often planted under greenhouse benches.

The Wandering Jew roots with great ease from cuttings and grows in any fairly good soil that is well drained. The soil should be kept always moist and specimens that have filled their pots with roots benefit from feeding regularly

A variegated-leaved variety of Tradescantia fluminensis.

with dilute liquid fertilizers. Some shade from very strong sun is desirable and the plants grow well in considerable shade. To induce branching and bushiness the tips of the shoots of young specimens should be pinched out occasionally.

T. fluminensis has white flowers and, in its normal form, has plain green leaves, the leaves being this color both above and on their undersides. Varieties known as variegata, albo-vittata and aurea have their leaves variously striped with white or yellow. It is important not to confuse this Wandering Jew with Zebrina pendula, known by the same common name. In the Zebrina (which see) the leaves are dark red or purple beneath and the flowers are pink. Yet another group of plants that is likely to be confused with these is Setcreasea. See Setcreasea.

T. albiflora albo-vittata has beautiful bluish-green leaves striped and margined with white. T. albiflora laekensis Rainbow has leaves striped with green, white and purplish rose. Both of these kinds have white flowers.

Tradescantia Blossfeldiana is a trailing kind that thrives in sunny window gardens and greenhouses and, in mild climates, out of doors. It has small clusters of pink or lavender-pink flowers.

An Erect Grower. Tradescantia Reginae is a very handsome kind from Peru. It thrives best in a warm, moist greenhouse but also has value as a house plant. Its stems grow erect and are furnished with lance-shaped leaves that measure to about 6 in. long. They are purpled-red on their undersides, and above are green with a purplish-crimson area at the leaf center and silvery areas at the edges. The leaves on the young, new shoots are more intensely marked than they are when they are older.

Tradescantia Reginae needs a rich, moist soil, a temperature between 60 and 70 degrees and shade from strong direct sunshine. It is readily propagated by cuttings planted in sand, vermiculite or other rooting medium.

Some Other Tender Spiderworts. T. Blossfeldiana, a native of the Argentine, is a creeping kind suitable for growing in window gardens and greenhouses. The plant, except for the upper surfaces of the leaves, is covered with long,

This low-growing plant with handsomely marked leaves is Tradescantia fuscata, a native of tropical Brazil.

whitish hairs. The stems are deep purple, the flowers pink or lavender towards the tips of the petals, white at their centers. This plant thrives in a temperature of 45-60 degrees. T. Blossfeldiana variety variegata has cream-striped leaves.

T. fuscata has a short, brown-hairy stem, or sometimes none at all, and leaves 6-8 in. long covered with conspicuous crimson hairs. The leaves are green above with a silvery stripe down the center of each and are deep crimson beneath. This handsome tropical plant is a native of Brazil and adjacent territory. It requires the same culture as T. Reginae. It is easily increased by division. This Tradescantia is also known as Siderasis fuscata and Pyrrheima Loddigesii.

T. navicularis, from Peru, is a distinct and interesting kind for growing in a window garden or in a greenhouse. It thrives under drier conditions than the other kinds mentioned here and prospers under the kind of cultivation that suits Cacti and other succulents. A temperature of 50-60 degrees is satisfactory and shade from sun is unnecessary. An important point in grow-

Graceful, and lovely both in foliage and flower, is Tradescantia Warscewicziana, a kind sometimes called Spironema Warscewiczianum.

A Cotoneaster trained as an espalier against a wall.

ing this plant is to keep it quite dry during its resting period from December to March. This kind is a tight-growing creeper. Its flowers are pink.

T. Warscewicziana is now known as Spironema Warscewiczianum, which see.

TRAGOPOGON. The botanical name of Salsify or Vegetable Oyster (Tragopogon porrifolius). Its cultivation is dealt with under the heading of Salsify, which see.

TRAILING ARBUTUS. Epigaea repens, which see.

TRAINING. The term training, as applied to plants, refers to growing them in some more or less formal manner and is accomplished by pinching, pruning and tying the stems and branches into place.

A simple form of training, not always thought of as such, is the pinching out of the tips of the shoots of young plants, as is often done with Ageratums, Coleus, Heliotropes, Snapdragons and many other kinds, to encourage branching and bushiness. Sometimes, as with Coleus and Chrysanthemums, the branches that result from the first pinch are later pinched themselves, and this may be repeated several times to secure plants of the desired shape and bushiness.

Young trees and shrubs are trained in their early years to form well-spaced and structurally strong trunk and branch systems. This is done by careful pruning (see Pruning).

Trees, shrubs and vines grown against walls, or on trellises or other supports are trained by arranging their branches so that the available space is covered uniformly and each branch receives adequate light. Fruit trees, especially dwarf kinds, may be similarly trained as espaliers.

Geraniums, Heliotropes, Lantanas, Fuchsias, Genistas, Chrysanthemums, Jasminums, Bay Trees and many other plants are often trained to standard (tree) form by encouraging a single stem to develop to a height of 2-6 ft. (all side shoots are pinched off this stem while they are yet small), then pinching out the tip of the

The branches of these young espaliered Apple trees are trained by careful pruning and tying to wires.

Espaliered Apple trees that have been developed by appropriate training over a period of more than thirty years.

These Apple trees trained as espaliers are in full bloom.

Grapes are trained to cover these ornamental fences at Colonial Williamsburg, Virginia.

main stem and allowing branches to develop only from near its top. These branches are, in turn, pinched to develop a bushy head or crown.

Chrysanthemums are trained in various other forms by tying their stems to a wire framework as they grow, and as "cascades" by training the branches to stakes set at an angle in the pots and later removing the stakes and allowing the

Many kinds of plants can be trained as standards (in treelike form). This grafted specimen of Forsythia viridissima bronxensis has been trained in this interesting form.

A charming garden of Boxwood, the result of training by shearing regularly.

stems to hang downwards over the side of the pot.

Many vines are trained into formal shapes by tying their stems to wire frameworks, stakes or other supports. Among plants that can be so grown are English Ivy, Akebia, Bougainvillea, Dipladenia, Thunbergia, Passiflora, Trachelospermum, Stephanotis and Clerodendrum.

Many evergreens and some deciduous trees and shrubs are trained into formal shapes by clipping or shearing. When the shapes so attained are fanciful, the art of training is known as topiary. See Topiary Work.

TRANSPLANTING. This term refers to lifting plants and replanting them elsewhere. Because the operation normally involves the destruction of a proportion of roots, certain precautions must be taken to ensure success. If too many of the roots are destroyed in relation to the amount of leaves the plant is carrying (or

By frequent shearing, hedges of Yew, Boxwood and some other evergreens may be trained to maintain interesting patterns such as this.

Transplanting Lettuce seedlings with a trowel. The young plants should be well watered with a fine spray immediately after they are planted.

A depression or saucer should be left around newly transplanted trees and this should be filled with water two or three times as soon as planting is finished.

will shortly carry) serious harm usually results.

To guard against this, it is advisable to transplant many kinds of plants while they are dormant or nearly so; thus early spring, and just before the leaves drop naturally in fall, are favored seasons for moving perennial plants, trees and shrubs from one location to another. When transplanting these, as many of the roots as can be preserved should be retained and every care taken to see that they do not become dry at any time.

Evergreens, except very small propagations (baby plants) should always be moved with a good ball of soil firmly attached to their roots; deciduous (leaf-losing) trees and shrubs may be moved with a ball of soil or, if dormant, bare-rooted.

Young leafy plants of annuals, biennials, perennials and vegetables are usually transplanted from pots, flats, cold frames or outdoor seedbeds while they are in full growth. They should be thoroughly watered a few hours before they are moved and should be lifted in such a way that as many as possible of the roots are preserved.

Balled and burlaped trees do not have to be planted immediately but they should receive regular watering.

After lifting, they should be replanted as soon as possible and every precaution taken to keep the roots moist (by wrapping them in wet moss, hay, newspaper or other convenient material if necessary) during the time they are out of the ground.

If the roots are of necessity damaged to an extent that is likely to prove harmful, the damage can be reduced to a minimum by pruning the top before or immediately after transplanting and in this way reducing the amount of foliage that the roots are called upon to support.

A large tree balled and burlaped in readiness for transplanting.

With plants in leaf at the time of transplanting it is important, if possible, to carry out the operation in cool, moist, dull weather and to water the newly moved plants thoroughly as soon as they are installed in their new locations.

When bare-rooted plants such as this young tree are transplanted it is important not to allow the roots to dry.

Plants devoid of leaves at planting time do not need watering after planting if the soil is reasonably moist.

Mulching the soil about newly transplanted trees and shrubs is an effective way of conserving moisture and encouraging new root growth. Peat moss, compost, leaf mold and other organic materials are ideal mulches for the purpose.

Shading from bright sunshine and spraying the foliage with water 2 or 3 times a day helps newly transplanted specimens in leaf to recover more quickly from the shock of moving.

Available from dealers in garden supplies are special sprays which, if used just before or just after transplanting, reduce the loss of moisture from the foliage and thus make success surer. Out of the best transplanting season, these sprays are especially useful on evergreens and other leafy plants that have to be moved.

In advance of transplanting, the soil should be thoroughly prepared by digging and fertilizing in a manner appropriate to the plant or crop that is to be set into it. The holes into which the plants are set should always be of ample size to accommodate the roots without crowding. The plant should be placed at the correct depth (in most cases very slightly deeper than it has been before), the roots spread out in a natural position and good soil worked among them and made firm.

TRANSVAAL DAISY. Gerbera, which see.

TRAPA—*Water Chestnut* (Tra'pa). Floating aquatic plants from Asia and southern Europe, which belong to the Evening Primrose family, Onagraceae. T. natans, the principal kind, has roundish, floating leaves averaging 3 in. in diameter, which are in large rosettes and beautifully variegated. It also has long, slender, submerged leaves which serve the function of roots. The small, white, four-petaled flowers, which appear in summer, are inconspicuous. They are succeeded by top-shaped, hard-shelled fruits (seeds) 1 in. in length and furnished with four large spines. The name Trapa is abridged from *calcitrapa,* the Latin name of an instrument of war which had four large hooklike projections.

Trapa natans is hardy and is naturalized in eastern North America. It may be grown in pools or large tubs containing a few inches of loamy soil and filled with water. The plants are simply laid on the surface of the water. Propagation is by sowing the seeds in the mud at the bottom of the tub. These must be kept in water before they are sown; they soon lose their power of germination when taken out of the water.

The Chinese kind, T. bicornuta, has fruits which in shape resemble a bull's head with two prominent horns. In China it is called Ling and the fruits are eaten. Another Asiatic kind is T. bispinosa. This, also, has usually only two horns. It is a native of Ceylon and is called Singhara Nut. The fruits are eaten. The Asiatic species of Trapa require the same culture as T. natans but are less hardy. For the plant called Chinese Water Chestnut, see Eleocharis dulcis.

TRASHY CULTIVATION. A system of surface cultivation employed in orchards and for some other crops that is intermediate between clean cultivation (the elimination of all weeds and grass by frequent stirring of the soil with a hoe or cultivator) and the maintenance of grass sod or other low ground cover. Under the trashy cultivation system the development of heavy sod is discouraged by using a disc harrow, but the sod is not turned under. As much should be left on the surface as is needed to prevent erosion and to act as a light mulch also.

TRAUTVETTERIA (Trautvetter'ia). A small group of herbaceous plants that are natives of North America and northern Asia and belong to the Buttercup family, the Ranunculaceae. The name honors the Russian botanist, Ernst Rudolph von Trautvetter.

Trautvetterias are of modest horticultural importance. They are suitable for planting in moist, shady places in wild gardens. They may be raised from seeds sown in humus-rich soil and by division in early spring or in fall.

T. carolinensis attains a height of about 3 ft., has clusters of small white flowers and occurs as a native from Pennsylvania to Florida and Missouri. T. grandis is similar to T. carolinensis and by some botanists is regarded as a variety of it. It grows naturally from Montana to California and British Columbia.

TRAVELER'S-JOY. Clematis Vitalba, which see.

TRAVELER'S-TREE. See Ravenala.

TREE-FELLING. This work is carried out by one of two methods: sawing or chopping the trunks off as near as possible to the ground and leaving the roots undisturbed, or by grubbing —that is, digging a trench around the tree, cutting through the roots, and felling the tree with the roots attached. The roots are afterwards cut off and taken away.

Trees grown under forestry conditions are usually sawed or chopped off and the butts or roots are left in the ground, because this is a much cheaper method of felling than grubbing. Moreover, the butts decay and add humus to the ground. On hilly or mountainous land the butts protect the steep slopes from erosion, whereas if the butts were taken out, erosion would be assisted by storm water washing away the loosened soil.

Felling by Sawing. When felling by sawing is practiced, the workmen should cut the tree near the ground. By leaving roots in the ground some risk to future trees is run, for various kinds of fungi, which are at work destroying and breaking down the roots, may spread to young trees. This is noticeable in the Honey Fungus (Armillaria mellea), which is present on old roots and sometimes spreads to young trees.

How the Work Is Done. In sawing off trees it rarely happens that the heads of the trees are removed before the trees are felled, but this may be necessary when there is danger of the branches injuring another tree or building in falling.

As a rule, a lip is cut with an axe in the base of the tree, facing the direction in which the tree is to fall. If the tree is a heavy one, a rope may be attached to the trunk at a point at least two thirds of the height above the ground, facing the direction in which the tree is to fall. Any large buttresses or surface roots are cut off with an axe, parallel with the bark, then the tree is sawed through by means of a crosscut saw.

Care must be taken to saw immediately behind the lip, and if the tree has a slight lean in any direction the cut must be so arranged as to correct the lean as the tree falls.

As sawing proceeds, the weight of the trunk may settle a little and cause the saw to run badly. When this happens, drive an iron wedge in the saw-cut behind the saw. Use a mallet or sledge hammer for this purpose, not the head of an axe, for a good axe may soon be ruined if used to drive iron wedges.

Trees of moderate size can usually be made to fall, when cut far enough through, by means of a push from behind; heavy trees may have to be pulled down by means of the rope. You must keep a sharp watch on the tree to make sure that it does not fall before you are ready. Where large trees have to be felled it is best to call in experts to do the job.

Felling by Grubbing. Grubbing should be practiced whenever possible when trees have to be felled on home grounds and in gardens. The butt is much easier to remove from the ground when attached to the trunk than it is afterwards. The leverage available during the fall of the tree is very considerable, and it helps to lift the heavy butt out of the ground. Then by carefully filling in the ground behind, and propping the butt into position before it is cut off, a good deal of labor can be saved in its removal.

The reason why grubbing should be practiced on home grounds and in gardens is that once a tree is removed it almost invariably follows that the ground is wanted for some garden purpose, and the grubbing of a large butt from which the trunk has been removed is a costly and laborious task. Moreover, if the site is not immediately required for some other purpose, the butt takes a long time to decay and often a good deal of fungus is produced during that time. Further, in some instances, decay may go on unnoticed until suddenly the ground gives way and a hole appears.

Lopping the Branches. When commencing to fell a tree with a heavy head by grubbing, it is wise to lop the branches. There is no need to cut the branches close to the trunk except on the side that is destined to fall on the ground; they are cut off at a convenient point a foot or two from the tree. On the side that will fall on the ground the branches should be cut close; otherwise the snags will be buried in the ground and cause difficulty in removing the trunk.

After the removal of the branches, secure a rope to the top of the tree facing the direction in which the tree is to fall. Then proceed to dig a trench around the tree and cut through the roots. The proper tool for cutting roots is a grub-axe or mattock, unless a thick root clear of soil and stones is encountered, when an ordinary axe may be used. An ordinary axe would soon be ruined if it were used to cut through roots intermingled with soil and gravel.

Should the tree lean in a particular direction, leave a large root uncut on the opposite side to counteract the effect of the lean as the tree falls. When a trench has been dug to the depth of the lowest main roots, undermine the side facing the direction in which the tree is to fall, and as soon as the undermining has been carried far enough, haul on the rope and overbalance the tree. If a root is left uncut a man with an axe should stand behind it in order to cut it, if it is offering too much resistance. During undermining operations workmen must be careful to see that the tree does not lose its balance before they are ready.

Once the tree is on the ground, cut off the snags of branches parallel with the trunk, secure the butt in position, saw it off and remove it, after clearing away as much soil as possible. If the trunk cannot be removed bodily, it should be sawed across by means of a crosscut saw into as many sections as is desirable.

Tree Surgery. *(Left)* cleaning and shaping wound; *(Right)* painting wound.

TREE FERN. A name given to those tall Ferns which have trunklike stems and are suitable for cultivation in a greenhouse or, in exceptionally mild regions, out of doors. The chief kinds are Alsophila, Blechnum, Cibotium, Cyathea Dicksonia and Sadleria, which see.

TREE GUARDS. When isolated trees are planted in areas to which horses, cattle and sheep have access, or where rabbits or deer abound, it may be necessary to erect iron or wooden guards to protect the trees from the animals; similar guards are sometimes needed to ensure the safety of trees planted along sides of roads and in other public places. Such guards are rarely needed throughout the life of the trees, but only until the bark has become hard and the higher branches are out of reach.

Cattle and horses may always be expected to eat some of the lower branches and leaves of trees, particularly when grass is becoming scarce, and it is rarely necessary to protect such branches; the trunk and leading shoots are, however, important.

Protection from Cattle and Rabbits. When rabbits are a menace it is necessary to use chicken wire to enclose the lower part of the guard used to exclude cattle, deer and horses.

Iron Tree Guards. There are many kinds of both iron and wooden tree guards. All are more or less unsightly, but, if the trees are to remain uninjured they must be used. They vary in width from 1 to 3 ft. or sometimes wider when built of wood. The height is variable, usually about 6 ft., with the upper rails of iron guards turned outwards for several inches. Iron guards should be built in two sections that can be bolted together, and have strong feet that can be driven 12 in. into the ground.

The bars are upright with bands of iron near the bottom and top and sometimes in the middle. The upright bars may be 3 in. apart, but in some strong wire guards they are much closer. With fairly widely spaced bars it is possible to insert the hand for weeding purposes.

Guards should be examined annually and painted when necessary. They should not be left in position long enough to injure the base of the tree; there is always a tendency for the living wood to enclose the iron when contact is made, and this must be guarded against.

Wooden tree guards are easy to make. They may be triangular, round or square, and must be substantial enough to withstand cattle rubbing against them. The rails can be made of any easily split wood, the posts of any strong wood that is resistant to decay. The lower parts should be treated with a wood preservative before being placed in the ground.

Cleft rails look better than sawed ones, although for special positions people sometimes go to the trouble of using guards of planed wood.

The vertical rails must be close enough to prevent an animal from getting its head through, and strong enough to withstand the weight of an animal rubbing or leaning against the guard.

Trees are sometimes secured to guards in order to dispense with stakes. When this is done, a rubber band should be placed around the tree and a triangle of ties used so that the tree cannot be blown against the guard. The ties should be examined after every violent storm, but in no case should they be allowed to go more than a year without attention.

Trees on the sides of roads or streets can sometimes be guarded sufficiently by driving in a triangle of stakes a few inches from the trunk, or a small guard of strong wire may be used to protect the base from knocks.

TREE HEATH. Erica arborea, which see.

TREE IVY. A name used to distinguish the mature type of English Ivy, which, when it has reached the top of its support, becomes bushy and bears flowers and fruits. See Hedera.

TREE LUPIN. Lupinus arboreus, which see.

TREE MALLOW. Lavatera, which see.

TREE OF HEAVEN. See Ailanthus.

TREE ONION. See Onion.

TREE PEONY. See Paeonia suffruticosa.

TREE POPPY. See Romneya.

TREE SURGERY. This term refers primarily to the pruning and repairing of wounds and structural weaknesses of trees, but modern tree surgeons concern themselves with much more than that. They undertake fertilizing, disease

Despite the loss of most of the interior of its trunk this ancient Apple tree lives. Its trunk is braced with iron bars and exposed surfaces are painted regularly with tree-wound paint.

and pest control, protecting trees from the adverse effects of changes in grade, and indeed every phase of work that promotes the health of trees. They also undertake the removal of unwanted trees and are especially skilled in taking

Injured by being run into by a truck, this tree is healing after the wound was cleaned and shaped and given two coats of tree-wound paint.

down specimens that occupy difficult locations and may be a danger to life or property.

Except in minor matters it is not wise for the amateur to engage in tree surgery, especially work that involves felling trees, cutting off large branches, bracing and filling cavities. Such activities call for specialized knowledge and experience, and felling and pruning in particular are likely to be extremely dangerous when undertaken by untrained individuals. Before engaging a tree surgeon it is well to check up on his reputation and reliability, even as you would that of a medical doctor. Trees are valuable assets; their care should not be entrusted to unreliable operators.

The home treatment of cavities is best confined to cleaning them out down to sound wood, shaping the cavity in such a way that water drains readily from it, and painting the exposed wood surface with tree-wound paint immediately after the operation and about once a year thereafter. This is usually better than attempting to fill the cavity with cement or other material. See Pruning, also Tree-Felling.

TREE TOMATO. See Cyphomandra betacea.
TREFOIL. Trifolium, which see.
TREFOIL, BIRD'S-FOOT. See Lotus.
TRELLIS. Many gardens can be improved by the use of a trellis—to increase the height of existing fences, provide screens to shut off one part of the garden from another, to cover walls, or to serve as a convenient framework on which to train climbing plants. Artistic screens

In this garden a light wooden trellis gives support to a variety of vines.

Figure 1

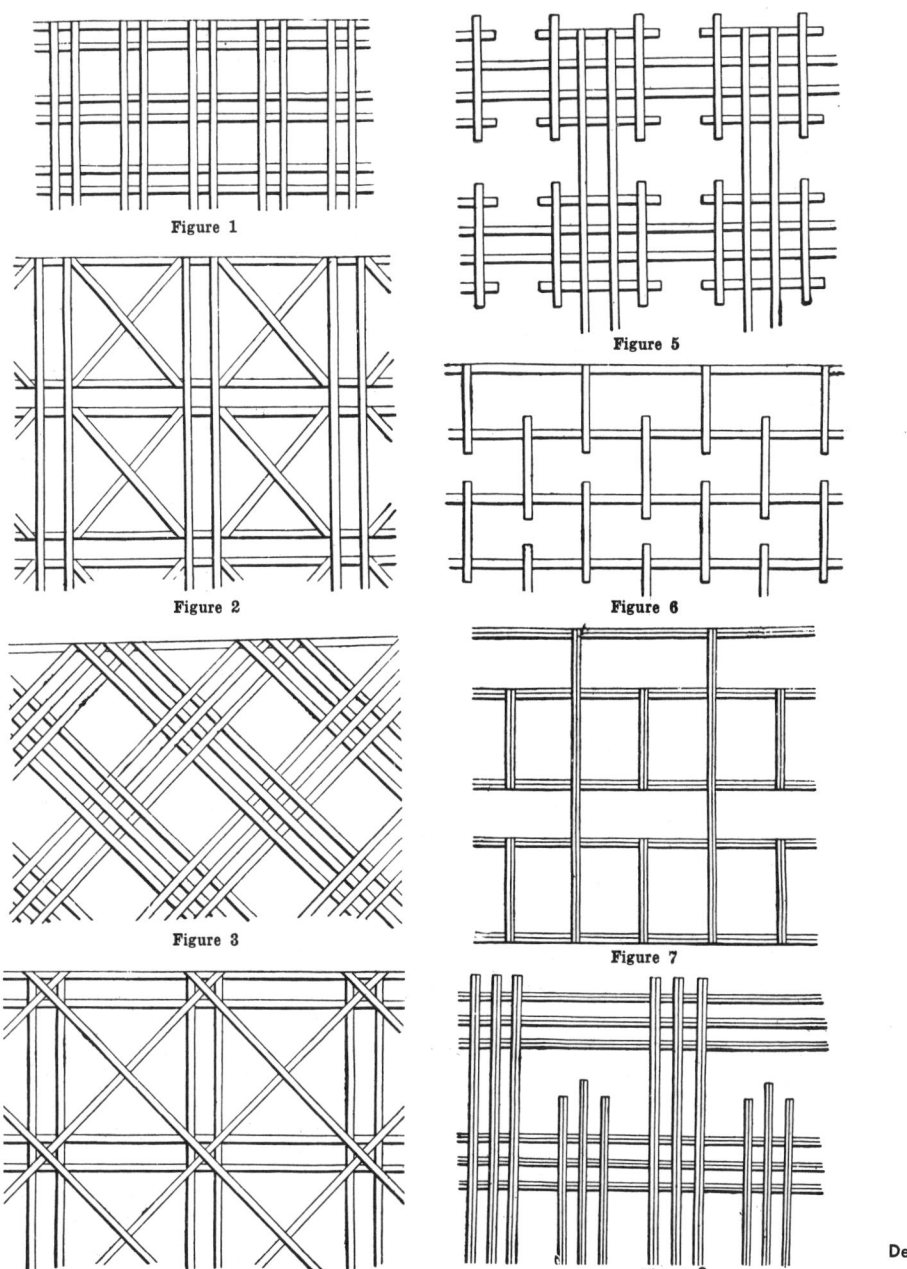

Figure 2

Figure 3

Figure 4

Figure 5

Figure 6

Figure 7

Figure 8

Designs for trellises.

and trellises can be obtained ready made, or they can be made by anyone who is handy with saw and hammer.

The most convenient materials to use are builders' laths, 1 in. wide and $\frac{1}{4}$ in. thick. These are stout enough for most purposes, yet sufficiently pliable to permit the slight bending that some trellis designs necessitate.

The first task is to construct and fix in position simple rectangular frames of 1-in.-square wood to carry the trellis design. At the corners and at all joints the wood is halved and jointed to give the finished frame a flat surface on which the trellis can be fixed.

Where the design allows, the frames should be made to coincide with one or another of the uprights and horizontals of the design, so that they are invisible from the front of the complete trellis. If a fence or screen is to be constructed, the frames will need to be fixed in 2-in-square posts, bedded into cement in the ground for stability.

The actual trellis is not constructed directly on the frames, but is built separately in sections of a convenient size to handle, then nailed or screwed into position on the frames. If a continuous design, such as that shown in Nos. 1, 3 and 6, is chosen, there is no difficulty about dimensions. If the design is composed of separate and distinct patterns, as for example in Nos. 2, 4 and 5, the space to be filled must first be measured and the patterns made of a size that will give an exact number of complete patterns in the finished job; otherwise the result will look haphazard and unbalanced.

The simplest and quickest way to work is to count up how many pieces of lath of each length will be required, then saw up the necessary quantity of each before commencing the assembling. This is less wasteful than cutting each length of lath as it is wanted. One-inch wire nails are used for joining the laths; one driven in wherever a lath crosses another is sufficient. Drive all the nails from the same side of the trellis, so that as each section is completed it can be reversed and the projecting points of the nails clinched over, to make the whole secure. The sections of trellis are then treated with wood preserver or painted and put aside to dry.

If it is decided to nail, rather than screw, the trellis to the frames, hold an old flatiron or some other heavy object with a flat surface at the back of the wood which is being nailed. This will prevent it from springing under the hammer blows.

The designs illustrated do not exhaust the possibilities of trellis; numerous others will suggest themselves. No. 1 is a simple design suitable as a fence or to cover a wall against which climbing plants are to be trained. If this design is to be fixed on a wall the 1-in. framework may be dispensed with. Wooden blocks 1 in. thick nailed to the wall at intervals will be sufficient to carry it.

No. 3 is suitable for increasing the height of an existing fence. It is more attractive than the plain square or diamond-meshed trellis so commonly used for this purpose. Nos. 2 and 4 are reminiscent of classical wrought ironwork. They are most suitable for complete screens, on which annual or deciduous (leaf-losing) climbing plants are to be trained. A screen in either of these designs looks handsome and dignified, even when it is bare of foliage and flowers.

No. 5 is a close-worked design that permits little to be seen through it. It is suitable for screening off, say, the vegetable garden, or for hiding the laundry yard. No. 6 is suitable for heightening a wall. For this purpose, too, a length of No. 2. or No. 4, one pattern high, is effective.

The special use of No. 7 is where a screen running east to west is necessary. Climbing or rambler Roses may be trained on its north side to face a house, or for other reasons. Yet, being an open design, it permits the plants to receive air and sunshine freely.

No. 8 is inspired by a Japanese garden screen. In the original it is made of bamboo. It looks particularly effective in bamboo (secured by crosswise lacing wherever the uprights cross the horizontals), but would be somewhat more expensive than if laths were used.

TREMANDRA (Treman'dra). Tender evergreen flowering shrubs which are rarely cultivated and are chiefly to be found in botanical collections. They are natives of Australia and belong to the Tremandra family, Tremandraceae. The name is derived from *trema,* a hole, and *andra,* anther, and refers to pollen bursting through holes in the anthers.

The only kind of Tremandra recognized by most botanists is T. stelligera, a shrub 2 ft. in height, with ovate leaves, 1½ in. in diameter, and small, purplish, five-petaled flowers. When grown in a greenhouse, it requires a minimum winter temperature of 45 degrees and a . soil compost of sandy peat. Repotting is done in March, when the plants are transferred to slightly larger pots. Pruning consists of shortening the shoots of the previous year's growth by two thirds in spring.

This shrub is grown in a well-lighted, airy greenhouse, which is shaded only from the fiercest rays of the sun. The soil is moistened only when it becomes moderately dry.

[13—6]
Vegetable Garden

[13—6a]
*White-flowered Madagascar Periwinkle
(Vinca rosea alba) bordering Cannas*

[13—7]
Mullein
(Verbascum)

[13—7a]
Mother-of-Thyme
(Thymus Serpyllum variety)

[13—7b]
European Cranberry Bush
(Viburnum Opulus)

[13—7c]
Viburnum Sieboldii

Propagation is by inserting cuttings, which are made from half-ripened shoots in August. They are placed in finely-sifted sandy peat, and are covered with a bell jar until roots are formed. Afterwards, the plants are set in 3-in. pots and eventually they are transferred to larger pots. This plant is suitable for cultivating outdoors in southern California.

TRENCHING. A method of digging, now rarely employed, which involves turning over and loosening the soil to a depth of 2½-3 ft.

TREVESIA (Treve'sia). A small group of trees and shrubs, natives of tropical Asia, suitable for cultivation in a warm greenhouse having a minimum winter temperature of 55 degrees and for planting outdoors in the deep South. They belong to the Aralia family, Araliaceae. The name commemorates an Italian family. Very few of these shrubs are grown in other than botanical gardens.

These plants have deeply cut leaves and bear umbels or flattish bunches of flowers in spring. They thrive under the usual conditions afforded warm greenhouse plants, and should be grown in a compost of two thirds loam and one third leaf mold or peat moss with a sprinkling of sand. A moist atmosphere and shade from strong sunshine are needed. Propagation is by cutting and by air layering.

The chief kind is Trevesia palmata, which in India, its native country, reaches a height of 12-20 ft.; it has large handsome leaves, and the flowers, which are white tinged with green, open in spring. The plant cultivated under the name T. Micholitzii is, apparently, a variety of T. palmata with leaves more deeply cut than those of the typical kind. T. sundaica, a native of Java, is an attractive small tree with glossy leaves and thorny stems.

TREVORIA (Trev'oria). A small group of Orchids with extraordinary flowers. Only one kind has so far flowered under cultivation, T. Lehmannii. (chloris), which is found wild in Colombia. The plant is epiphytal (grows on trees) and has small, clustered, ovate pseudobulbs, each with a single evergreen leaf. The spikes bear from three to five blooms each; the color is greenish-yellow, with the exception of the disc and base of the lip, which are white. The name Trevoria was given in commemoration of Sir Trevor Lawrence, onetime President of the Royal Horticultural Society of England.

These plants are grown in Orchid baskets, using a compost of three parts of osmunda fiber and one part of sphagnum moss, drainage (broken crocks) being so placed as to allow for the flower spikes to push through. Rebasketing, when absolutely necessary, should be done in the spring. Water may be given freely in summer; a warm, moist atmosphere is necessary at that season. In winter, water is needed occasionally; the temperature should not fall below 60 degrees. The flowering season is late summer.

TRIAS (Tri'as). Small Orchids which are found wild, chiefly in Burma, and are epiphytal (grow on trees). The small, almost globose pseudobulbs are set closely together, and each has a single evergreen leaf. The single-flowered stems are produced in profusion, generally in autumn or early spring. The flowers have spreading sepals, which are larger than the petals, and a thick, tonguelike lip. The name is from *treis,* meaning three, and was given on account of the three prominent sepals.

These Orchids are easily grown in a moderately warm greenhouse with a minimum winter temperature of 60 degrees. Owing to the creeping habit of the plants, flower pans are preferable to pots; they should be suspended near the glass. Shading is needed in very bright weather. A potting compost of osmunda fiber, Tree Fern fiber, Fir bark or of Redwood bark is suitable, and free drainage is required. Water should be given freely in the summer, less frequently in winter.

Repotting is done when growth begins in spring. The plants should be disturbed as seldom as possible, the compost being renewed when necessary; they can be allowed to creep over the sides of the flower pans.

T. picta is most frequently met with. Its flowers are 1 in. across, yellowish, densely spotted with red. T. disciflora is similarly colored, but larger. T. oblonga has much smaller and less attractive flowers.

TRICHINIUM (Trichin'ium). A group of subshrubs and herbaceous perennials, natives of Australia, a few of which are grown outdoors in warm parts of the United States and in greenhouses. They belong to the Amaranth

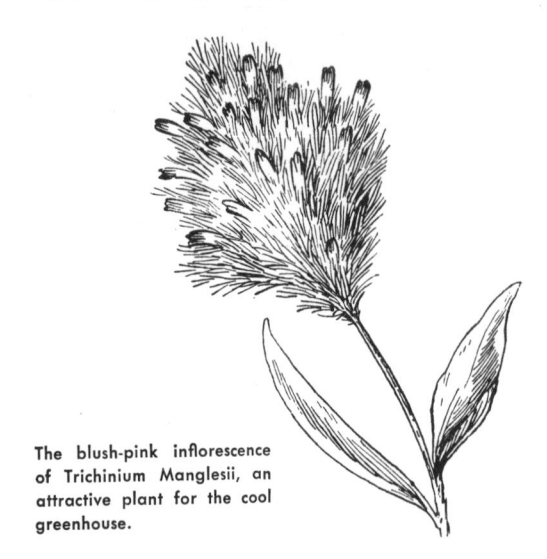

The blush-pink inflorescence of Trichinium Manglesii, an attractive plant for the cool greenhouse.

Trichocaulon Dinteri.

family, Amaranthaceae. The name is derived from *trichinos,* hairy, and alludes to the flowers.

These plants are suitable for cultivation in a greenhouse in which the temperature in winter does not fall below 45 degrees. Loam with a little leaf mold or peat moss and a free scattering of sand makes a suitable compost. Trichiniums need cool, airy conditions during the summer months, and at that season the soil must be kept moist; but during the autumn and winter very little watering is needed. Propagation is by dividing the roots in early spring.

Few kinds have been introduced into cultivation. The chief ones are T. exaltatum, 2½ ft., yellow and red; T. Manglesii, 8 in., blush; T. spathulatum, prostrate, yellowish; and T. Stirlingii, 2 ft., pale yellow and pink. All bloom during summer.

TRICHOCAULON (Trichocaul'on). A group of small African succulent plants belonging in the botanical family Asclepiadaceae, the Milkweed family. The name is derived from *trichos,* a hair, and *caulon,* a stem, and refers to the bristles on the tubercles of some kinds.

These are curious plants that appeal chiefly to the fancier of succulents. They require essentially the same care as Cacti, which see. The plant body consists of a stout, more or less obese stem covered with small projections or tubercles, each tipped, usually, with a spine or bristle.

Kinds likely to be cultivated are T. cactiforme, flowers pale yellow spotted red; T. Delaetianum, flowers brownish-yellow; T. Dinteri, flowers buff-yellow with reddish-brown dots; T. Engleri, flowers pale yellow or greenish with red or purple dots; T. keetmanshoopense, flowers greenish with reddish spots; T. meloforme, flowers yellow spotted with dark purple; T. piliferum, flowers dark purplish-brown.

TRICHOCENTRUM. (Trichocen'trum). Epiphytal evergreen Orchids with very small pseudobulbs, from the American tropics. The flower stems are short and each bears one or more flowers; these have spreading sepals and petals and a rather flat lip, the base of which is protracted into a long spur. These Orchids bloom at various times, but usually in the late summer and autumn. Trichocentrum is supposed to be derived from *trichos,* a hair, and *kentron,* a spur, possibly an allusion to the slender spur of some kinds.

All these Orchids need a greenhouse with a winter night temperature of 60 degrees. Owing to their small size, flower pans suit them better than pots, and some of the small-growing sorts succeed equally well when attached to pieces of cork or blocks of wood. Shading is required from early spring to late autumn, and care in watering is necessary throughout the year. The atmosphere must be moist, yet the plants quickly suffer if the compost becomes sodden.

A suitable potting compost consists of cut osmunda fiber, Tree Fern fiber, or of Fir bark or Redwood bark. If pans are used, crushed crocks or a little charcoal may be added. Repotting, when necessary, should be done about March.

T. albococcineum (albopurpureum) has flowers about 2 in. across, with tawny sepals and petals and a purple and white lip. T. porphyrio has larger flowers in which the lip is magenta-purple. T. tigrinum has yellowish-green sepals and petals, and a white and purple lip with yellow crest. Others are T. maculatum, T. orthoplectron, T. Pfavii and T. pulchrum.

TRICHOCEREUS (Trichocer'eus). A group of mostly tall, branched, columnar Cacti from South America. They belong to the Cactus family, Cactaceae. The name is derived from *trichos*, a hair, and Cereus, the name of a group of Cacti. These plants thrive under the general care recommended for Cacti, which see. They are suitable for planting outdoors in the Southwest and also for growing in greenhouses.

Many kinds are known to botanists and are likely to be found in the collections of Cactus fanciers, among which are the following: T. Bertramianus, 5-6 ft., flowers yellowish; T. Bridgesii, 15 ft., flowers white or whitish; T. chiloensis, 25 ft., flowers white, tinged red; T. peruvianus, 12 ft., flowers white; T. strigosus, 3 ft., flowers white; T. Terscheckii, 40 ft., flowers white.

TRICHODIADEMA (Trichodiade'ma). A group of South African succulent plants formerly included in Mesembryanthemum and belonging in the Aizoaceae, the Carpetweed family. The name is derived from *trichos*, a hair,

Trichodiadema densum, showing the crown of hair at the end of each leaf, the feature for which the plant is named.

and *diadema*, a diadem or crown.

These are small, shrubby plants with more or less cylindrical leaves. They require the same culture as Mesembryanthemum, which see.

Kinds that may be cultivated include T. barbatum, 4 in., flowers reddish; T. bulbosum, 6-8 in., flowers red; T. densum, 3 in., flowers violet; T. mirabile, 3 in., flowers white; T. stellatum, 4 in., flowers violet-red.

TRICHOGLOTTIS. (Trichoglott'is). A small group of Orchids of no great horticultural importance. All are epiphytal (grow on trees), without pseudobulbs, and have evergreen leaves. They are found wild in Sumatra and the Philippines. The name Trichoglottis is derived from *trichos*, a hair, and *glottis*, a tongue, and alludes to the hairs in the throat of the lip.

A greenhouse with a humid tropical atmosphere in the summer and a winter temperature of 60-65 degrees is needed. A suitable potting compost is cut osmunda fiber, Tree Fern fiber, Fir bark or Redwood bark. The pots should be well drained. The compost must be renewed in spring, but annual repotting is not necessary. Shading and abundance of moisture are required in summer. Water may be given freely in summer but less abundantly in late autumn and winter.

T. Joiceyana has spikes 3 ft. long, bearing numerous small, whitish-purple or rose-purple flowers. T. Wenzelii has long-lasting fragrant flowers with greenish-yellow, red-barred sepals and petals, and a white, purple-marked lip. It flowers in winter and is much smaller than T. Joiceyana. T. philippinensis brachiata, which some botanists place in the genus Stauropsis, is the so-called Black Orchid. Its fragrant blooms are blackish velvety crimson with the lip pinkish purple with a yellow blotch.

TRICHOMANES — *Killarney Fern, Filmy Fern* (Trichom'anes). Beautiful cool greenhouse and hothouse Ferns with finely divided semi-transparent foliage. The lovely Killarney Fern, T. radicans, is found wild in Ireland, where it inhabits moist, shady nooks by waterfalls. A closely related kind, T. Boschianum, occurs wild in North America as far north as Kentucky and some other species also occur in the Southeast. Other kinds are found wild in the West Indies, tropical America, tropical Asia,

Africa, and in New Zealand and Australia.

These Ferns differ greatly in the size and shape of their fronds; some have large fronds, 18 in. in length, while in others the fronds are but a few inches long. The fronds of some are simple (undivided), and of others are multipinnate, or very finely divided. The multipinnate kinds are the most beautiful, their finely cut, pellucid fronds being quite distinct from most other Ferns. The name Trichomanes is derived from *trichos,* a hair, and *manos,* soft.

Culture. Except for the temperature, all require the same treatment. A minimum winter temperature of 55 degrees is necessary for the hothouse kinds and 45 degrees for the cool greenhouse kinds. Their chief requirements are complete shade and a very moist atmosphere. The best soil compost consists of 1 part each of peat moss, loam, and leaf mold, and 1 part of equal proportions of sand, crushed charcoal and sandstone. The Ferns may be grown in deep pans covered with bell jars or planted out in a bed of soil in shady, moist corners of the greenhouse.

After potting or planting, the Ferns are not disturbed for many years, but are kept growing vigorously by top-dressing them with fresh compost annually. Only when they show signs of deterioration should they be disturbed; they should then be lifted, in spring, and planted or repotted in fresh compost. The soil must be kept moist at all times and the atmosphere maintained in a very moist condition by damping the floors and walls.

The Killarney Fern, T. radicans, and the closely related T. Boschianum are best grown in a cool greenhouse or cold frame. The frame must be placed in a shaded location and the sash kept closed or nearly closed to maintain the necessary moist atmosphere. The plants may be grown either in deep pans or in a bed of soil among pieces of sandstone. New plants are obtained by separating the old ones into small sections at potting or planting time, or they may be raised from spores. (See Ferns.)

The chief kinds are the following (the measurements refer to the length of the fronds). For the tropical greenhouse: T. alatum, 3 ft.; T. capillaceum (trichoideum), 6 in.; T. maximum, 12 in.; T. Bancroftii, 4 in.

For the cool greenhouse: T. radicans, 6 in.; T. Boschianum, 8 in.; T. reniforme (kidney-shaped leaves), 4 in.; T. auriculatum, 9 in.

TRICHOPILIA (Trichopil′ia). Epiphytal Orchids found wild in Mexico, Central America, Peru and Brazil. Most kinds have evergreen leaves and short stems which bear two or more large flowers with rather narrow, sometimes twisted sepals and petals and a large lip. Spring and summer are the principal flowering seasons, but a few bloom in late autumn and winter.

The name Trichopilia is from *trichos,* a hair, and *pilion,* a cap. The column has a hoodlike pronged termination.

Orchids for a Warm Greenhouse. Though most of these Orchids require a minimum winter temperature of 60 degrees, T. fragrans and its variety nobilis, and T. sanguinolenta (also known as Helcia sanguinolenta) are better suited by a slightly cooler temperature.

In nearly all kinds the pseudobulbs are fairly hard and the plants need watering only occasionally during winter. In summer, when they are in full growth, water may be given freely. Shading is necessary in bright weather. A position near the glass suits them.

Repotting should be done when the young growths are seen, usually in spring. If pots are used, they must be well drained with broken

Trichopilia suavis.

crocks; flower pans suit them better. The potting compost may be cut osmunda fiber, Tree Fern fiber, or Fir bark or Redwood bark. A few decayed leaves may be added, together with crushed crocks. The compost should be so placed as to be slightly above the rim of the flower pan and highest in the center. Repotting is not necessary every year.

The Chief Kinds. T. suavis, which bears large, scented flowers, white, spotted and blotched with rose-pink, is very handsome. A white variety is also known. Both bloom in spring.

T. crispa has crimson, white-margined sepals and petals, and a crimson lip. T. marginata has sepals and petals that are pale brown or reddish, margined with green or white; the lip is crimson on its inside and whitish on the outside. T. Galeottiana has smaller flowers, soft yellow in color. T. fragrans and T. Backhousiana have white flowers on erect spikes. T. sanguinolenta has small pseudobulbs; the flowers are over 2 in. across, with olive-green sepals and petals and a white lip marked with red-purple. T. tortilis has large cattleya-like flowers which are pale yellowish-green with reddish-brown centers.

TRICHOSANTHES (Trichosan'thes). Tender, climbing plants with ornamental fruits and flowers. They are slender cucumber-like plants with five-lobed leaves and climb by means of tendrils. They bear clusters of small white flowers with fringed petals, and produce curious, cucumber-like twisted fruits, 3-6 ft. in length.

These plants are natives of tropical Asia, India and Japan, and belong to the Gourd family, Cucurbitaceae. They are grown in North America as curiosities. In India the fruits of T. Anguina, the Serpent, Snake or Club Gourd, are eaten. The name Trichosanthes is derived from *trichos,* a hair, and *anthos,* a flower, and refers to the flowers' being fringed with fine hairs.

Raising Seedlings. The plants are raised annually from seeds sown in pots of sandy soil in spring. The seedlings are potted separately in 3-in. pots and later, after the weather is really warm and settled, are planted outdoors; or seeds may be sown directly outdoors when the weather is warm. The best soil is one that is well supplied with organic matter, is fertile and well drained. Stakes, wires, trellises or other supports for the plants to climb up must be provided. During the summer plenty of water is needed.

The chief kind is T. Anguina, a native of India. Other kinds are T. cucumeroides and T. japonica, both from Japan.

TRICHOSPORUM (Tricho'sporum; Trichospor'um). A group of tropical, woody climbers or trailers that are sometimes known by the name of Aeschynanthus and are often so called in gardens. They are natives of Asia and are suitable for cultivating in warm, moist greenhouses. These plants belong to the Gesneria family, the Gesneriaceae. The name is derived from *trichos,* a hair, and *spora,* a seed.

Trichosporums root readily from cuttings inserted in sand, sand and peat moss, or vermiculite in a close propagating case where a bottom heat of 70-75 degrees is maintained. When rooted, the cuttings should be potted individually in small pots and kept growing in warm, humid conditions with shade from strong sunlight provided. When they are a few inches tall, their tips may be pinched out to induce branching.

As soon as the young plants have filled the small pots with roots, they may be planted, several together, in 6-in. pans or in hanging baskets. The soil should be coarse, loose and well drained. A satisfactory mixture can be made of

Scarlet-flowered Trichosporum Lobbianum is an easy-to-grow vine that is suitable for warm, humid greenhouses.

turfy loam, half-rotted leaves, peat moss and coarse sand in equal proportions, with a little broken charcoal added.

A minimum night temperature of 60 degrees should be provided and daytime temperatures may exceed this by 10-15 degrees. In summer, temperatures will, of course, naturally be higher. At all times the atmosphere should be humid; shade from summer sunshine is needed. The plants should be watered freely from spring through fall, more sparingly in winter. Well-established specimens benefit from feeding regularly with dilute liquid fertilizer. The plants should be syringed on all bright days.

Old plants do not need repotting every year; in years when they are not repotted they should be top-dressed in March. Pruning consists of shortening the shoots to a length of about 6 in. in February or March.

Kinds include T. Lobbianum, flowers scarlet, a native of Java; T. marmoratum, flowers green, spotted brown, of unknown origin; T. pulchrum, flowers scarlet with a yellow throat, a native of Java.

TRICHOSTEMA—*Blue-Curls* (Trichostem'a). North American annuals and herbaceous perennials that are sometimes planted in wild gardens and rock gardens. They belong to the Mint family, the Labiateae. The name is derived from *trichos,* a hair, and *stemon,* stamen, and refers to the fact that the filaments of the stamens are very slender. Some kinds are good bee plants. They are chiefly cultivated in the Southwest. The kinds worth growing in gardens are not hardy in the North.

Trichostemas are easy to grow. They prosper in full sunshine and thrive in hot summer. They may be propagated by seeds and, the perennial kinds, by division.

Kinds likely to be grown in gardens are T. dichotomum, an annual, 2 ft. tall, flowers blue, pink or white; T. lanatum, perennial, 3-4 ft., flowers covered with blue or purple woolly hairs; T. lanceolatum, an important bee plant, flowers blue.

TRICUSPIDARIA. Crinodendron, which see.

TRICYRTIS—*Toad Lily* (Tricyr'tis). A group of mostly hardy herbaceous plants, natives of the Himalayas, Japan and China, and belonging to the Lily family, Liliaceae. The plants have creeping rhizomes. The name is from *treis,* three, and *kyrtos,* convex, from the three outer petals or perianth segments which have sacs or pouches at their bases.

The Japanese Toad Lily, Tricyrtis hirta, a hardy herbaceous plant with stem-clasping leaves and white flowers with purple markings.

The flowers have a rough resemblance to Lily flowers in form, and a curious resemblance to some Orchids in their strange markings and purplish colorings. They combine extraordinary form and lurid coloring with a somber beauty to a remarkable degree. They are increased in spring by careful division of the roots, or by seeds sown in a pan of loam, peat moss or leaf mold and sand in a cold frame.

Chief Kinds. Tricyrtis hirta, the most common kind of Toad Lily, has erect stems, 1-3 ft. tall, with pointed stem-clasping leaves on the lower portion and rather large flowers in the upper portion. The flowers are white with purple markings and are produced in fall.

Tricyrtis macropoda grows 2-3 ft. tall, with handsome flowers, whitish-purple with darker purple dots. It flowers in summer, an advantage over the other sorts, which often flower so late in the year that they are destroyed by frost before they have reached full beauty. T. macropoda is a native of China and Japan.

Tricyrtis maculata (pilosa), the Spotted Toad Lily, grows 2-3 ft. tall, the leaves slightly clothed with silky hairs. The flowers are remarkably handsome, being white, marked with purple blotches in a most striking manner. It was introduced into cultivation from the Himalayas in 1851.

Tricyrtis stolonifera, a native of Formosa, grows about 2 ft. tall and has purple flowers marked with cream-colored blotches.

The Toad Lilies should be given light loam and a rather sheltered position. Although they are generally hardy, they all flower so late, except T. macropoda, that they are worth cultivating in pots of sandy loam and leaf mold in the alpine house or cool greenhouse.

TRIENTALIS — *Starflower* (Trienta'lis). A group of two species only of small, hardy herbaceous plants, belonging to the Primrose family, Primulaceae, and natives of Europe, northern Asia and western North America. The name is of Latin origin; it means one third of a foot in height, and refers to the height of the plant.

Trientalis europaea is a pretty little plant. It has underground running stems, and in June or July sends up a number of erect, wiry, slender stems, 3 or 4 in. high, each carrying at the summit several ovate, pointed leaves arranged in a whorl. Rising above the whorl of leaves are one or two white or pale pink starry flowers, each on a threadlike stem.

The American species of Starflower, T. borealis (americanum), occurs as a native from Labrador to Virginia and Illinois. It grows naturally in rich woods and bogs and is sometimes known as the Chickweed Wintergreen. It reaches a height of about 9 in. and in June bears white, star-shaped flowers, which rise from a collar of leaves located at the top of the stem.

For the Rock Garden. These dainty plants are well worth a place in the rock garden or wild garden. They should be planted in a mixture of loam, and leaf mold, good compost or peat moss in a fairly shaded location; they flourish in the peaty ground that suits Rhododendrons. The soil should be fairly moist.

Starflowers are propagated by seeds sown in pans of moist, sandy, peaty soil in a cold frame in the fall and also by division of the roots in fall or in early spring.

TRIFOLIATE. A botanical term meaning having three leaflets, as, for example, the Clover leaf.

TRIFOLIATE ORANGE. See Poncirus.

TRIFOLIUM—*Clover* (Trifo'lium). A large group of hardy annuals and herbaceous perennials, natives of the temperate and subtropical regions of the Northern Hemisphere, also of the mountain regions of tropical America, Africa; and non-tropical South America. The name is from *treis,* three, and *folium,* a leaf, most of the species having leaves consisting of three leaflets. Trifolium belongs to the Pea family, Leguminosae.

The Trifoliums, of which there are about one hundred and fifty distinct kinds, are richer in useful plants than in ornamental ones, although there are a few charming alpine and border kinds. Chief among utility Trifoliums are kinds valuable as fodder plants and as green manure crops.

Four-leaved Clovers are supposed to be lucky and rare, though they are more common than is usually supposed.

The White Clover or White Dutch Clover, as it is often called, Trifolium repens, is often used in mixture with lawn grass seeds. This is the kind, too, which is most generally accepted as the "true" Shamrock, although differences of opinion exist as to which particular plant St. Patrick selected to illustrate the doctrine of the Trinity.

There is a variety of the White Clover, Trifolium repens atropurpureum, in which the base of each leaflet is stained with a purple blotch. Trifolium repens variety purpureum has leaves wholly bronzy-purple. The Trifoliums are usually propagated by seeds but some may be increased by division. They are all sun lovers.

A Fragrant Rock-Garden Clover. Trifolium alpinum, which is found abundantly in the European Alps, is an attractive rock-garden plant. In nature, it is found growing at considerable altitudes, always on nonlimy formations, where it forms wide mats in the close alpine turf. The trifoliate leaves are only an inch or so high, and the heads of pale lilac-pink flowers are equally dwarf. The whole plant emits a pleasing aromatic rose-like scent when the sun shines, scenting the alpine air far and wide with a delicious fragrance. The roots are used by the peasants medicinally, and the plant is used also in flavoring certain cordials and liqueurs.

Trifolium alpinum is easy to grow. It requires a light, nonlimy soil, well drained, and exposure to full sun. The root is a long, woody taproot, and the plant is best increased by seeds, sown in a pan of light loam and sand in a cold frame in spring; the seedlings should be potted at an early stage and planted out in their permanent quarters while small.

Other Attractive Kinds. Trifolium Parnassi, from Mount Parnassus, is a dwarf carpeting plant with heads of fine pink pealike flowers. It is a decorative rock-garden plant for open sunny, well-drained locations. Trifolium caespitosum resembles T. Parnassi, but is considerably larger in all its parts.

Trifolium rubens, from central and southern Europe, grows a foot high, and bears heads of carmine or purple-red flowers in summer.

Trifolium uniflorum, from Syria, is a charming dwarf, mat-forming plant for a sunny position in light, well-drained soil in the rock garden, or for the alpine house. It forms close, flat mats of leaves, studded in spring with little single, almost stemless clover-like flowers with rose-pink standards and white keels. It is increased from seeds sown in a pan of sandy loam in a cold frame in spring, or by careful division in spring.

Trifolium badium is a pretty, hardy perennial from the Alps, 6 in. or so tall, with charming, compact heads of golden-yellow flowers, fading with age to chocolate-bronze. It is easily raised from seeds sown in a pan of loam and sand in a cold frame in spring.

TRIGONELLA — *Fenugreek* (Trigonel′la). Uncommon hardy herbaceous plants of little horticultural value. Although there are upwards of four dozen species, very few are cultivated, and these are principally found in botanical collections. They are natives of Europe, Africa, Asia and Australia. Trigonella belongs to the Pea family, Leguminosae, and is closely allied to Trifolium (Clover). The name is derived from *treis,* three, and *gonu,* an angle, and refers to the three-angled appearance of the flowers.

These plants have small trifoliate leaves and narrow, pea-shaped flowers. The principal kind, T. caerulea, grows 2 ft. in height and has blue flowers. T. Foenum-Graecum (Fenugreek) is 18 in. high, with white flowers. The seeds of this kind are used medicinally and the plant is grown for forage in the Mediterranean region.

The Trigonellas are treated as hardy annuals, the seeds being sown out of doors in April in the locations in which the plants are to grow. Light, well-drained, ordinary soil and a sunny position are necessary.

When the seedlings are 2 in. high they are thinned to 8 in. apart, after which no further attention is required, beyond the ordinary routine of watering, weeding and stirring of the surface soil between the plants.

TRIGONIDIUM (Trigonid′ium). A small group of Orchids found wild in Brazil and Honduras. All are epiphytal (grow on trees) and have small, compressed pseudobulbs, which bear one or two evergreen leaves. The flowers are borne singly on erect stems produced from the base of the bulb. They open at various times of the year. Trigonidium is derived from *trigona,* a triangle, and *eidos,* like, and alludes to the three-sided tube formed by the sepals.

A greenhouse with a moderately warm, moist atmosphere in summer is required, and a winter temperature of about 60 degrees. Shading is necessary in summer. Though these Orchids may be watered freely in summer, care is needed in winter, for a sodden compost causes root decay. Well-drained pots, as small as possible, should be used, and a suitable potting compost consists of cut osmunda fiber, Tree Fern fiber, Fir bark, or Redwood bark.

T. tenue has greenish-yellow flowers; T. acuminatum is straw-yellow lined with reddish-brown, and T. obtusum is brownish-yellow with touches of white and rose.

Some botanists include Trigonidium in Laelia.

TRILISA (Tril′isa). Eastern North American herbaceous perennials closely related to Liatris and belonging to the Daisy family, Compositae. The name is an anagram of Liatris.

Although not of great garden merit, these plants may be grown in wild gardens and sometimes in flower borders. They are easily cultivated and may be propagated by seeds.

T. odoratissima, the Carolina Vanilla, has foliage that is vanilla-scented when it is bruised. It grows 3 ft. tall and has rose-purple flowers in fall. It is native from North Carolina to Florida and Louisiana. T. paniculata, native from Virginia to Florida, differs from T. odoratissima chiefly in having sticky stems. Its flowers are purple or white.

TRILLIUM—*Wake Robin* (Trill'ium). A group of hardy perennial plants belonging to the Lily Family, Liliaceae. They are natives of North America, the Himalayas and Japan. Woodland plants with fleshy rhizomatous roots, they bear solitary flowers on the summits of their erect stems. Each flower has three conspicuous petals and below each flower are three broad, green leaves. The name Trillium is from *trilex,* triple, and refers to the triple arrangement of the parts of the flowers and the leaves.

In gardens Trilliums require a shady or half-shady location and a loamy soil to which peat moss, compost or leaf mold has been added freely. They are beautiful for planting in rock gardens and in wild gardens and are especially appropriate for naturalizing in half-open woodland. Trilliums increase slowly, but established clumps may be lifted and divided in spring, or seeds may be sown in pans of loam, leaf mold and sand in the cold frame, as soon as they are ripe.

T. cernuum, the Nodding Trillium, grows 1-1½ ft. in height. The white flowers are carried on drooping stalks and are often hidden or partly hidden by the leaves.

T. erectum grows 9-15 in. high and has flowers with erect, brownish petals and an unpleasing odor. Its popular names are Bethroot, Birthroot and Purple Trillium. T. erectum variety album has white flowers. T. erectum variety flavum has yellowish-green flowers.

The Most Beautiful Kind. T. grandiflorum is without doubt the most beautiful and the most satisfactory of all the Trilliums. It grows 9-18 in. tall, with three handsome, rich green leaves surmounted by a white flower of great size and purity. As the flowers age they fade to a delicate rose-pink. T. grandiflorum is a grand woodland plant, only requiring loam and leaf mold and a cool, half-shady location; where its simple requirements are met it will establish itself and increase. Its common or popular name is Great White Trillium; it is sometimes called Trinity Lily. A double-flowered variety of T. grandiflorum is sometimes cultivated.

T. nivale, the Snow Trillium is, in effect, a miniature edition of T. grandiflorum, growing only 3-6 in. high, with pure white flowers. It does best in a cool mixture of leaf mold and loam in the rock garden or in a sheltered place in the woodland garden. T. petiolatum grows to 6 in. tall and has purple flowers.

T. pusillum is a dainty pink-flowered kind, reaching 6-8 in. in height.

T. sessile is an early-flowering species with handsome marbled foliage and large flowers of a dark chocolate-purple, placed close down upon the three leaves. The petals are carried in upright position. There is a variety called rubrum with redder flowers, and a white-flowered variety, album, has been described. T. undulatum is like a smaller T. grandiflorum, only 4-6 in. high, with very fine, white flowers that are veined with purple. This is a difficult kind to cultivate; it requires a wet, acid soil.

TRIPTERYGIUM REGELII (Tripteryg'ium). A hardy, leaf-losing shrub from eastern Asia that grows about 6 ft. tall and is handsome. It belongs in the Staff Tree family, the Celastraceae. The name is derived from *tri,* three, and *pteryx,* wing, and refers to the three-winged fruits.

Tripterygium Regelii grows without difficulty in any reasonably good soil and may be propagated by seeds or cuttings. It has attractive bright green foliage which contrasts well with its

The charming Wake Robin named Trillium grandiflorum. It is a native of eastern North America and blooms in spring.

red-brown stems. In July or August it bears conspicuous terminal clusters of white flowers.

TRITELEIA. Brodiaea, which see.

TRITHRINAX (Trithri'nax). Dwarf Palms from Brazil, which are planted outdoors in southern California and other warm parts of the United States. T. brasiliensis is the principal kind. It grows up to 15 ft. in height.

This Palm has a short stem and long-stalked, fan-shaped, deeply divided leaves. The leafstalks are furnished with stout spines. The name Trithrinax is derived from *treis,* three, and Thrinax, a species of Palm, and refers to the leaves being more deeply divided than in Thrinax.

Palms for a Warm Greenhouse. These Palms are adaptable for growing in warm greenhouses. A minimum winter temperature of 55 degrees and a compost of two parts of loam, one part of peat and a liberal sprinkling of sand, are necessary. For the first few years, the plants are repotted annually in March into larger pots, but older specimens need only to be top-dressed with rich compost.

The general treatment consists of maintaining a moist atmosphere by damping the floor and benches, syringing the foliage daily and shading the plants from strong sunlight. Established plants require abundance of water in summer, but during the winter the soil is only moistened when it becomes moderately dry.

Raising Seedlings. Young plants are obtained by sowing seeds, but these must be fresh because they quickly lose their powers of germination. They should be soaked in tepid water for 48 hours to soften the seed coats, and then sown 1 in. deep in a pan of sandy soil, set in a greenhouse propagating case with a bottom heat of 70-75 degrees. The soil is kept moist, and when the first seed leaf is 2 in. high the plants are potted separately in 3-in. pots.

Watering must be done very carefully in the early stages. It is a great advantage to keep the pots in the propagating case until the plants are well rooted; afterwards they may be hardened off, set on the open benches, and transferred to larger pots as becomes necessary.

TRITOMA. Kniphofia, which see.

TRITONIA (Trito'nia). Tender bulb plants, related to Freesia, and requiring the same culture.

Tritonia deusta is an elegant cool-greenhouse plant.

The Tritonias are found wild in South Africa and belong to the Iris family, Iridaceae. The name is derived from *triton,* a weathercock, and refers to the stamens, which are arranged differently in the various species.

The principal kind is Tritonia crocata, with brilliant orange-yellow flowers.

By growing a number of corms in pots, a brilliant display of flowers is assured in the greenhouse in late winter or spring. Drain well a sufficient number of 5-in. pots, and prepare a soil of two parts of sandy loam, one part of leaf mold, and one part of sand and decayed manure. Fill the pot to within 2 in. of the rim with the compost; press it firmly and set six bulbs in each pot. Cover them with an inch of compost and place the pots on a layer of ashes in a cold frame. Potting is done from September to November.

Very little watering is required until growth becomes active, but the soil must be kept moist. When the shoots are 2 in. in length, remove the plants to a greenhouse with a minimum temperature of 40 degrees, and set them in a sunny location. As growth becomes active, more water will be required and, after the pots are well filled with roots, weekly applications of dilute liquid fertilizer will prove beneficial. After flowering, when the foliage begins to turn brown, the supply of water should be lessened;

when the foliage has completely died down, the soil is kept dry until November, when the corms are shaken out and repotted.

Several varieties of T. crocata are listed, notably Orange King, orange; coccinea, scarlet; purpurea, purple; and sanguinea, blood-red.

Other Tritonias suitable for the cool greenhouse are T. deusta, 12 in., orange with chocolate-colored blotches; T. hyalina, 12 in., light orange; T. rosea, 12-18 in., bright rose-pink; T. squalida, 24 in., pale rose.

TROLLIUS—*Globeflower* (Trol′lius). A group of ornamental herbaceous perennial plants belonging to the Buttercup family, Ranunculaceae. The name Trollius is said to be from the German word *trol*, a globe. They are natives of the temperate and frigid regions of the Northern Hemisphere. Trollius europaeus, the common European Globeflower, is a beautiful kind which has been used in the raising of many of the fine garden hybrids. In Trollius the showy petal-like parts of the flowers are not true petals, they are sepals which are petal-like in appearance. The true petals are small and inconspicuous and are concealed within the flowers.

For Deep Moist Soil. All of these plants enjoy rich loamy soil and ample moisture at the roots. Many are superb plants for the flower border as well as for the bog garden, for pond and poolside planting; the more dwarf kinds may be planted in the rock garden. Globeflowers, too, are invaluable as cut flowers, lasting well.

Trollius may be increased by division of the roots in spring or autumn, or by seeds which should be sown as soon as harvested in a pan of loam, leaf mold, and sand in a cold frame. They are usually slow in germinating, the seedlings often taking a year or more to come up, though they are fairly certain germinators in the end.

The Globe Flower, Trollius europaeus, blooming by the side of a pool. In addition to their value for garden display Globe Flowers are excellent as cut flowers.

The European Globeflower. Trollius europaeus occurs naturally in damp places and is abundant in alpine meadows, where it makes a superb show in summer. It grows 18-24 in. tall, with erect branched stems carrying large, globe-shaped, clear citron-yellow flowers. The stems of this flower are curiously smooth, and feel as though they had been smeared with a greasy substance.

Other Attractive Kinds. Trollius acaulis is a

dwarf plant from the Himalayas, growing about 6 in. tall, with large, golden, wide-open flowers like handsome Buttercups carried singly on erect stems. It grows best in rich loam in the rock garden.

Trollius albiflorus is native from Colorado to British Columbia. It grows to a height of about 1 ft. and has charming white flowers that measure about 1½ in. across.

Trollius altaicus, the Altaian Globeflower, grows 12-18 in. high and has pale yellow sepals arranged like a wide-open Buttercup.

Trollius asiaticus is closely related to T. europaeus, but the stems are unbranched, the flowers rich golden-yellow and more loosely globe-shaped than in T. europaeus; the leaves are tinged with a dark bronze shade. It grows about 18 in. high. There is a much larger form of T. asiaticus known variously in gardens as T. giganteus, T. Fortunei and T. Loddigesii.

T. chinensis, with deep golden flowers, is an Asiatic species that grows about 2 ft. tall. T. japonicus has large golden flowers like Buttercups. It grows 9-12 in. high. T. Ledebouri grows 18-24 in. high and has golden flowers. It is a native of Siberia.

T. laxus grows to a height of 2 ft. and inhabits bogs and swamps in the eastern United States. Its flowers, measuring to 2 in. across, are yellowish-green.

T. lilacinus (also known as Hegemone lilacina), native to the Altai Mountains, is rare in gardens, and reputedly difficult to cultivate, though a most beautiful and interesting plant. It requires gritty, stony loam and abundant moisture at the roots during the growing period. It grows 4 in. high, and has very large flowers, 2 in. across, of a lovely lilac-blue color.

T. patulus is one of the Asiatic species with handsome, wide-open buttercup-like flowers of rich gold on 9-12-in. stems; it is a good plant for rich loam in the rock garden. T. pumilus is another of the buttercup-flowered Asiatic kinds, growing some 6-12 in. high; it is most attractive in the rock garden and easily managed. There is a larger form called T. pumilus variety yunnanensis.

The Choice Hybrid Globeflowers. T. hybridus is a name which covers a fine race of crossbred Globeflowers. They range from palest yellow to deep orange, and grow 18 in. to 3 ft. tall. They are fine for the flower border, the bog garden, and for cutting, and well repay the gardener who gives them plenty of manure or rich compost and fertilizer. Among the best-named varieties are Earliest of All, yellow; Excelsior, Goldquelle, orange-yellow; Orange Globe, Fire Globe, Giganteus, Sunburst, pale yellow; and Lemon Queen.

TROPAEOLUM—*Nasturtium* (Tropae'olum). A group of between thirty and forty tender annual and perennial herbs which belong to the Tropaeolum family, Tropaeolaceae, and are native from Mexico to Chile. The name is from *tropaion,* a trophy, from the resemblance of the leaves to a buckler, and the flowers to a helmet.

Some of the dwarf annual kinds are extremely showy plants for summer beds, and the annual climbers are very useful and brilliant for covering fences, arbors and walls. The tuberous-rooted tender kinds are charming for training up the rafters inside a cool greenhouse, or for training to stakes or pieces of twiggy brushwood. They should be grown in pots of loam, leaf mold and sand, and be dried off by gradually withholding water from them, after flowering, and stored safe from frost until they are about to start into growth naturally the following spring. These kinds may be cultivated outdoors in mild climates but they do not thrive where the summers are very hot.

The seeds of the large-flowered annual Nasturtiums, both dwarf and climbing, if picked green, make a pleasant pickle, and the leaves may be used in salads and sandwiches. The popular name Nasturtium (Latin for Cress) was given on account of the biting, pungent flavor of the leaves, which resembles the flavor of Watercress, the Nasturtium officinale of botanists.

The Common Nasturtium. T. majus is the well-known common garden Nasturtium, so popular for planting in gardens, window and porch boxes and pots to produce summer bloom. There are both single- and double-flowered varieties; the singles are to be had in both climbing and dwarf forms in endless shades of color. There are also varieties, both tall and dwarf, with variegated leaves.

Tropaeolum majus is naturally a perennial, though it is convenient to treat it as an

A single-flowered form of the common Nasturtium, Tropaeolum majus.

annual. True double-flowered varieties set no seeds, and so must be increased by cuttings, which root readily under glass with a little bottom heat. These annual Nasturtiums are best grown in sandy soil that is not too rich. Too much fertilizer tends to make them run to leaf at the expense of flower.

In addition to their value for summer bloom outdoors, varieties of T. majus, the Common Nasturtium, are excellent for growing in pots in sunny, cool greenhouses to flower indoors. From seeds sown from September to January, and from cuttings rooted during that same period, plants are produced that bloom profusely over a very long season in late winter, spring and summer. A night temperature of about 50 degrees with a daytime rise of 5-10 degrees suits them well and they need very well-drained soil. When the pots in which they are to flower are filled with healthy roots the plants benefit from weekly applications of dilute liquid fertilizer.

Tall and Dwarf Varieties. Tall-growing varieties of T. majus are invaluable for covering arbors, fences and walls, and are to be had in many lovely and brilliant shades of orange, yellow, red, etc. The dwarf sorts have an even wider range of color, and there are varieties with dark, purple-tinged leaves.

One of the most striking of all is the variety Golden Gleam, which is of moderate growth, usually compact, but sometimes assuming a vigorous climbing habit, and bears semidouble, fragrant flowers of golden-yellow color. Scarlet Gleam, and the Gleam Hybrids, are showy developments from Golden Gleam. Many other fine varieties are offered in seed catalogues.

These various forms of T. majus are extremely sensitive to frost. They may be raised under glass in spring and planted out in the garden when all danger of frost has passed, or they may be sown in the open in spring, in the positions where they are to flower.

Canary-Bird Flower. T. peregrinum, the Canary-Bird Flower or Canary Creeper, is a very pretty climber with yellow flowers in summer. It is an annual and is treated in the same

A variety of the common Nasturtium, Tropaeolum majus, that bears double flowers.

The Canary-Bird Flower, Tropaeolum peregrinum, is a fast-growing annual climber that bears pretty yellow flowers.

way as T. majus. It is a rapid climber, running up to a height of 6-10 ft., and is invaluable for using as a screen. It requires only brushwood or strings to cling to. It is a native of Peru and Ecuador.

Some Perennial Kinds. T. azureum, a native of Chile, is an extremely pretty, tuberous-rooted, tender climber, 6-10 ft. tall, with flowers the shape and color of Violets. It is most attractive when trained up strings on the rafters of a cool greenhouse. T. Beuthii is a tender, tuberous-rooted species from Bolivia with pretty yellow flowers.

T. brachyceras is a tender, tuberous-rooted plant from Chile, with golden-yellow flowers in summer. It is a graceful, slender climber, suitable for growing as a pot plant in the greenhouse, where it is trained up strings under the rafters. It grows 6-8 ft. tall.

T. Deckerianum, from Venezuela, is a striking and beautiful tender climber. The flowers have a conspicuous scarlet spur and blue petals. T. edule is a tender climber from Chile with orange and green petals. It flowers in March and is suitable for the cool greenhouse.

T. peltophorum (Lobbianum) is a handsome Tropaeolum from South America, with large orange-colored, long-spurred flowers.

T. pentaphyllum is from the Argentine and has striking flowers, colored dull purple, green and vermilion. The stems and leafstalks are purplish; the root is a large tuber. The plant climbs by twisting its leafstalks about its support.

T. polyphyllum is a handsome, tuberous-rooted species from Chile, where it grows on desolate stony screes at an altitude of from six to nine thousand feet in the Andes. The rather thick stem, 18-24 in. long, is prostrate and clothed with gray-blue leaves, and bears numerous handsome nasturtium-like flowers ranging from pale yellow through golden-yellow to orange. In the garden it enjoys light, stony soil and a raised position, being particularly happy on sunny banks. It flowers in summer. It is increased from seeds, sown in a pan of loam and sand in a cold frame in spring, or by division of the tuberous roots in spring. Once established, it is best left alone. The tuberous roots are edible and have a pleasant flavor.

The Flameflower. T. speciosum, the Flameflower, from Chile, is a brilliant perennial climber, ascending to a height of 15 ft. or more, with trailing slender shoots clothed with delicate apple-green leaves; in late summer it bears nasturtium-like scarlet flowers. These are followed by dull red seed capsules exposing lovely turquoise-blue seeds as large as peas.

The Flameflower is difficult to establish in most gardens. In favored climates it becomes a positive weed, although an exquisitely beautiful one, spreading rapidly and clambering over choice shrubs and half-strangling them. The Pacific Northwest affords climatic conditions best suited for the growth of this plant. In most parts of the United States it is difficult or impossible to grow. It tolerates neither cold winters nor hot summers.

Cultivation of the Flameflower. To make the plant happy, the long white thonglike fleshy roots should be planted in a bed of peaty soil, or of leaf mold, mixed with broken sandstone. The bed should be on the north side of a hedge, at the foot of a cool wall, or by some low evergreen shrub, any of which will shelter it from sunshine and give it the support it requires. The roots should be laid horizontally on the bed, and covered with 4 or 5 in. of the special soil.

Seeds may also be sown in the prepared bed where the plants are to flower, but this is a slower method than putting out plants. The Flameflower is particularly beautiful growing over a Yew hedge, its fresh green foliage and scarlet flowers contrasting splendidly with the dark somber green of the Yew.

An Exquisite Perennial. Tropaeolum tricolor is an exquisite tender, tuberous-rooted perennial from Chile, growing 6-10 ft. tall, with slender climbing stems, light green leaves, and spurred flowers of curved trumpet shape, with orange-red, yellow and purplish-black or green coloring. It is a delightful climber for training on strings up the rafters in a cool greenhouse, where it flowers in summer. It is increased by seeds, or cuttings of the growing shoots may be rooted in a propagating case, forming tubers.

The Peruvian Nasturtium. T. tuberosum, the Peruvian Nasturtium, is a tender, tuberous-rooted species from Peru, growing 6-10 ft. tall, with pretty orange and yellow, spurred flowers.

In mild climates it may be grown in the open and trained against a wall or over a porch, to flower in September. The tuberous roots are edible when cooked.

TROUGH GARDENING. This subject is dealt with under Sink Gardening, which see.

TROUT LILY. See Erythronium.

TROWEL. One of the most useful of the smaller garden tools. It is invaluable for planting small plants, and does the work far more satisfactorily than a dibble, which is often used by experienced vegetable gardeners instead of a

Planting young Chrysanthemums with a trowel. This illustrates the way to hold a trowel for its most effective use.

trowel. By using a trowel, it is possible to make a hole of suitable size so that the roots of a plant can be spread out if necessary, and provided with friable (crumbly) soil in which they will form roots more quickly than in ground which has been compressed by a dibble.

TRUFFLES. Truffles are edible fungi which grow under the ground and are consequently hard to find. They have a characteristic odor, and so dogs or pigs can be trained to hunt for them. The man in charge of the animals must dig out the truffles when located.

True Truffles are species of Tuber (Tuber aestivum and Tuber melanospermum) which belong to the family Ascomycetes. Another group of fungi simulates them in general character and they are therefore called False Truffles. These are allied to the Puffballs: some of them are edible, but greatly inferior to true Truffles.

Most Truffles sold commercially come from France, where they are usually found under Oak trees. Small poodles are specially trained to search them out. About one third of the crop is exported. Truffles also grow wild in America.

TRUMPET, ANGEL'S. Datura arborea, which see.

TRUMPET CREEPER. Campsis, which see.

TRUMPET FLOWER. Bignonia capreolata, which see.

TRUMPET HONEYSUCKLE. Lonicera sempervirens, which see.

TRUMPET LILY. Lilium longiflorum, which see.

TRUMPET VINE. Campsis radicans, which see.

TRUNCATUS. A botanical term meaning ending abruptly or bluntly, as if broken off.

TRUNK. The main stem of a tree.

TSUGA—*Hemlock, Hemlock Spruce* (Tsu'ga). Evergreen trees, natives of North America, the Himalayas, China and Japan. Most are hardy. They share with other Conifers a dislike for atmospheric impurities, and are unsuitable for gardens in or near towns where the atmosphere is laden with smoke or chemical fumes. They thrive in gardens where climatic conditions are on the moist side, and give excellent results in mountain valleys and in valleys near the sea. But they also thrive in other gardens, forming very fine and graceful trees. They stand partial shade.

The Carolina Hemlock, Tsuga caroliniana, is one of the most decorative and graceful of evergreen trees.

The Eastern American Hemlock, Tsuga canadensis.

Hemlocks are trees for somewhat sheltered locations; in wind-swept places their foliage is apt to "burn" (turn brown at the tips of the leaves) and they do not prosper. They stand shade much better than most Conifers. Tsuga belongs to the Pine family, Pinaceae. The name is a Japanese one for a native Japanese kind.

Graceful Conifers for Gardens. The Tsugas are first-rate trees and shrubs for decorative planting, being peculiarly graceful in outline. They must, however, be given plenty of space so that they will not be crowded by other trees, either during development or at maturity.

As hedges the Hemlocks are very satisfactory and stand shearing well. When planting a Hemlock hedge it is advisable to set out young plants, not more than 1-3 ft. tall, in deeply spaded soil that has been enriched by mixing with it compost, leaf mold, rotted manure or some other bulky, decayed organic material, in really generous amounts. The plants should be spaced not more than 18-24 in. apart.

Shearing should be done each year just before new growth begins in spring and, if desired, once again about midsummer.

Established hedges benefit from being given a mulch of manure or a dressing of a complete fertilizer each spring.

Raising Trees from Seeds. The tree kinds are best increased by seeds, which may be sown in prepared beds of soil out of doors in spring, or in pans or flats of light soil in cold frame or

Sargent's Weeping Hemlock, Tsuga canadensis pendula, forms a large billowy shrub with drooping branchlets.

Hemlocks, when sheared regularly, form splendid hedges. Here, hedges of the Eastern American Hemlock, Tsuga canadensis, are used to secure a measure of privacy from the public road.

greenhouse in late winter. Young plants should be grown in nursery rows until they are large enough for permanent planting. Generally, it is advisable to set comparatively small plants in their permanent places rather than attempt to move large plants, although, if carefully handled, quite large specimens can be transplanted successfully.

Early autumn or spring are good times to transplant. Except when it is desired to clear the lower part of the trunk of branches, only sufficient pruning is needed to keep plants in shape; that may be done in summer. It is not advisable to remove many lower branches at once; take off a few each year until the desired height of clean trunk is attained.

Taking Cuttings. There are a number of distinct varieties that cannot be raised true from seeds; they are usually increased by cuttings of short, half-ripe wood inserted in a propagating case in a greenhouse in late summer or fall. These varieties can also be increased by grafting, in a greenhouse, on stocks of their respective types in winter; stocks previously established in pots are used.

The newly grafted plants are placed in a close propagating case until the union between stock and graft is complete.

The Eastern American Hemlock, T. canadensis, is a native of eastern North America from Nova Scotia to Alabama. It is the hardiest kind. In the wild state it sometimes attains a height of 100 ft. but it is usually lower in gardens. It is a very graceful tree, especially when its branches droop somewhat, as they do at maturity.

A number of varieties of T. canadensis have been given distinct names, such as T. canadensis pendula (Sargent's Weeping Hemlock), which forms a broad, dwarf tree to 12 ft. high with drooping or "weeping" branches; T. canadensis albo-spica, with shoots tipped with white; T. canadensis microphylla, with very small leaves; T. canadensis macrophylla, with large leaves; T. canadensis Fremdii, of stiff, erect habit; T. canadensis nana, a dwarf form; and T. canadensis gracilis, a slow-growing plant of peculiarly graceful outline.

The Carolina Hemlock, T. caroliniana, grows as a native in the mountains from Virginia to Georgia. It does not grow so tall as T. canadensis but does make quite as graceful a tree, or perhaps an even more graceful one. It thrives in gardens and is well suited for planting as a single specimen or in groups. It is hardy as far north as New England. A variety, T. caroliniana compacta, is more dwarf, denser, and round-topped, and is a slow grower.

The Mountain Hemlock, T. Mertensiana, is a very handsome tree of western North America, where it occurs from Alaska to California. It often exceeds 100 ft. in height. It has rather soft, bluish-green leaves, and its cones are much larger than those of other North American Hemlocks, being often 1½-2 in. long, whereas those of other kinds rarely exceed ¾ in. The variety argentea has bluish-white leaves. Both are excellent lawn trees for regions where plenty of summer moisture is assured, but they often fail to thrive in the East because of lack of this.

The Western American Hemlock, T. heterophylla, is a handsome kind. In western North America it reaches a height of 220 ft. This tree is of pyramidal habit, and the almost horizontal branches divide into numerous very fine branchlets, clothed with small, dark green leaves.

The Japanese Hemlock, T. diversifolia, seldom attains a height greater than 80 ft. and is usually lower in cultivation. It is a splendid evergreen and is hardy as far north as New England. It forms a pyramidal-shaped tree of dark green color.

Another Japanese species of considerable merit is T. Sieboldii, which grows to a maximum height of about 80 ft. and has wide-spreading horizontal branches. It is somewhat less hardy than T. diversifolia but grows in southern New England.

The Himalayan Hemlock, T. dumosa (T. Brunoniana), is a handsome tree 50-120 ft. high in its native habitat, with drooping branches and long, slender leaves. In the United States it may be grown only in the warmer sections.

Two other kinds that are somewhat less hardy are T. chinensis and T. yunnanensis. They are closely related; both are natives of western China. They may be expected to succeed as far north as New Jersey and southern New York.

TUBA ROOT. See Derris.

TUBER. Swollen, underground parts of plants, serving for food storage and vegetative propagation. Stem tubers, such as those of the

A clump of Dahlia tubers. For later identification, a label is tied on them after they are dug up in the fall.

The largest of all tubers is that of Amorphophallus Titanum. Such tubers may exceed one hundred pounds in weight.

The huge calla-like inflorescence ("flower") of Amorphophallus Titanum.

Potato and Jerusalem Artichoke, are swollen parts of the underground stems which originate in the axils of the leaves close to the base of the plant. Each "eye" of a Potato is really a scale (vestigial) leaf, bearing a bunch of buds in its axil. Thus any portion of a Potato tuber which bears an "eye" can be made to grow into a new plant; even the peelings will behave in this way.

Root tubers are those of the Dahlia and Salvia patens, for instance. They are thickened roots and bear no buds, but can easily be used for propagation purposes if each tuber is cut away with a portion of the old stem base attached. It is the latter which bears the necessary buds.

TUBEROSE. Polianthes, which see.

TUBS. Wooden tubs are commonly used in place of flowerpots for the cultivation of plants that need considerable root room. Bay trees, Palms, Cycads, Agaves, Agapanthus, Aloes, Acacias and Citrus trees are examples of plants

Stout tubs such as this one made of heavy rot-resistant lumber and secured with iron bolts are excellent for Bay trees, Orange trees and similar plants.

Ornamental tubs made of reinforced concrete last indefinitely and are suitable for many purposes.

Inexpensive tubs such as these, made of pine and bound with wire, are much used by florists for plants that will not remain in them for more than a year or two.

Because it is well constructed and made of Redwood, this ornamental tub, bound with copper bands, will last for many years.

that are often grown in tubs in conservatories and greenhouses and for the decoration of terraces, patios and similar outdoor areas. In general, it is best to use a tub if the diameter of the container must be 12 in. or more, and often tubs 9 to 11 in. in diameter are preferred to flowerpots of the same sizes. In place of wooden tubs, tubs made of concrete are sometimes used for plants on terraces and in outdoor locations.

Tubs may be round or square. Usually, they are slightly wider at the top than at the bottom and they must have holes in their bottoms to permit the escape of excess water.

Comparatively inexpensive tubs of light construction and made of pine or other wood that does not last long when filled with moist soil, are offered for sale and are much used by commercial growers, who sell their plants before they have been in the tubs long. These tubs are of little use as receptacles in which to grow plants for a period of many years.

The best tubs are made of Cypress, Redwood or other water-resistant lumber of fairly heavy grade. They are well constructed and are bound around with stout bands of steel or, in the case of square tubs, the sides are bolted together with steel rods. The outsides of the tubs may be painted with any ordinary paint, the insides treated with asphaltum paint or a wood preservative, such as Cuprinol, that is non-toxic to plants, or may be charred by burning to increase resistance to decay. Under no circumstance should creosote be used on the insides of tubs, because it is deadly to plant life. Most often the tubs are used without treating their insides in any way.

Tubs in which plants are growing should be fitted with short legs or should be stood on 3 bricks or other supports that raise them slightly off the floor. If a tub is set directly on the ground or floor, its base will decay much more quickly than otherwise and free drainage of excess moisture may be impeded.

For Aquatics. Water Lilies and other vigorous aquatics, such as Euryale, are often grown in wooden tubs filled with soil and then entirely or partially submerged (depending upon the need of the particular kind of plant).

Tubs as Pools. Tubs 1-2 ft. deep may be used as miniature pools in which to grow aquatic plants. Such tubs must be watertight and so are made without drainage holes. They are sunk in the soil almost or quite to their rims.

Rockwork may be built up to hide the rims, or the tubs can be sunk level with the soil and surrounded by paving. Such a miniature pool can be made very attractive, and is practicable for a sunny town garden, where a pond would be out of the question. Miniature Water Lilies may be grown in the tub, and around the damp edges many flowering plants can be grown, such as the Siberian and Japanese Irises, Marsh Marigold, yellow and orange Globeflower and brilliant red Lobelia cardinalis.

Tubs for Plant Cultivation. Old barrels should be cut in half, and filled with straw or shavings which are then burned to char the inside and render it durable, the outside being protected by three coats of paint, preferably green, and the hoops painted black. Several holes are bored in the bottom of the tub and covered with an inch or two of broken crocks, broken bricks or gravel to ensure good drainage; the tubs are filled with loamy soil.

Plants to Grow in Tubs. Some of the most suitable shrubs and plants for cultivation in tubs are Bay Trees (Laurus nobilis), Lemon Verbena, Hydrangea, Sedum spectabile, Agapanthus umbellatus, Hostas and hardy Ferns. During summer they may be filled with Ivy-leaf Pelargonium, Verbena, Petunia and other bedding plans, and climbing annuals. Climbing Roses, Clematis and Honeysuckle are also suitable for cultivation in tubs.

TUFA. A light-weight rock of a very porous, spongy nature, valuable for rock-garden work.

TUFTED PANSY. Viola cornuta, which see.

TULBAGHIA (Tulbagh'ia). A group of African rhizomatous or somewhat bulbous, tender herbaceous perennials, most of which emit

Tulbaghia fragrans is an attractive and fragrant-flowered bulbous plant that is a native of South Africa.

an onion-like odor when bruised. They belong in the Lily family, Liliaceae, and are named in honor of a former Dutch governor of the Cape of Good Hope, Ryk Tulbagh.

These attractive plants are suitable for planting in the outdoor garden in mild climates such as that of California, and for growing as pot plants in greenhouses and window gardens. They thrive in any reasonably fertile garden soil that is well drained and require full sun. Tulbaghias are very easily propagated by division and by seeds. When they are cultivated indoors, a minimum night temperature of 45 degrees is sufficient; at all times they should be grown under cool, airy conditions. Specimens that have filled their containers with healthy roots benefit from regular applications of dilute liquid fertilizer during their season of active growth.

Kinds include T. fragrans, 12-18 in., rosy-lavender flowers that are sweetly fragrant, the plant without any onion-like odor when bruised; T. violacea, 12-24 in., flowers have deep rosy-violet color and they are somewhat unpleasantly scented.

TULIP. See Tulipa.

TULIPA or TULIP
Most Colorful of All Spring-flowering Bulbs

Tulipa (Tu′lipa). A genus of hardy bulbs which provide some of the most brilliant flowers of spring and early summer. They are natives of various parts of Europe, western Asia and northern Africa. The name is said to be derived from the Turkish word *tulbend,* a turban, and refers to the shape of the flower. These plants belong in the Lily family, Liliaceae.

Tulips are bulbs for cool climates; they need a period of comparatively low winter temperatures. They do not thrive in the far South and can be grown there only if the bulbs, after their purchase in fall, are subjected to several weeks of cold storage at a temperature of about 40 degrees F. before they are planted.

Tulips owe their popularity, partly at least,

Beds of May-flowering Tulips are gay in spring gardens.

Tulips are excellent for planting in borders in groups between perennials.

Rows of Tulips planted in the cutting garden give long-stemmed blooms for use in flower arrangements.

to the use that is made of them in public parks and gardens. Both the Early-flowering and the May-flowering Tulips are massed in beds and borders. The May-flowering are especially popular, for their large blooms on tall strong stems make an exceptionally fine display.

Tulip "Breaking." "Broken" Tulips are varieties in which the flower shows striping or variegation; this takes the form of long stripes of white or pale color (or sometimes darker shades of the ground color) and feathering is frequently seen near the edge. Some of the patterns are very attractive and, since the bulbs always come true, useful new varieties have been obtained in this way. Broken varieties are not now so popular as the self-color types, but they were formerly highly prized, and existed as long ago as 1640.

Broken Tulips that have their color patterns on a pink or cerise background are called "Roses"; if the markings are violet or purple on a white background they are called "Bybloemens"; if the markings are brown, or red or purple on a yellow background they are called "Bizarres."

It has been shown in recent years that "breaking" is caused by a virus disease and under suitable conditions is infectious. The "breaking" can be transmitted artificially by grafting a piece of a diseased bulb on to a healthy one and by aphids. In nature it is partially spread by aphids feeding on the bulbs in storage; if a variety like Clara Butt is allowed to become infested with aphids when the bulbs are in storage, a large percentage of "broken" flowers will appear next season.

Other varieties such as Bartigon are much less susceptible, but "breaking" can be induced in all of the varieties and species of Tulip.

Very frequently the leaves are also affected, showing pale green stripes and mottling. The plant is also reduced in size and will not give such a large crop of flowers or of bulbs as a normal healthy plant.

"Broken" varieties never recover, although they may produce a few healthy offsets. If aphids are kept down in storage, there is no danger of the disease spreading, but it is also advisable to discard plants which bear broken flowers if it is desired to keep this condition from spreading to bulbs that bear unbroken flowers.

Classification of Tulips. All Tulips are classified into two groups, the Early-flowering and the May-flowering. The Early-flowering normally bloom in April outdoors, the May-flowering in May. These groups are subdivided into 16 divisions according to characters of the flowers and the habits of growth of the plants.

Early-flowering Tulips comprise divisions I to V and some of the species included in division XVI. May-flowering Tulips comprise divisions VI to XVI and some of the species included in division XVI.

The recognized names of the divisions and brief descriptions of the characters by which they are distinguished follow. Each division consists of many named varieties. (Recommended ones are listed at the end of this article.)

Division I: Duc Van Tol, 6 in., very early.

Division II: Single Early, 9-16 in., April.

Division III: Double Early, 9-16 in., April.

Division IV: Mendel, 16-26 in., resembling Darwins, but blooming two weeks earlier, some double flowered.

Division V: Triumph, 16-26 in., resembling Darwins, slightly earlier than Mendels and somewhat stouter, some double flowered.

Division VI: Cottage, all Tulips, including Lily-flowered varieties, that do not fall into other classes.

Division VII: Dutch Breeders, flowers oval or

Masses of the beautiful pink-flowered Darwin Tulip Clara Butt beneath a flowering Cherry tree.

cupped, brown, purple, red or bronze, base white or yellow generally stained blue or green.

Division VIII: English Breeders, flowers forming one third to one half of a hollow ball when fully expanded, base white or yellow without other color.

Division IX: Darwin, lower part of flower usually rectangular in outline, flowers of good substance, tall, strong stems.

Division X: Broken Dutch Breeders, same as division VII but with color feathered or striped, usually on white or yellow ground.

Division XI: Broken English Breeders, same as division VIII but with color striped or feathered usually on white or yellow ground.

Division XII: Rembrandt, broken Darwin Tulips.

Division XIII: Broken Cottage Tulips.

Division XIV: Parrot, varieties with slashes and fringed petals.

Division XV: Late Doubles.

Division XVI: Species and first crosses between species.

Outdoor Culture

As subjects for growing outdoors, the ordinary garden varieties of Tulips are most valued for massing in formal beds and borders, for planting in groups in perennial borders and for growing to supply cut flowers. They are also planted in window boxes and porch boxes. The species or botanical Tulips are most useful for growing in rock gardens, and the strongest-growing kinds, such as Tulipa Clusiana, T. Eichleri, T. Fosteriana, T. Gregei and T. Kaufmanniana, for planting at the fronts of perennial borders.

Although some kinds of Tulips, such as Tulipa persica, may persist and flower regularly in gardens for many years, occasionally as long as twenty or more, this is not generally the case under North American conditions. As a rule, in most localities, the bulbs gradually deteriorate and after a few seasons reach a stage where they flower sparsely or not at all. For the very best results and to assure uniformity in time of blooming, size of flowers, heights of stems, etc., newly purchased bulbs of good quality must be planted each fall. This is the recommended procedure for the production of grand mass effects of floral color in formal beds and borders.

When this plan is followed, the old bulbs need not be discarded after their first flowering; rather, they should be lifted, dried and stored as described below, and planted in fall in a less formal part of the garden or in a cut-flower garden, there to produce flowers of less uniform height and quality in succeeding years.

Location. Tulips are sun lovers. They will stand a little light shade during the hottest part of the day and the flowers will remain in good condition longer if they are afforded this, but they are not suitable for really shaded locations.

Tulips cannot be expected to compete successfully with the roots of trees, shrubs and vigorous perennials, such as Asters, Phlox, Iris and Heleniums; therefore they should be planted sufficiently far away from these to eliminate any serious problem.

The Soil. Tulips thrive best in well-drained, fertile, sandy loam. They do well for one season in almost any garden soil, but may prove disappointing in succeeding years, unless the soil is made suitable for them by draining; by the incorporation of decayed organic matter, sand, or heavier soil; or by whatever other measures are necessary to bring about the most desirable condition for the cultivation of Tulips. If the soil is very clayey or very sandy and is not modified as suggested above, it is doubtful whether it is worth while keeping the bulbs of Early-flowering Tulips for a second year.

Even in comparatively unsuitable soils the May-flowering Tulips are more satisfactory. Provided they are lifted annually when the leaves have died down, and dried and stored until autumn, most of them will bloom well, at least in their second year.

When the soil is prepared for Tulips it should be dug deeply and fertilized moderately. It must be remembered that the roots grow downwards from the bases of the bulbs and thus it is more important to have agreeable soil beneath the bulbs than above them. It is fatal to plant the bulbs of Tulips in infertile subsoil or to set them so that there is little other than that beneath them.

Fertilizers for Tulips. When preparing the ground for Tulips it is unwise to use animal

In preparation for planting Tulips, fertilizer is spread over the ground surface.

The ground is forked over deeply and the fertilizer well mixed with the soil, after which the surface is raked level.

The next step consists of setting the Tulip bulbs on the ground surface at the desired spacing.

The bulbs are then planted at a uniform depth with a trowel.

A few months after planting, the bed is a blaze of color.

If mice or other rodents are likely to eat the bulbs, the bed should be lined and covered with wire net.

manure unless it is thoroughly decayed, and then it should be set about 10 in. below the surface of the ground. Well-rotted compost may be substituted for manure. Bone meal is excellent for Tulips; it should be scattered on the surface of the ground, before planting, at the rate of 2 oz. per square yard, and be mixed in deeply with the garden fork.

A beneficial effect is obtained through the application of a complete garden fertilizer, such as one of 5-10-5 analysis, made in spring when the shoots are an inch or two high and cultivated shallowly into the surface soil. Such fertilization is especially important for bulbs that are left in the ground more than one year.

Planting the Bulbs. The best time to plant the Early-flowering Tulips is in October; the bulbs of the May-flowering Tulips should be planted late in October or early in November.

Bulbs of the Early-flowering Tulips are covered with 3-4 in. of soil on heavy land, and with 4-5 in. of soil on light land; they are set about 5-6 in. apart if they are used without other plants between them, 8-9 in. apart if they are interplanted with Pansies, Forget-me-nots, Primulas or other spring bedding plants.

Bulbs of May-flowering Tulips should be covered with 4 in. of soil on heavy land, and with 5 in. of soil on light land; they should be set 6 in. apart if they are planted without other plants between them, 9-12 in. apart if interplanted with spring bedding plants.

Rodent Damage. A serious problem in some localities is damage done to the bulbs by mice and other rodents. The best preventative is to line the outsides of the beds, to a depth of 9-10 in. with fine wire mesh and to cover the bed surface in fall (it may be removed in late winter) with the same material. Small groups of bulbs may be planted in baskets of wire mesh.

Winter Protection. In cold climates it is advisable to cover the Tulip beds, after the soil has frozen to a depth of an inch or so, with salt-marsh hay, leaves, evergreen branches or other suitable winter protection. Manure, compost or other compact materials that exclude air should not be used for winter covering.

Spring Care. When the shoots appear above ground in late winter or spring and danger of really hard freezing is past, the material used for winter covering should be removed, not all at once, but gradually in two or three operations spaced a few days apart. If practicable, dull, humid days, rather than sunny, windy ones, should be chosen for uncovering.

When the shoots are about 2 in. high, the spring application of fertilizer (see Fertilizers for Tulips, above) should be made and the ground between the plants should be stirred occasionally with a hand cultivator.

To protect small groups of Tulips from rodents, baskets of wire net may be sunk in the ground and filled with soil and the bulbs planted in them.

Bulb planters such as these are especially suitable for planting Tulips.

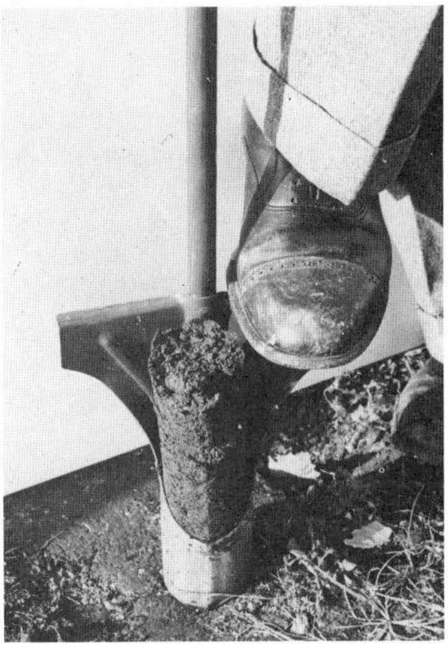

The bulb planter, pushed into the ground with the foot and withdrawn, lifts out a neat plug of soil.

If long periods of dry weather occur between the time when the shoots break through the ground and the final turning brown and dying down of the foliage, it is important to soak the ground thoroughly with water at whatever intervals are necessary to keep it from drying out. Dry soil conditions are likely to result in short stems, small flowers and poor bulb development.

Cutting the Blooms. When Tulips are taken as cut flowers, only the uppermost leaf on the

A Tulip bulb is dropped into each hole made by the bulb planter.

After the bulb is dropped into the hole, the plug of soil is replaced to cover it.

When Tulip flowers are cut, the leaves should be left.

As soon as Tulip flowers have faded, the tips of the flower stems should be cut off to prevent seed from forming.

stem (which is a small one) should be cut with the blooms if the bulbs are expected to flower the following year. If the larger lower leaves are cut off, the plants' ability to prepare food materials to store in the bulbs in preparation for the following season's growth is destroyed or greatly diminished.

Flowers that are not cut while fresh should be removed as soon as their petals drop, to prevent the formation of seed pods. This latter activity reduces the plants' ability to store food in the bulbs. When faded blooms are removed, they should be cut just below the flower, leaving most of the flower stalk intact.

Lifting and Storing the Bulbs. There are two distinct methods of caring for Tulips during their summer season of dormancy. One is to leave the bulbs in the ground undisturbed, the other to dig them up after they have flowered and store them in a cellar or other cool place and replant them in the fall.

In most gardens the lifting and storing method is considered the better one, and it must be practiced if the beds are to be dug over and fertilized in preparation for planting such summer-flowering plants as Geraniums, Heliotropes, Begonias, Coleus, Cannas, Lantanas and Dahlias. If the bulbs are left in the ground it is practicable, after the leaves have died and been removed, to sow such annuals as Sweet Alyssum, Portulaca, Thymophylla, Gypsophila and Sanvitalia directly where they are to bloom, after first cultivating the surface soil shallowly and improving it by stirring into it a dressing of bone meal or complete fertilizer.

When flower beds must be prepared in late May or early June for replanting with summer bedding plants, it becomes necessary to remove the Tulips before they have died down naturally and completely, even though this is somewhat harmful to them. When this premature digging must be done, every effort should be made to give the bulbs an opportunity to complete their ripening process by replanting them, with their leaves attached, in a shaded place. They should be taken up with as little damage to the roots as possible and replanted close together in shallow trenches about 3 in. deep. They should be well watered after transplanting.

After such treatment the leaves are likely to die off earlier than they would if the bulbs had not been disturbed. When the leaves have died down the bulbs should be lifted, set out to dry under cover for a few days, and then stored as described below until fall. A better way of managing Tulip bulbs, and one that can be carried out when they do not have to be replaced quickly by summer-flowering plants, is to leave them undisturbed until the leaves have died down completely, and then to lift, dry and store them.

When digging the bulbs, great care must be taken not to pierce them with the fork or bruise them in other ways. They are dried by spreading them out in a shaded, dry, airy place for a few days. Then old roots and other debris are

Clearing old dead foliage from Tulips that are to be left in the ground through the summer.

cleaned off and the bulbs are graded according to size, dusted with sulphur and stored in thin layers in well-ventilated shallow trays (preferably with bottoms made of wire screening or mesh), paper bags or old nylon stockings suspended from a roof or other convenient support. The place of storage should be comparatively cool, dry, well ventilated and shaded from direct sun.

Propagation. An increased stock of special varieties can be obtained by removing the offsets when the bulbs are lifted in summer after the leaves have died down; the offsets are stored and replanted in autumn. Tulips may also be raised from seeds sown as soon as they are ripe, in flats of sandy soil in a cold frame. The seedlings will not, however, bloom for several years. When the seedlings are well developed they should be planted in a bed of sandy soil made up in the frame.

Most gardeners buy bulbs from commercial sources rather than propagate their own Tulips. Success with raising propagations to flowering size is only likely where soil and climate are particularly suitable. In the vicinity of Holland, Michigan, Tulips are propagated and grown for commercial bulb production, but such cultivation is not practicable in most parts of North America. The vast majority of Tulip bulbs planted in American and Canadian gardens are produced in the Netherlands.

Culture Indoors

Tulips are among the most satisfactory bulbs for forcing into early bloom indoors, both in greenhouses and in homes. By making a suitable selection of varieties, flowers may be had from Christmas until Tulips come into bloom in the outdoor garden. Forced Tulips are attractive as pot plants and useful for cutting.

To ensure success it is necessary to obtain top-quality bulbs and to plant them early, from September to November. Those that are to bloom first should be planted first and the later-blooming ones in succession. For cultivation as pot plants Single Early and Double Early varieties are very satisfactory and are the easiest to grow in ordinary dwelling houses; they may be had in bloom from January onwards. The Mendels may also be had in bloom in January. Where a greenhouse is available, taller-growing kinds such as Darwins, Dutch Breeders, Cottage and other May-flowering types may be grown and had in flower from February onwards. These kinds are rarely satisfactory to raise in the house because if they do not receive full sunshine and, if the temperature is higher than they need (and it almost always is), they grow tall and weak-stemmed and bear inferior flowers.

The very earliest forced Tulips are produced from "prepared" bulbs—that is to say, from bulbs which have been subjected to special treatment in Holland to make them suitable for early forcing. To flower prepared bulbs calls for careful control of temperatures and other environmental factors that is beyond the facilities and skill of most amateurs; these bulbs are not adaptable for cultivating in houses. It is from prepared bulbs that flowers are produced in greenhouses in December and January.

Planting. Tulips for forcing may be planted in pots or deep flower pans measuring 6-10 in. in diameter or in 4-in.-deep flats; the latter are used when the objective is flowers for cutting. These receptacles should be drained so that superfluous moisture can escape and should then be filled to a suitable level with light, loamy, porous soil. A mixture of good topsoil (lightened with some sand if it is of a heavy nature) and a moderate amount of organic matter such as well-rotted compost, peat moss, leaf mold or humus is satisfactory. The soil should be firmed lightly but not packed hard and should be at such a level that when the bulbs are stood on it their tips are level with or slightly below the level of the rim of the container.

Set the bulbs so closely together that they almost, but not quite, touch each other, then fill in with soil and, with the tips of the fingers, press this as firmly as possible. The finished surface should be smooth and even, with the tips of the bulbs slightly buried or just peeping out of the soil. After planting, water thoroughly.

Rooting Period. After planting, Tulips need a period of several weeks (10-12 or more) in cool, moist, dark conditions to stimulate root growth; it is fatal to success to place the newly planted bulbs in a greenhouse or living room

In preparation for planting bulbs to be forced, crocks are placed in the bottom of the pans or pots to insure good drainage.

Top-quality Tulip bulbs are set on the soil so that their tips will barely show when planting is finished.

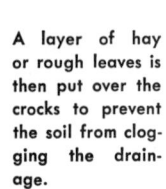

A layer of hay or rough leaves is then put over the crocks to prevent the soil from clogging the drainage.

A pan of Tulips before planting is completed. The bulbs almost touch each other.

Next, a fertile, porous soil mixture is added and lightly firmed.

The bulbs are next almost covered with soil, and this is made quite firm with the finger tips.

right away. One satisfactory method of providing the needed conditions is to bury the pots or flats outdoors under a 6-8-in. layer of sand or sifted coal ashes or—and this makes getting them out easier in frosty weather—they may be buried in a cold frame under several inches of sand, sand and peat moss, peat moss or sifted coal ashes. After the top inch of the covering material has frozen, the frame sash may be placed over them and this may be further protected with mats, straw or other insulating material in very severe weather.

Instead of being buried outdoors or in a cold frame, the newly planted bulbs may be stored in a cool, moist, frost-free root cellar or similar building. Where they are placed matters little, so long as the essential environmental conditions are provided. Even moisture, darkness, a temperature in the neighborhood of 40 degrees, or as near that as outside conditions permit,

After planting, the pots of bulbs may be placed outdoors or in a cold frame and covered with 6-8 in. of sand, coal ashes or some similar material. The bulbs remain covered for several weeks.

After Tulip bulbs to be forced have rooted well under cool conditions and have produced shoots 1-2 in. high, the pots may be brought indoors. At first they are kept out of strong light and in a fairly cool temperature.

When the shoots have made a little more growth and have become green the pots may be moved into stronger light and warmer temperatures.

With light and warmth, growth is very rapid and flower buds soon begin to appear.

The fully developed flowers will last longer if the plants are kept in a moderately cool location.

move from the container) a sample potful and examine the condition of the roots. When roots emerge freely from the bottoms of flats in which Tulips are planted and when roots can be seen in quantity on the surface of the soil, it indicates that the bulbs are well rooted and ready for forcing.

When first brought indoors, Tulips should be shaded from strong light, but gradually, as the shoots turn green, they should be given more light and, as soon as they are of a normal green color, they should be exposed to all and freedom from actual freezing are the conditions required. After the bulbs are well rooted, the containers are brought into the house or greenhouse where they are to be forced into bloom.

Before they are brought in, the shoots from the tops of the bulbs should be 1-2 in. long but, most important of all, healthy white roots should fill the pots, pans or flats. To make sure that this is so, it is usual to "knock out" (repossible sunshine. Because Single Early and Double Early Tulips naturally have short stems and because they are likely to be extra short when they are forced early, they may be kept in complete or almost complete darkness during most of the forcing period, and given light only after the flower buds are well up and the stems have lengthened considerably.

Although it is better to start the forcing of Tulips in a fairly cool (45-50 degree at night) temperature and gradually increase this to 55-65 degrees at night with a few degrees increase in the daytime permitted, Single Early and Double Early varieties will respond if put into forcing temperatures of 60-70 degrees right away. Other types of Tulips must be grown cooler throughout the forcing period. For them a beginning night temperature of 45-50 degrees, later increased to 50-55 degrees with a few degrees' increase in the daytime allowed, is best; but if quick results are desired, these bulbs may be started in a temperature of 60 degrees and have this reduced to 50-55 degrees when the flowers begin to show color.

During the forcing period ample supplies of water are necessary; if the roots become dry the flowers "go blind"—that is, they fail to develop and eventually dry up. The application of diluted liquid fertilizer at weekly intervals is beneficial.

Staking and tying may be needed to keep the flowers well arranged. Do this neatly, using thin bamboo or wire stakes and inconspicuous tying material. As soon as the flowers approach full development, move the pots or other containers to a somewhat cooler location; this will delay opening slightly but will result in finer blooms of firmer texture.

To have a long succession of bloom it is necessary to plant some varieties that are most suitable for early forcing and some that are naturally later flowering. It is also essential to bring successive batches of rooted bulbs from the location where they have been rooting into the home or greenhouse. Batches may be brought in about every ten days to ensure a continuous display of flowers.

It is important not to allow bulbs under the sand to develop their shoots too much before they are removed from the ashes or other covering material. Examine them and, when the shoots are 2 in. long (usually before mid-February), remove the pots, pans or flats containing the bulbs from the covering material. If they are not yet needed for forcing, place them in a cold frame and protect them from freezing by using heavy mats or other suitable protection at night. In the daytime, give them all light possible (except for the first few days) and ventilate the frame freely in mild weather.

Timing. Single Early, Double Early and Mendel Tulips may be had in flower in 3-4 weeks from the time they are brought indoors. Darwin, Breeder and Cottage types take longer. These are had at their best if given 8-9 weeks indoors to bring them into bloom, although by "pushing" them a little with somewhat higher temperatures than are recommended here they may be brought into flower in 6-7 weeks. All Tulips force more quickly later in the season than early—that is, as the time of their natural season of flowering outdoors is approached.

The best varieties for forcing include the following:

Single Early Tulips: Crown Imperial, Cullinan, Fred Moore, General de Wet, Keizerskroon, Mon Trésor, Pink Perfection, White Hawk, Yellow Prince.

Double Early Tulips: El Toreador, Marechal Niel, Mr. van der Hoef, Murillo, Peach Blossom, Schoonoord, Tea Rose.

Mendel Tulips: Amidonette, Athleet, Brightling, Her Grace, Hildegarda, Krelage's Triumph, Orange Wonder, Pink Gem, Weber, White Sail.

Triumph Tulips: Elmus, Glory of Noordwijk, Kansas, Korneforos, Paris, Red Giant, Telescopium.

Cottage Tulips: Advance, Albino, Carrara, Dido, Lemon Queen (Mothers' Day), Mongolia, Rosabella.

Breeder Tulips: Cherbourg, Indian Chief, Limnos, Tantalus.

Darwin Tulips: Adoration, Demeter, Glacier, Insurpassable, King George V, Rose Copeland, Pride of Haarlem, The Bishop, Venus, William Copland, William Pitt.

History of Tulips

Few flowers have caused such a sensation,

[13—8a]
Venidium fastuosum

[13—8]
Vanda caerulea

[13—8c]
Royal Water Lily
(Victoria regia)

[13—8b]
Venidium decurrens

[13—9]
Eastern American Hemlock
(Tsuga canadensis)

[13—9a]
Wake Robin
(Trillium grandiflorum)

[13—9b]
Viburnum Carlesii

[13—9c]
American Cranberry Bush
(Viburnum trilobum)

when first introduced, as the Tulip. Nothing is known of its history before 1550, beyond the fact that before that date it was in cultivation in Turkey, though for how long is unknown. Busbecq, Ambassador of the Emperor Ferdinand I to the Sultan, mentioned in a letter written in 1554 that in a garden between Adrianople and Constantinople he saw Tulips flowering in profusion. The Tulips, he said, were "flowers with little or no smell, but are admired for their beauty and variety of color."

The first record of a Tulip flowering in Europe is that made by Conrad Gesner, the famous botanist. The flowers he saw were growing in a garden in Augsburg. In his *De Hortis Germaniae* he states, "In this year of our Lord, 1559, at the beginning of April in the garden of the ingenious and learned Councillor, John Henry Herwart, I saw there a plant which had sprung from seed which had been procured from Byzantia, or as some say from Cappadocia. It was growing with one large reddish flower, like a red Lily, having eight petals of which four are outside and just as many within, with a pleasant smell, soothing and delicate, which soon leaves it."

Tulips were introduced into England before 1582, but the exact date is unknown. Writing in that year, Richard Hakluyt says in his *Remembrance of Things to Be Endeavoured at Constantinople,* "And now within these foure years there have been brought into England from Vienna in Austria divers kinds of flowers called Tulipas and these and others procured thither a little before from Constantinople by an excellent man called Carolus Clusius." Clusius, or de l'Ecluse, was the celebrated Belgian botanist who went to Leyden as Professor of Botany in 1593. Although the Tulip mania did not begin for another thirty years, de l'Ecluse made a small fortune by selling his bulbs.

Introduction of Tulips into America. We have no precise record of the earliest date of the introduction of Tulips into America but we are quite certain that the early colonists grew them about their homes. Certainly from 1640 onwards the Dutch settlers in New York (then New Amsterdam) grew Tulips. Adrian Van der Donck, who visited New Amsterdam in 1642, later reported upon "the flowers in general which the Netherlands have introduced" and specifically included "different varieties of fine Tulips."

The tulipomania, as it is commonly known —a period of fervid interest and speculation in Tulip bulbs—began in Holland between 1620 and 1623. Nicholas Wassenaer, writing in 1623, records that a variety called Semper Augustus had sold for thousands of florins, and that in 1625 the sum of three thousand florins was refused for two bulbs.

By 1634 the tulipomania was at its height. Collegiums or clubs were formed and inns became "Tulip exchanges." In a rare print of the period entitled "The Fools' Wagon," Flora, the Goddess of Flowers, is depicted holding a horn of plenty filled with Tulip blooms in one hand and three blooms in the other. The three florists with her, named Eager Rich, Good for Nothing, and Tippler, are adorned with Tulips. People trampling on weaving looms, etc., run after the wagon crying: "We will all sail with you." The tulipomania subsided by 1637.

In England, Tulips became the most highly esteemed spring-flowering bulbs. Parkinson, in his *Paradisus* (1629), says that flower lovers were "more delighted in the search, curiosity and rarities of these pleasant delights than any age I thinke before. But indeed this flower above any other deserveth his true commendations and acceptance with all lovers of these beauties, both for the stately aspect and for the admirable varieties of colours that daily does arise in them. . . .

"But above and beyond all others the Tulipas may be so matched, one colour answering and setting of another that the place where they stand may resemble a piece of curious needlework or a piece of painting: and I have known in a Garden the Master as much commended for this artificial form in placing the colours of Tulips as for the goodnesse of his flowers or any other thing. . . . But to tell you of all the sorts of Tulipas (which are the pride of delight) they are so many and as I may say almost infinite doth passe my ability and as I believe the skill of any other . . .

"Besides this glory of variety in colours they carry so stately and delightfull a forme and do abide so long in their bravery that there is no

Lady or Gentlewoman of any worth that is not caught with this delight."

In 1733 and 1734 there was a mild revival of the tulipomania in the Low Countries. As late as 1836, 16,000 francs, in those days a large sum, was paid in Amsterdam by an amateur grower for a new variety, the "Citadel of Antwerp."

The earliest mention of securing Tulips in flower before those in the open garden is to be found in Gervase Markham's *English Husbandman* (1615). He states that Tulips and other spring-flowering plants, such as Narcissi and Columbines, were sometimes planted in boxes of earth placed on wheels, and that these boxes were left in the open during the daytime and wheeled under cover at night, so that they stood "warme and safe from stormes, windes, frosts, dewes, blastings, and other mischiefs which happen in the Sunnes absence."

Varieties of Tulips

Not all of the 16 divisions into which Tulips are officially classified (see Classification of Tulips, above) are equally popular in gardens in North America, nor is the official classification always strictly followed in dealers' catalogues. For example, varieties belonging in division I, Duc Van Tol Tulips, are seldom listed and rarely grown, neither are those belonging in division VIII, English Breeders, division X, Broken Dutch Breeders, division XI, Broken English Breeders and division XIII, Broken Cottage Tulips. Varieties of division VII, Dutch Breeders, are usually listed simply as Breeders. The Lily-flowered Tulips, which are officially classed in division VI, Cottage Tulips, are most commonly listed separately in catalogues.

Catalogues often list Tulips belonging in division XVI, species and first crosses between species, as Botanical Tulips.

Single Early Tulips. These do not grow so high as the May-flowering Tulips. They are well adapted for forcing indoors, and when massed in outdoor beds make gorgeous displays of color. They usually appear at their best when planted alone, but they may be interplanted with early spring-blooming plants such as Pansies and Polyanthus Primulas with good effect also.

The following are good varieties: Couleur Cardinal, red; Crown Imperial, mahogany-red with a broad yellow band; Cullinan, soft pink; DeWet, golden-orange; Fred Moore, terracotta tinged with golden buff; Ibis, pink; Keizerskroon, red and yellow; Mon Tresor, yellow; Pink Beauty, rose pink; Pink Perfection, white, flushed pink; Prince of Austria, orange-scarlet; Sunburst, golden-yellow; Van der Neer, purple-mauve; Vermilion Brilliant, vermilion-scarlet; White Hawk, white; Yellow Prince, canary yellow.

Double Early Tulips. The remarks made above under Single Early Tulips apply to Double Early Tulips also. The flowers of the double-flowered kinds usually last a little longer in good condition than those of the single-flowered varieties.

The following are good double-flowered varieties: Couronne d'Or, yellow, flushed orange; Dante, blood-red; Electra, carmine-pink; El Toreador, salmon and orange; Maréchal Niel, yellow and orange; Mr. van der Hoef, pure yellow; Murillo, soft pink; Orange Nassau, orange-red; Peach Blossom, rose-pink; Schoonoord, white; Tea Rose, primrose yellow shaded with pink; Vuurbaak, orange-scarlet; Willemsoord, carmine, edged white.

Mendel Tulips. The varieties in this division

Single Early Tulip Keizerskroon, scarlet and yellow.

One of the loveliest Double Early Tulips, the yellow, orange-shaded Maréchal Niel.

normally bloom 10-14 days earlier than Darwin Tulips and later than Single Early Tulips and Double Early Tulips. Most varieties force well indoors.

The following varieties are recommended: Amidonette, lilac-rose with white margins; Athleet, pure white; Brightling, rose-pink flushed with orange; Her Grace, pink and white; Hildegarda, deep red; Krelage's Triumph, dark red; Orange Wonder, bronze-scarlet shaded orange; Pink Gem, white edged with pink; Scarlet Admiral, red with black center; Weber, white margined with lilac-rose; White Sail, cream white changing to pure white.

Triumph Tulips. These are a race of handsome Tulips characterized by vigorous growth, tall, strong stems and large flowers of fine quality. They were originated by hybridizing Single Early Tulips with Darwin, Breeder and Cottage varieties. The blooming season of Triumph Tulips is intermediate between those of the Single Early varieties and Darwin, Breeder and Cottage varieties. Most varieties force well.

The following Triumph Tulips are an excellent selection: Bandoeng, mahogany-red and yellow; Bruno Walter, golden-brown with purple tinge; Elisabeth Evers, carmine-rose; Elmus, cherry-red edged with white; Glory of Noordwyk, lilac-rose; Johanna, deep salmon-pink; Kansas, pure white; Korneforos, cerise-red; Paris, orange-red and yellow; Piccadilly, cherry-red with white margin; Princess Beatrix, orange-scarlet edged gold; Red Giant, bright red; Telescopium, reddish violet.

Cottage Tulips. The varieties in this division have mostly been grown for very long periods in the cottage gardens of Great Britain and France. They are tall and vigorous, and usually have long pointed flowers. They bloom in May and may be forced earlier indoors. Officially, the Lily-flowered Tulips are included in the Cottage Tulip division, but, because they are quite distinct and are listed separately in catalogues, they are treated separately here (see Lily-flowered Tulips, below).

Good varieties of Cottage Tulips are: Advance, orange-scarlet; Arethusa, lemon-yellow; Belle Jaune, golden-yellow; Carrara, white; Dido, pink, yellow, orange; Geisha, pink; Golden Harvest, golden-yellow; Grenadier, orange; Ivory Glory, cream-white changing to pure white; Jeanne Désor, soft yellow, edge orange; Marshal Haig, scarlet; Mrs. John T. Scheepers, yellow; Mrs. Moon, yellow; Perseus, orange; Rosabella, pink; Rosy Wings, salmon-pink.

Lily-flowered Tulips. Officially, Lily-flowered Tulips are included in the Cottage Tulip division but they differ considerably in appearance and are usually listed separately in catalogues. They bloom at the same time as or slightly earlier than other Cottage Tulips and are distinguished by having pointed petals that curve outwards markedly at their ends.

The following selection of varieties is suggested: Alaska, yellow; Capt. Fryatt, ruby-purple;

Cottage Tulip.

pointed in outline. They may be had in a great variety of brilliant colors and are excellent for forcing as well as for planting outdoors. Some of the newer Darwin varieties are sometimes catalogued as Ideal Darwin Tulips.

The following is a good selection of Darwin varieties: Adoration, flesh-pink; Afterglow, rose-amber; Bartigon, cochineal-red; Bleu Aimable, lavender; Charles Needham, brilliant red; City of Haarlem, scarlet; Demeter, violet-blue; Farncombe Sanders, scarlet; Giant, purple; Glacier, pure white; Golden Age, deep yellow; Helen Madison, pink; Insurpassable, lilac; King George V, carmine-red; King Harold, blood-red; La Tulipe Noire, maroon-black; Mahogany, deep mahogany; Niphetos, deep cream; Pride of Haarlem, carmine-rose; Pride of Zwanenburg, rose-pink; Princess Elizabeth, deep pink;

The Lily-flowered Tulips are characterized by reflexed petals that are pointed at their tips.

Dyanito, vermilion; Ellen Willmott, primrose-yellow; Florestan, crimson; Gisela, soft pink, shaded with yellow; Mariette, salmon-pink; Painted Lady, yellow and orange-red; Picotee, white, edge rose; Stanislaus, orange; White Duchess, white; and White Triumphator, pure white.

Dutch Breeder Tulips. Commonly listed as Breeder Tulips, the varieties in this division are similar in general appearance to Darwin Tulips. They bloom at the same time as Darwins, have large flowers carried on long stout stems and are available in a glorious variety of "art" colors, most of which do not occur in other kinds of Tulips.

Good varieties of Dutch Breeder Tulips are the following: Bacchus, violet; Barcarolle, blue-purple; Chappaqua, cherry-pink; Cherbourg, old gold and bronze; Dillenburg, salmon-orange; Dom Pedro, coffee-brown; Indian Chief, red-brown; J. J. Bouwman, mahogany and bronze; Limnos, salmon-pink and orange; Louis XIV, violet and bronze; President Hoover, orange-scarlet; Tantalus, light yellow shaded with violet; Velvet King, royal purple.

Darwin Tulips. Deservedly one of the most popular groups, Darwin Tulips are remarkable for their vigorous growth, long, sturdy stems and large flowers, which are squarish rather than

The pink Darwin Tulip Princess Elizabeth.

Prunus, salmon-pink; Queen of Bartigons, pink; Rose Copeland, pink; Scarlett O'Hara, scarlet; Smiling Queen, pink; The Bishop, purple, Venus, silvery-rose; White Giant, white; William Copeland, mauve-lilac; William Pitt, strawberry-red; Yellow Giant, yellow; Zwanenburg, white.

Rembrandt Tulips. Darwin Tulips that have broken (see Tulip "Breaking," above) comprise the group called Rembrandt Tulips. They are distinguished by having varicolored flowers, beautifully striped, feathered and blotched, after

Attractively feathered Rembrandt Tulips.

the manner of those so often depicted in old Dutch paintings.

Among the best of the Rembrandts are the following: American Flag, rose-red and white; Clara, pink, scarlet and white; Cordell Hull, white and rose-red; Kathleen, pink and white; Madame de Pompadour, white and lilac; Paljas, white and scarlet; Pierrette, white and violet purple; Refinement, white and red.

Parrot Tulips. The Parrot Tulips, which bloom in May, are extremely showy, but they are scarcely suitable for massing in formal flower beds; the large, shaggy, artistic blooms are, in most varieties, weak-stemmed, and are therefore liable to be blown down in windy weather. A sheltered place should be chosen for them.

The following are some of the loveliest Parrot Tulips: Black Parrot, maroon-black; Blue Parrot, lavender-mauve; Fantasy, pink and green; Firebird, scarlet and green; Gadelan, purple-mauve; Orange Favorite, orange and green; Orange Parrot, mahogany and gold, very fragrant; Sunshine, golden; Texas Gold, golden-yellow; Therese, rose-red and scarlet; Van Dijck, pink, similar to Fantasy.

Late Double Tulips. This modern race of Tulips is sometimes catalogued as Peony-flowered Tulips. They are of sturdy growth and produce large, many-petaled flowers on long stems that last well. They flower in May. Among the best are the following varieties: Eros, old rose; Golden Lion, golden-yellow; Clara Carder, clear pink; Livingstone, cherry pink; Mount Tacoma, white; Nizza, cream, marked crimson; Pavo, rose-pink; Uncle Tom, deep wine-red.

Botanical Tulips. Among the "botanical" Tulips (as dealers usually term the wild types or Tulipa species) there are many beautiful kinds suitable for planting in the rock garden and in other locations where they may be left undisturbed, and for growing in pans in the alpine house.

A few of the loveliest, which are offered by bulb specialists, are: T. Batalinii, pale yellow, 4 in., May; T. biflora, pale and deep yellow, 5 in., March; T. chrysantha, yellow and cherry-rose, 6 in., April; T. Clusiana, the Lady Tulip, rose-red and white, 8 in., April; T. Eichleri, vermilion and yellow, 10 in., April; T. Fosteriana, 12 in., scarlet, April; T. Greigii, 8-10 in., vivid scarlet, April; T. Hageri, 5 in., copper-red, April–May; T. Kaufmanniana, cream and carmine, 6 in., March or April; T. linifolia, 4 in., scarlet, May; T. patens (persica), 3 in., yellow-bronze, fragrant, May; T. praestans, 8 in., dazzling orange-scarlet, April, and its brilliant variety Fusilier; T. pulchella, the Crocus Tulip, 6 in., rose-purple, February; T. tarda (dasystemon), 3 in., primrose-yellow, April-May; T. viridiflora, 24 in., May formosa.

Tulipa Kaufmanniana Hybrids are often

The shaggy-flowered pink and green Parrot Tulip Fantasy.

The charming Lady Tulip, Tulipa Clusiana, white and rosy red.

Flowers of the lovely Water-Lily Tulip, Tulipa Kaufmanniana.

cent, brilliantly colored April-flowering Tulips, 12-18 in. tall, are developed from the vivid Oriental-scarlet T. Fosteriana. They have huge flowers in vivid scarlet and vermilion shades. Some of the most striking are Feu Superbe, red with yellow base to flower; Galatea, orange-scarlet; Holland's Glory, enormous blooms of glowing orange-red; Princeps, vermilion red; Red Emperor, large bright red blooms; Red Matador, vivid orange-red; Red Riband, brilliant red; Rockery Beauty, brilliant red, plant very dwarf.

called Water Lily Tulips. These have been developed from the species Tulipa Kaufmanniana and have large blooms of striking form and coloring, produced in March or early April on 6-in. stems.

The many fine varieties include: Aurora, deep yellow and red; Brilliant, red and gold; Edwin Fischer, yellow, red and carmine; Johann Strauss, cream and red; Mendelssohn, yellow and carmine-rose; Robert Schumann, chrome-yellow and crimson; Scarlet Elegance, and Vivaldi, cream-yellow and deep pink.

Tulipa Fosteriana Hybrids. These magnifi-

An unusual green-flowered Tulip named Tulipa viridiflora. This kind grows about 2 ft. high and has large light green petals which are yellow at their margins.

TULIP, GLOBE. See Calochortus.

TULIP ORCHID. See Anguloa.

TULIP POPLAR. Liriodendron Tulipifera, which see.

TULIP POPPY. Papaver glaucum, which see.

TULIP POPPY, MEXICAN. Hunnemannia fumariaefolia, which see.

TULIP, STAR. See Calochortus.

TULIP TREE. Liriodendron, which see.

TUNG OIL TREE. Aleurites Fordii, which see.

TUNIC. A loose, outer covering or skin possessed by some corms and bulbs. Bulbs and corms that possess a tunic, such as Tulips, Onions and Crocuses, are said to be tunicated.

TUNICA (Tu'nica). A small group of hardy annual and perennial plants, natives mostly of southern Europe and western Asia. The name Tunica is from *tunica,* a coat, from the overlapping arrangement of the floral envelope. They belong to the Pink family, Caryophyllaceae.

Tunica Saxifraga, the Tunic Flower, is the only kind in cultivation. It is a pretty dwarf perennial for the rock garden, wall garden, or for the crevices of paved paths, and forms a mass of slender wiry stems, 6-9 in. tall, covered during summer with a mass of small, pale pink or white flowers resembling those of Gypsophila. It is easily raised from seeds, which are freely produced, sown in a pan of loam, leaf mold and sand in spring. Tunica is easily grown in light loamy soil and a sunny position, and is a popular rock plant.

Two double-flowered varieties, pink- and white-flowered, are in cultivation, but they are somewhat weak in constitution and have never become very popular. These double-flowered varieties are propagated by cuttings.

TUNICATED. See Tunic.

TUNIC FLOWER. Tunica Saxifraga, which see.

TUPELO. Nyssa, which see.

TUPISTRA (Tupis'tra). A small group of perennial herbaceous plants that are natives of northern India, Burma and Malaya. They belong in the Lily family, Liliaceae. The name is derived from *tupis,* a mallet and refers to the form of the stigma.

Tupistras somewhat resemble Aspidistras. Their long, broad leaves spring directly from underground rhizomes. Their yellowish or purple bell-shaped flowers are borne in dense spikes near to the bases of the plants. Each flower has 6 or more rarely 8 lobes or segments.

Tupistras are suitable for growing in moist tropical greenhouses and probably would be suitable for planting outdoors in southern Florida. They thrive in rich, moderately moist soil and are easily propagated by division at the beginning of their growing season. They endure well in the shade.

The Chief Kinds are T. grandis, flowers purple; T. nutans, flowers lurid purple and greenish; T. tupistroides flowers dark purple.

TURBAN BUTTERCUP. Ranunculus asiaticus, which see.

TURBAN RANUNCULUS. See Ranunculus asiaticus.

TURF. As used by gardeners, the word turf is employed as a noun for a dense, low, matted growth of grasses or other herbaceous plants that are naturally low or are kept low by frequent mowing. It is also used to describe a slab or sod of such material, usually 2-4 in. thick, that is cut from a lawn, pasture or other turfed area. Turf is also sometimes employed as a verb to describe the operation of laying turfs to form a new lawn or turfed area; when used in this way, to turf is synonymous with to sod. All good lawns consist of good turf. See Lawn: the Perfect Setting for Garden Flowers.

So far as is known, the use of turf for making lawns, seats, etc., is not of very ancient origin. Little information has been preserved of the green plots of classical times, and it is doubtful whether turf was used in making them.

In medieval gardens turfed plots were a conspicuous feature, but unlike modern lawns, they were planted with flowers. They were, in fact, imitations of the natural meadow. A flowery mead of this kind is described in Boccaccio's *Decameron:* "What seemed more delightful than anything else was a plot of ground like a meadow, the grass of the deepest green starred with a thousand various flowers . . . in the center of the green plot a carved fountain of pure white marble."

One will find numerous illustrations in medieval missals, romances, Books of Hours, etc., of turfed plots of this kind, among the best-known being the garden miniature in the fifteen-century copy of the *Romance of the Rose* in the British Museum. In Pinturicchio's fresco, in the Vatican, Susannah and the Elders are depicted in a garden which is all turf thickly planted with flowers. Sometimes lawns were planted with grass only and no flowers. A lawn of this type is described by Albertus Magnus in his *De Vegetabilibus*—"a plot of grass carefully weeded and trampled under foot, a true carpet of green turf with no projections on the uniform surface."

Turf-topped seats were a marked feature of gardens, not only in the fourteenth and fifteenth centuries, but also in Tudor and Stuart times. Gardening manuals of later times show that it was customary to plant Violets, Camomile, Daisies, etc., on them. It was also customary to make these turfed seats inside arbors.

Turfed seats were also made around trees and illustrations show they were supported by wattle fencing or brick.

The sporting green plots of Tudor times were similar to the flowery meads of medieval times, but apparently they had ceased to be planted with flowers. Gervase Markham gives full directions for the making of "a sporting green plot for Ladies and Gentlewomen to recreate their spirits in"; or "a place whereunto they may withdraw themselves if they would be solitary and out of sight." Turfed walks were important and well kept, and Markham enjoins that sanded alleys should always be bordered by grass as broad on each side as the breadth of the path.

Leonard Meager says: "In Orchards curious green walks kept short by Mowing and Rolling in Summer are of good esteem, and such may be raised so above the common surface that the wet may have little influence in staying on this, even in Winter after a shower of Rain is past."

Camomile lawns were as common as those made with turf. The majority of seventeenth-century gardening books give directions for the making and upkeep of Camomile lawns. These lawns were made even in nineteenth-century gardens. Full directions are given in Charles Marshall's *Introduction to the Knowledge and Practice of Gardening* (1805). Considerable stretches of the lawns in Buckingham Palace Garden are now still planted with Camomile.

In the late seventeenth century and still more during the eighteenth century, lawns occupied the greater part of the garden. In the most detailed plan of a seventeenth-century garden that has come down to us, that of Wilton, in England, by Isaac de Caux—the lawn occupies a third of the whole. In John Rea's *Flora* (1665), lengthy instructions are given for the making of lawns and the painting of the wooden rails with which it was customary to surround them. The custom of surrounding lawns with low, painted rails survived well into the eighteenth century.

Bowling greens in the eighteenth century were variously turfed. The author of *The Solitary or Carthusian Gardener* (1706) gives as alternatives Turfs, Spanish Clover-Grass, Hayseed, Sainfoin, Medick Fodder. Turf he considered the best. Bowling greens were usually placed where they could be overlooked from the windows of the house, or the garden house. The bowling green at Chatsworth House in England was the central feature of the garden.

In the eighteenth century the word "lawns" applied not only to lawns proper, but to deer parks, groves, etc. In John Reid's *Scots Gardener*, the first book on Scottish gardens, a deer park is described as a lawn. A later writer, Alexander McDonald, speaks of "a lawn eight acres or more in extent." One of the most important eighteenth-century gardening books, Batty Langley's *New Principles of Gardening* (1728), is almost wholly devoted to the subject of lawns and there are numerous plans of them.

English lawns were generally acknowledged during the eighteenth century to be the finest in the world. Le Blond says; "Their Grass plots are of so exquisite a beauty that in France we can scarce ever hope to come up to it."

The great difficulty was apparently the lack of good seed. The author of *The Gardener's New Kalendar* (1758) says: "There is great difficulty in getting good seed, for that from a common haystack is by no means proper." But even in the early nineteenth century hayseed was still commonly used, although laying turf was considered a better method.

Alexander McDonald, in his *Gardening Dictionary*, states: "A man will cut from three to five, six, or seven hundred [turfs] a day or more of very soft, easy cutting turf with a person to race them out and roll them up as they are cut." He is the earliest author to suggest obtaining grass seed from a seedsman.

The essential difference between the methods of making and maintaining lawns in older times and now is that formerly their perfection depended entirely on the skill and labor of the gardener, but modern lawns are largely the result of the careful use of mechanical equipment and of up-to-date fertilizers, weedicides and pesticides.

The quickest way to make a lawn is to lay turf, a subject dealt with under Lawns, which see.

TURKEY BEARD. Xerophyllum, which see.

TURKEY OAK. See Quercus Cerris.

TURK'S-CAP CACTUS. Melocactus communis, which see.

TURK'S-CAP LILY. Lilium Martagon, which see. The American Turk's-cap Lily is L. superbum.

TURMERIC. A substance, largely used in East Indian cookery, which is obtained from the dried and ground underground stems of Curcuma. See Curcuma.

TURNERA (Turn'era). A group of herbaceous plants, subshrubs and shrubs which are natives of South America, the West Indies, Africa and Madagascar and of which only one, T. ulmifolia, is likely to be cultivated. Turnera belongs in the Turneraceae, the Turnera family, and was named in honor of the fourteenth century herbalist, William Turner.

T. ulmifolia, a native of the West Indies, Mexico and South America, is a much-branched shrubby plant, 2-4 ft. high, and bears large yellow potentilla-like flowers from early summer to fall. It is suitable for planting outdoors in frost-free climates and for growing in greenhouses. It thrives in any good soil in a sunny location. It should be watered freely from spring through fall, more sparingly in winter. A minimum greenhouse temperature of 55 degrees suits it well. Propagation is very easily effected by cuttings and by seeds.

TURNIP. This familiar vegetable belongs to the Mustard family or Cruciferae; its botanical name is Brassica Rapa. It is of value chiefly in early summer, in autumn, and early winter.

Turnips, thinned out to allow for their development.

During hot weather the roots become hot to the taste and stringy, and are not nearly so palatable then as at other seasons.

Turnips must be sown on soil that is fertile, for it is necessary that they shall grow quickly if the roots are to be of good flavor. It should be dug over and enriched with compost several weeks before seed sowing and a dressing of a 5-10-5 or other complete fertilizer should be forked in about a week before sowing.

When to Sow Seeds. The best time to make the first sowing out of doors is in early spring, as soon as the ground is dry enough to be broken down to a fine, crumbly condition with fork and rake. Drills ½ in. or so deep are drawn 12 in. apart. If the weather is dry, they should be watered just before seed sowing. The seeds are sown thinly, and the seedlings are thinned out gradually until they are about 4 in. apart. The soil between the rows must be hoed or cultivated frequently to keep down weeds and stimulate growth. A second sowing may be made about two weeks after the first to provide a succession.

Autumn and Early Winter Turnips. Turnips are a good late-season crop. To harvest roots in

Turnera ulmifolia has attractive yellow flowers.

fall and early winter, seeds are sown in July in rich and well-tilled ground. The drills should be 15 in. apart, and the seedlings thinned to 5 or 6 in. from each other. Care must be taken to keep down weeds and encourage growth by hoeing. When the Turnips are well developed they may be lifted, the tops cut off and the roots stored in a root cellar or, where winters are not severe, they can be left in the ground to be lifted as required. If seeds are sown in mid-July, and again at the end of the month, a succession of roots for fall and winter use will be assured.

Turnip tops, for use as winter greens, are provided in mild climates by sowing seeds broadcast in early September; passing the rake over the soil will cover them deeply enough.

Varieties. For sowing in spring, suitable varieties are Early White Milan and Early Purple Top Milan. For sowing in July, Purple Top White Globe is a good variety. The yellow-fleshed Turnips are rather stronger in flavor than the white-fleshed ones; Golden Ball is one of the best varieties. Shogoin is an excellent variety to sow to produce Turnip greens; it has good-quality white roots also. For the so-called Swede or Swedish Turnips, see Rutabaga.

TURNIP, INDIAN. Arisaema triphyllum, which see.

TURNIP-ROOTED CELERY. Celeriac, which see.

TURNIP-ROOTED CHERVIL. Chaerophyllum bulbosum, which see.

TURNIP-ROOTED PARSLEY. See Parsley, Hamburg.

TURNIP-STEMMED CABBAGE. See Kohlrabi.

TURTLEHEAD. Chelone, which see.

TUSSACIA (Tussac′ia). A few tender herbaceous plants that are natives of tropical America and the West Indies and which belong to the Gesneria family, the Gesneriaceae. The name honors the French botanist F. Richard de Tussac.

T. pulchella, from the West Indies, attains a height of 12-18 in. and in summer bears yellow flowers whch have red calyces. It requires the same general culture as Corytholoma and Smithiantha, which see.

TUTCHERIA (Tutcher′ia). Two tender evergreen trees which are natives of southeastern China and are closely related to Camellia. The name commemorates William James Tutcher of the Botanical and Forestry Department of Hong Kong. Tutcheria belongs in the Tea Family, Theaceae.

Tutcheria spectabilis is the only kind known to be in cultivation. It is a small tree with slender-pointed, ovate-lanceolate leaves and slightly fragrant white flowers which measure 3 in. in diameter and are decidedly attractive. Tutcherias are, presumably, about as hardy as Camellias and require the same general culture.

TUTSAN. Hypericum Androsaemum, which see.

TWAYBLADE. See Liparis and Listera.
TWEEDIA. See Oxypetalum.
TWELVE APOSTLES. Neomarica, which see.
TWINBERRY. Mitchella repens, which see.
TWINFLOWER. Linnaea borealis, which see.
TWINLEAF. See Jeffersonia.
TWINSPUR. Diascia, which see.
TWISTED-STALK. Streptopus, which see.
TYDAEA. Isoloma, which see.

TYING the stems of plants to stakes or other supports is often necessary to keep them neat and orderly, to prevent breakage by storms and other causes and to train them in particular forms. The tying materials most commonly used are raffia, soft twine, special florists' thread and thin wires wrapped around with a softer material which are sold as "twistems." Tying should always be done well in advance of likely harm that may occur as

With many-stemmed plants such as Phlox and Chrysanthemums more than one stem can be secured with each length of string from the stake.

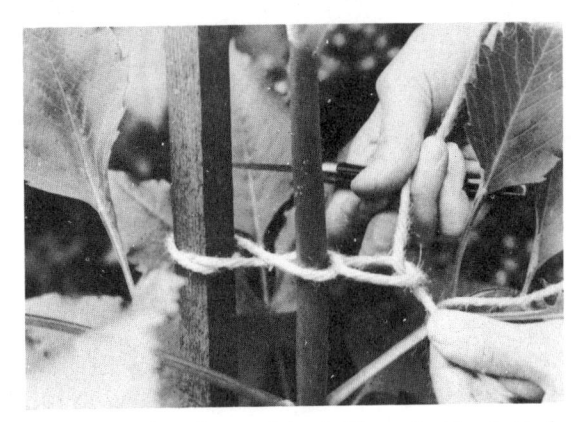

For tying succulent plants such as Dahlias, soft string is ideal. Note the crossover of the string between the stake and the stem.

a result of not attending to this detail. The ties should be made in such a way that they will not pull open easily and so that they will not bind or cut into stems either when made or at a later date after the stems have become thicker.

TYPHA—Cattail, Reed Mace (Ty'pha). Vigorous aquatic plants which are found wild in rivers and ponds in many temperate and tropical regions. They belong to the Cattail family, Typhaceae, and the name is an ancient Greek one.

Typha latifolia, the tallest of the Cattails, has long, narrow, smooth green leaves, several feet in length, and produces flower stalks which rise well above the leaves and are terminated by a cylindrical spike of densely packed flowers in summer. These spikes are 9 in. or more in length, the flowers opening dark brown and changing eventually to brownish-black. If cut and dried in early autumn, they may be used for winter decoration. T. angustifolia is similar to T. latifolia but the leaves are narrower and the flower heads are smaller. T. minima is a miniature plant, only 2 ft. in height.

For Ponds. The Typhas are suitable for planting in ponds or lakes, but because they spread very quickly by their underground rhizomes some thought should be given before introducing them to such bodies of water, for they may become a nuisance by occupying more area than is desired. When planted, the rhizomes are set 1 in. below the soil where the water is about 12 in. deep. They need no further attention beyond cutting out portions of rhizome which grow beyond their allotted space.

If it is desired to grow Cattails in a small pool, the rhizomes should be planted in a large wooden tub, or a portion of the pond may be partitioned off with concrete to prevent their spreading all over the pool.

Division of the rhizomes, which may be done in fall or spring, is the principal method of propagation.

The leaves of T. latifolia may be used for making mats, hassocks, and baskets. The down from the flower heads of T. angustifolia is used in Australia for stuffing mattresses, and cakes are reported to be made in New Zealand from the pollen of T. angustifolia.

TYPHONIUM (Typho'nium). A group of tuberous perennial herbaceous plants that are mostly natives of tropical Asia, Australasia and the Pacific Islands. They belong in the Arum family, the Araceae. The name is an ancient Greek one for an unidentified plant that was named in honor of Typhon, a mythological giant.

Typhoniums are suitable for growing as foliage plants in warm and temperate humid greenhouses. They require a soil that contains an abundance of organic matter and which is kept moist throughout the season of active growth. After the foliage dies down naturally water should be withheld and the plants allowed to rest with the soil quite dry. When signs of new growth become evident the tubers should be shaken free of their old soil, repotted in new. Watering should then be begun again. Shade from strong sun is needed. Plants in active growth that have filled their pots with healthy roots benefit from weekly applications of dilute liquid fertilizers. Propagation is effected by division.

The chief kinds are T. filiforme, T. giganteum and T. Giraldii. T. filiforme, a native of Perak, requires tropical conditions. The other two, both natives of China, thrive in cooler temperatures.

TYPHONODORUM LINDLEYANUM (Typhonodor'um). An evergreen, treelike aroid up to 10 ft. tall from Madagascar and Zanzibar. It has a stout stem and very large hastate leaves. It belongs in the Arum family, Araceae. The name is derived from *tuphov*, a stormy wind and *doron*, a gift, but the relevance is not obvious. A tropical temperature, rich soil kept always wet and exposure to sun afford suitable cultural conditions. Propagation is by seeds and offsets.

U

ULEX—*Gorse, Whin, Furze* (U'lex). Intensely spiny, leaf-losing shrubs which appear to be evergreen by reason of the green young branches. They bear golden blossoms and bloom very freely for a very long season. A few kinds only are known, those being natives of Europe. One kind, U. europaeus, has become naturalized in sandy places along the coast from Massachusetts to Virginia and in parts of the Pacific Northwest.

In the Gorse's natural habitats in Europe, it is often possible to find flowers in some places at almost any time during the year, a phenomenon that led to the saying, "Kissing is out of fashion when the Gorse is out of bloom."

The beauty of the Gorse when in full bloom is one of the best sights of the British countryside; it is said to have appealed so powerfully to Linnaeus, the father of present-day botany, that when he first saw it at its best he fell down on his knees and thanked God for its loveliness.

Ulex belongs to the Pea family, Leguminosae, and the name was probably taken from the Celtic *uile-ex,* all prickles, but it is also said to have been the old Latin name for the plant.

Raising Gorse from Seeds. All the wild kinds are easily raised from seed. Care must be taken to collect the pods before they burst, otherwise the seed may be lost.

If it is desired to plant a favorable area with Gorse, the seed can be sown broadcast where the plants are to grow. Young plants may be transplanted, but older ones do not move well. There are several varieties, and these must be increased by cuttings. The most useful of these varieties is a form of the common Gorse, Ulex europaeus, with double flowers, called variety flore-pleno. This is superior to the common Gorse for planting in gardens, for it is of more compact habit and does not produce seed pods, which in the typical kind are unsightly after the flowers have faded.

Propagating Double Gorse from Cuttings. This double Gorse needs special care in propagation. Take side shoots 3-4 in. long in July or August, removing them from the main shoots with a slight heel of older wood. Trim off the leaves and spines from the lower half and insert them in a bed of sand in a cold frame or in a cool greenhouse propagating bench. Water them and leave them undisturbed until the following spring. They do not root well if placed in a warm greenhouse or frame.

About April, roots will have formed. The plants must then be lifted carefully and placed separately in small pots. They will be ready for permanent planting by autumn, or they may be placed in larger pots and be kept plunged out of doors for another year. If they are planted in nursery beds and again moved, many losses will occur at transplanting.

Soil and Location. The plants grow well in poor sandy or gravelly soil and give better results in firm than in loose ground. The object throughout must be to keep the plants dwarf and sturdy. No better place can be found than a sunny, gravelly bank where ordinary plants do not thrive. They must not, however, be planted in limy soil.

Pruning. Some pruning may be necessary to keep the plants dwarf, and that should be done as soon as the flowers fade. Do not prune back into very old wood, for such wood does not produce young shoots freely. As a rule, it is not wise to prune closer than near the base of the previous year's growth.

The Common Gorse. U. europaeus is the well-known common Gorse of western Europe. Although often seen as a bush 4-6 ft. high, it may attain a height of 18-20 ft. It withstands a good deal of exposure and is sometimes used in Europe for hedges and shelter clumps in wind-swept areas. In the Falkland Islands it has been found to be one of the best shelter bushes that have been tried in windy locations.

The variety flore-pleno is the best of several varieties; it is a very useful plant for gardens, parks and other conspicuous places, where the ground is poor. It associates well with Heather, Rosemary and various kinds of Cistus. The variety strictus, sometimes called Irish Gorse, is of stiff, erect habit, and is really no improvement on the type. The best flowering time for all of the U. europaeus varieties is late spring.

The French Gorse. U. Gallii, the French Gorse, flowers during late summer and early autumn. It forms dense tufts, 9-18 in. high, which at blooming time are covered with golden flowers. This kind is not quite so hardy as U. europaeus.

U. nanus is a dwarf, slender-branched plant of western Europe. It has golden-yellow flowers and is less hardy than U. europaeus.

ULMUS—*Elm* (Ul'mus). Leaf-losing, or sometimes subevergreen, trees, widely distributed in Europe; Asia, from the Himalayas northwards; and North America, east of the Rocky Mountains and as far south as northern Mexico.

Elms vary from small trees or shrubs to trees of very large size. They have small, often purplish, flowers which, in most kinds, appear in late winter or early spring well in advance of the leaves, but one or two kinds flower later in the year. The fruits are wafer-like, a seed occupying a more or less central position and being surrounded by a wide, papery wing. The seeds ripen during early summer, but sometimes a small percentage only are fertile.

The leaves vary a good deal in size; they are unequally elliptic, one side being much better developed than the other. It is not unusual to find two kinds of leaves on the same tree,

The American Elm, Ulmus americana.

the normal kind on the ordinary branches, and very large leaves, which may have deeply lobed margins, produced by vigorous shoots from adventitious buds on the trunks. Strong young shoots of some kinds have somewhat corklike bark; in one or two varieties this peculiarity has become permanent.

The Elm belongs to the Elm family, Ulmaceae. Ulmus is the old Latin name for the tree.

The American Elm, Ulmus americana, in winter, showing the characteristic vaselike branching system.

The English Elm, Ulmus procera.

The large-growing Elms are most decorative trees, growing 90-200 ft. high. They have been so widely used as shade trees in some areas, such as New England, that they have become a very definite feature of the landscape.

Unfortunately, Elms, especially American and European species and their varieties, are subject to a most serious disease (Dutch Elm Disease) and this should be considered before planting (see Pests and Diseases). The Chinese and Siberian Elms are resistant.

Propagation should be effected by means of seeds whenever possible; the different kinds come true to type only when the parent trees are isolated, for they readily hybridize when two or more kinds are growing together. Some produce suckers freely; these may be detached and planted as young trees. Layering may also be practiced, using specially cut-down plants in the nursery for the purpose. Rare varieties may be grafted on closely related understocks. Seeds should be sown out of doors as soon as they are gathered; sow them thinly in light soil. Young plants soon appear and make good growth before the end of summer. Yet another method of propagating rare varieties of Elms is by means of root cuttings taken from a desirable tree.

Elms are not fastidious regarding soil acidity; they thrive both where there is a good deal of lime and where little lime is present. Soil of a loamy character, however, is the best. Their adaptability leads to their use sometimes in places for which they are hardly appropriate.

Elm bark has some medicinal use, particularly the bark of the Slippery Elm of North America, U. fulva. This has diuretic, emollient, demulcent and pectoral properties, and is used in cases of inflammation, ulcers, etc. The bark of the English Elm, U. procera, has astringent, demulcent and diuretic actions.

Several name changes have been made among the Elms during recent years owing to the exigencies of the rules and regulations governing botanical nomenclature, and in order to avoid confusion the standard name and the better-known one (in parentheses) are given together in the following notes.

The American Elm. U. americana, the American Elm, also known as the White Elm and the Water Elm, grows to a large size, 100-120 ft. high, with a trunk 4-6 ft. in diameter. It is widely distributed, occurring natively from Newfoundland to Florida and westward to the Rocky Mountains. Without doubt this species is one of the most magnificent of native American trees. In many places it has been widely planted as a shade tree along streets and in parks and gardens and, in New England in particular, it gives special landscape character to numerous towns and villages.

The American Elm, at maturity, is beautifully vase-shaped in outline and, typically, has a trunk that divides, low down, into several huge, trunklike main branches that gradually arch outwards from their point of origin. The leaves are to 6 in. long, ovate-oblong and distinctly unequal at their bases. The bark is gray and is deeply fissured.

This tree tends to be quite variable and a number of the most distinct forms have been given variety names. Chief among these are U. americana variety ascendens, which has erect branches and a very narrow head; U. americana variety aurea, which has yellow or yellowish leaves; U. americana variety columnaris, which has erect branches and forms a narrow top (although not so narrow as that of the variety ascendens); and U. americana variety pendula,

The Weeping Wych Elm, Ulmus glabra pendula.

The Chinese Elm, Ulmus parvifolia.

which is characterized by having drooping or pendulous branches.

The trees known as the Lake City Elm and the Moline Elm are fastigiate (erect, narrow-headed) forms of U. americana.

The Slippery Elm, U. fulva, grows natively in eastern North America from Quebec to Florida and westward to the Dakotas and Texas and attains a maximum height of 60-70 ft. It forms broad, open-headed specimens and has spreading branches. In fall its leaves, which are 6-8 in. long, assume a dull yellow coloring. This tree is sometimes called the Red Elm, which name is also applied to U. serotina.

The Rock Elm, U. Thomasii (racemosa), forms a tree to 100 ft. tall with a more or less oblong, round-topped head and distinctly corky winged twigs. Its leaves are 4-6 in. long and turn bright yellow in autumn. This kind is a native from Quebec to Tennessee and westward to Nebraska.

Other American Elms. Several other species of Ulmus are natives of North America. One of these is U. alata, the Wahoo Elm, which grows natively from Virginia to Florida and westward to Illinois and Texas and is less hardy than the three American Elms discussed above. The Wahoo Elm grows about 50 ft. tall, has a

[13—10]
Vinca minor

[13—10a]
Verbena hortensis variety

[13–11]
Verbena peruviana

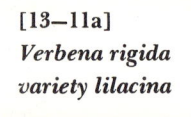

[13–11a]
*Verbena rigida
variety lilacina*

[13–11b]
*Moss Verbena
(Verbena laciniata)*

[13–11c]
*Chaste Tree
(Vitex Agnus-castus)*

round-topped head and is planted to some extent as a street tree in the South.

U. crassifolia, the Cedar Elm, is native from Mississippi to Texas and New Mexico and is sometimes planted for ornament in that region. It forms a medium-sized specimen.

U. serotina, the September Elm (also known as the Red Elm, a name applied to U. fulva, too) attains a height of 60-70 ft. and grows naturally from Georgia and Illinois to Alabama and Kentucky. It has a broad head and spreading or pendulous branches.

The English Elm. Ulmus procera (U. campestris), commonly called English Elm, is one of the best-known trees in western and southwestern Europe, including the southern part of the British Isles. It is often found from 70 to 100 ft. high, but may be much taller, with a stout trunk and spreading head of branches divided into many minor branchlets. In vigorous young shoots the bark may be of a corky nature. The coarsely toothed leaves are 2-3½ in. long, and up to 2 in. wide, rough above, very hairy beneath. The leaves turn golden-yellow in autumn. Flowers are borne freely in February but fertile fruits are rarely seen. This tree suckers very freely.

There is some doubt as to the origin of this tree; some people suggest that it is a native of southwestern Europe, introduced into Britain; others maintain that it is of hybrid parentage. There are many well-marked varieties, notably Louis Van Houtte, with golden leaves; purpurea, with purple-tinged foliage; purpurascens, with small purplish leaves; and Berardii, of bushy habit.

The Smoothleaf Elm. Ulmus carpinifolia (U. foliacea), the Smoothleaf Elm, is rather like U. procera, but the leaves are less harsh on the upper surface and the hairs beneath are confined to small tufts in the axils of the veins. It is not quite so large as the English Elm, although it may reach 100 ft. in height. It is a native of Europe and mid-Asia.

This Elm is very variable in habit and a number of forms have been selected for variety names. Some of them are pendula, with weeping branches; suberosa (Cork-barked Elm), in which the branchlets have definite corky ridges; gracilis, of slender habit; variegata, with silver-variegated leaves; sarniensis (Wheatleyi), Guernsey or Jersey Elm, of stiff, erect growth; and Webbiana, of stiff, erect growth, with small leaves.

U. carpinifolia variety cornubiensis, the Cornish Elm, is also of stiff erect habit. It forms rather short and not very heavy branches.

The Wych Elm. U. glabra (U. montana) is the Wych Elm or Scotch Elm. This tree is native from Great Britain, especially in the midlands and northern parts, to Siberia. When it grows with U. foliacea the two intercross very freely and there are many hybrids between the two in cultivation, some named, others not. It is distinguished by its large rough leaves, 3-7 in. long and 2-4 in. wide, which are coarsely toothed, rough above and downy beneath. The unequal lobes at the base may sometimes be split off into one or more distinct leaflets. The shoots are intensely hairy, and the tree may grow 100-120 ft. high with a large trunk. The Wych Elms should be raised from seeds taken from isolated trees. Both it and several of its varieties are planted freely in North America.

The Weeping Wych Elm. Of many varieties of U. glabra, pendula is popular by reason of the regularity of its weeping branches; it is a handsome shade tree for planting on lawns. The variety fastigiata, the Exeter Elm, is of stiff, erect habit with small branches, and is of slow growth; it is a very good kind for planting along the sides of streets and roads. U. glabra variety Camperdownii, the Camperdown Elm, is another variety with pendulous branches; the variety Wredei is of stiff habit with yellowish leaves; laciniata has the margins of the leaves divided into a number of lobes; lutescens has yellow leaves; nana and monstrosa are of dwarf, bushlike habit; and purpurea has purple leaves.

The Dutch Elm. U. hollandica (U. major), the Dutch Elm, is a hybrid between U. carpinifolia and U. glabra. It grows into a very large tree with a wide-spreading head, the leaves much larger than those of U. carpinifolia. It is a vigorous and free-growing tree.

The Huntingdon Elm. U. hollandica vegeta, the Huntingdon Elm, is another very vigorous tree of the same parentage as the Dutch Elm. It grows up to 100 ft. high with a trunk sometimes 5-6 ft. in diameter. It more closely resembles U. glabra than it does the other parent.

U. hollandica belgica, the Belgian Elm, is another of these hybrids, as are U. hollandica superba, a narrow-pyramidal kind, and U. hollandica Pitteursii, a strong-growing Elm with large leaves.

The Willow Elm. U. viminalis, the Willow Elm, is a small, narrowly branched tree of uncertain origin, but possibly a form of U. procera. It is often less than 25 ft. high with very slender branchlets and small leaves. The variety aurea has golden leaves, and variegata has white variegated leaves.

The European White Elm. U. laevis (U. pedunculata), the European White Elm, is a tree 90-100 ft. high, with a trunk 5-6 ft. in diameter. It is a late-flowering kind, the flowers appearing in April as the leaves are developing. Its leaves are as large as those of the Wych Elm but smoother and thinner.

The Chinese Elm, U. parvifolia, a native of China and Japan, is partially evergreen in mild climates but completely leaf-losing in winter in the North. It normally forms a small tree to about 45 ft. high but it may grow considerably taller. It has a rounded, broad head and has leaves 1-3 in. long. It may be distinguished from U. pumila, with which it is sometimes confused, by the fact that it bears its flowers (which, like those of all Elms, are relatively inconspicuous) in fall instead of spring. It is hardy in the North but not so far north as U. pumila, the Siberian Elm, described below. Like the Siberian Elm it grows fast and its wood tends to be weak, so that the tree is easily damaged by storms.

The Siberian or Dwarf Elm, U. pumila, grows to a maximum height of 75 ft. but is usually lower and sometimes is scarcely more than a shrub in parts of its native habitat, which is northern China, Manchuria and Korea. As known in cultivation in North America, this kind is a small tree closely resembling the Chinese Elm, U. parvifolia, from which it may be distinguished by the fact that it bears its inconspicuous flowers in spring instead of fall.

This tree grows quickly but its wood is so weak that the tree easily suffers from storm damage. It has been especially recommended for planting as a street tree and as a shade tree in arid parts of North America. It is perfectly hardy in the North.

UMBEL. An inflorescence of which the stalks arise from a common center, providing a flattish cluster of bloom.

UMBELLATE. A term used in reference to plants which bear flowers in the form of an umbel (which see).

UMBELLULARIA CALIFORNICA — *California Laurel* (Umbellular'ia). An evergreen tree which is a native of California and Oregon and grows to a height of 25-30 ft. It forms a spreading tree, clothed with glossy leaves, 2½-4 in. in length. The small yellowish-green flowers, which are produced in little clusters in spring, are followed by small, roundish, purple fruits. The name Umbellularia is derived from *umbella*, sunshade, and refers to the form of the flower clusters. It belongs to the family Lauraceae.

Umbellularia is only suitable for planting in mild climates, such as that of the Pacific coast. A moist location and ordinary soil are required.

No pruning is ordinarily required and propagation is by seeds. These should be sown in sandy soil in spring, the seedlings being potted separately in small pots, in which they should remain until they are large enough to plant outdoors. The foliage of this plant, when bruised, emits a strong, tangy, pleasant odor.

UMBILICUS — *Navelwort* (Umbil'icus). A small genus of succulent plants belonging to the Crassula family, Crassulaceae. They are somewhat tender but are attractive for rock gardens where the climate is not too severe. They are natives of northern Africa, southern Europe and the Orient.

The Navelwort or Pennywort, U. pendulinus, has rounded leaves and drooping spikes of yellowish-green flowers marked with reddish dots. It is sometimes called Cotyledon Umbilicus. It requires the same culture as Sedum and Sempervivum, which see.

UMBRELLA FERN. See Gleichenia.

UMBRELLA LEAF. See Diphylleia.

UMBRELLA PALM. Hedyscepe, which see.

UMBRELLA PINE. See Sciadopitys.

UMBRELLA PLANT. Cyperus alternifolius, which see.

UMBRELLA TREE. Magnolia tripetala, which see.

UMKOKOLA. See Dovyalis caffra.

UNDERSTOCK. That part of a grafted,

budded or inarched plant which includes the roots and into which the scion or bud of the variety to be propagated is inserted. It is often called, simply, the stock.

UNICORN PLANT. See Proboscidea.

UNIOLA (Uni′ola). Hardy perennial Grasses, natives of North America. They are sometimes grown for their large ornamental flower spikes. They reach a height of 2-6 ft., have long, narrow leaves and produce immense panicles of decorative flowers which may be cut and dried for winter decoration. Uniola belongs to the Grass family, Gramineae; the name is derived from *unus,* one, and perhaps refers to the united glumes (flower heads).

These plants are easily grown in ordinary garden soil in a sunny position. Planting may be done in spring or fall. Propagation is by division of the rhizomes at planting time and by seeds.

The chief kinds are U. latifolia, 4 ft., native from New Jersey and Illinois to Florida and Texas; and U. paniculata, Sea Oats, 6 ft., native from Virginia to Florida and Texas.

UNITED STATES DEPARTMENT OF AGRICULTURE. The United States Department of Agriculture is an administrative branch of the Government of the United States that renders diverse services of importance to all. Certain of these services, especially those that are of an informational character, are of particular interest to gardeners.

The Department engages in scientific research and conducts surveys and prepares analyses of problems and conditions affecting agriculture (including horticulture) in all its many phases. Soils, insect and pest control, weather forecasting, crop forecasting and numerous other fields of investigation and knowledge are covered.

The United States Department of Agriculture prepares and issues numerous publications of importance and interest to gardeners. These include circulars, bulletins, etc., some of which are free and for some of which a moderate charge is made. Current lists of such publications may be had from the Superintendent of Documents, United States Government Printing Office, Washington 25, D.C.

URCEOCHARIS (Urceocha′ris). Hybrids obtained by crossing Eucharis with Urceolina, hence the name Urceocharis. These bulb plants have broad leaves, 12 in. long and 6 in. wide, and produce attractive flowers, intermediate in shape between those of the two parents. The flowers are bell-shaped, 2 in. in diameter and white. They are produced in small clusters on the ends of stout stalks in summer.

Summer and Winter Management. A minimum winter temperature of 55 degrees is required, and repotting is done after the plants have flowered; this is not necessary every year, and should only be carried out when the plants decline in vigor.

The best potting compost consists of two parts of fibrous loam, one part of peat or leaf mold and one part of well-decayed manure with a scattering of sand. In autumn or early spring, several bulbs are placed in a well-drained 8-in. pot, the tips of the bulbs level with the surface of the compost. Water is applied freely to established plants during the summer, and dilute liquid fertilizer is given twice a week when the flower buds are forming. From October–April the soil is only moistened when it becomes very dry.

Propagation is by separating the young bulbs and potting them separately in spring.

The chief kind is U. Clibranii, 18 in., white.

URCEOLINA PENDULA — *Golden Urn Flower* (Urceoli′na). A tender bulb plant, introduced to cultivation from Peru in 1836. It was crossed with Eucharis grandiflora to produce Urceocharis (which see).

The bulbs of Urceolina urceolata (pendula) are roundish, and about 2½ in. in diameter. They produce large, smooth, ovate, deciduous leaves, 12 in. in length, and bear attractive flowers in summer. These are urn-shaped, yellow and green, and are formed in small clusters on the tips of stout stalks 12 in. in height in summer.

Urceolina belongs to the Amaryllis family, Amaryllidaceae. The name is derived from *urceolus,* a little pitcher or urn, and refers to the shape of the flowers. These bulbs require the same treatment as Eucharis, which see.

URGINEA—*Sea Onion* (Urgin′ea). Tender bulb plants from the Mediterranean region, and tropical and South Africa. They are closely related to Scilla and Ornithogalum. One species,

U. maritima (Scilla), is grown in large quantities in Europe for the bulbs, from which syrup of Squills, a medicine, is produced. Urginea belongs to the Lily family, Liliaceae; the name is derived from the name of an Arabic tribe in Algeria, who were probably the first to use the bulbs medicinally.

These plants have narrow, strap-shaped leaves, 18 in. in length and produce small, campanulate, white and green or white and purple flowers borne in short racemes on the ends of slender stalks, in summer. They are not very showy and are chiefly of interest to plant collectors. In mild climates they are hardy. They are sometimes cultivated in pots in greenhouses and window gardens.

Potting the Bulbs. The bulbs, which are 4-6 in. in diameter, are potted separately in 6-in. pots in March. The bulbs are half-buried in the soil, which should consist of equal parts of loam and leaf mold with sand added freely. They are set in a greenhouse with a minimum temperature of 45 degrees, and watered sparingly until growth commences. When roots have formed freely, the soil is kept moist until the autumn, when the supply is gradually reduced; during the winter the soil is only moistened when it becomes quite dry. A sunny, airy location in the greenhouse is necessary.

Propagation is by offsets and by seeds. The small bulbs are removed from the larger ones in spring and potted in small pots, to be grown on to flowering size. Seeds sown in spring in pots of sandy soil germinate freely in a temperature of about 60 degrees.

The Chief Kinds. U. maritima (Scilla maritima), 18 in., white and greenish-purple; U. altissima, 24 in., white and green; U. filifolia, 9 in., white and purple.

UROPEDIUM LINDENII (Uroped'ium). The name originally given to Cypripedium caudatum Lindenii, which has a third ribbon-like petal in place of the "slipper" common to the type.

URSINIA (Ursin'ia). A group of plants from South Africa and other parts of the African continent, few of which are in cultivation in North America. They belong to the Daisy family, Compositae. The name commemorates John Ursinus, a botanist. There are both herbaceous annual and shrubby kinds. The annuals are most commonly cultivated.

The brilliant orange-flowered annual Ursinia anethoides.

The most popular kind is Ursinia anethoides, an annual which reaches a height of 10-18 in. and bears brilliant orange-colored flowers. They provide a dazzling display during bright weather, and may be grown in pots in the greenhouse for winter and spring flowers or planted out of doors for the summer. Well-drained or light soil and a sunny position are required for the successful management of these plants.

When to Sow Seeds. For outdoor cultivation seeds are sown in a flat of sifted light soil in à greenhouse, temperature 50-55 degrees, in March. As soon as they are big enough to handle easily, they are transplanted to other flats, in

Ursinia pulchra.

which they are set 2 in. apart, and are hardened off in a cold frame and planted out of doors in May.

An alternative method is to sow the seeds outdoors in early spring, in the position where the plants are to bloom, and to thin the seedlings out so that they stand 6-8 in. apart. Ursinias do not prosper in really hot weather; therefore, in many sections of North America, it is very important to give the plants as early a start as possible so that they will bloom before conditions become too difficult.

To provide pot plants for the decoration of the greenhouse, seeds are sown from September to February; three seedlings are set in a 6-in. flowerpot filled with a compost of two parts of loam and one part of leaf mold, with a scattering of sand. They need cool, airy conditions after they have passed the seedling stage, and must be exposed fully to all possible sunshine, as they are essentially sun-loving plants.

There are several species and varieties, seeds of which are sold by seedsmen. U. anethoides has orange-colored flowers with a zone of dark purple at the base; in the variety Aurora the flowers are orange and crimson; those of anthemoides are lemon-yellow. There are several kinds of lower growth, attaining a height of only about 8 in. Of these the best are U. pulchra and the garden variety Radiance, with orange-colored flowers.

USAMBARA VIOLET. See Saintpaulia.

UTAH, GARDENING IN. See Regional Gardening.

UTRICULARIA—*Bladderwort* (Utricular'ia). Hardy and tender aquatic and terrestrial plants of botanical interest, but of little horticultural value. Utricularias belong to the Lentibulariaceae, the Bladderwort family. The name is derived from *utriculus,* a little bottle, and alludes to the bladders formed on the leaves.

The aquatic kinds, which are native of tropical America and Europe, have submerged leaves which are finely divided. They also produce small, bladder-like structures fitted with valves which only open inwards. Small insects which enter are therefore unable to escape. These plants are sometimes grown in indoor aquariums for the interest of their feathery foliage and their insect-catching valves.

The terrestrial kinds are quite different in habit, having lanceolate leaves, 6 in. long, and producing slender, wiry flower stalks, bearing, towards the tips, a raceme of yellow, blue or purple flowers.

These Bladderworts require a minimum winter temperature of 55 degrees and a soil compost of equal parts of fibrous peat, sphagnum moss, and broken bricks. They are set in well-drained pots, which are kept in saucers of water and placed under a bell jar in a shady position in the greenhouse. They are ventilated daily by tilting the bell jar a few inches each morning. During the summer months they are watered freely, but through the winter they are only moistened when the compost shows signs of becoming dry.

Repotting is done in March when the old compost is removed from the roots and they are placed in slightly larger pots, if necessary. New plants are obtained by sowing seeds on the surface of damp peat moss and sand in a seed pan. They are covered with a bell jar until large enough to pot separately in small pots, and afterwards set in larger pots.

The chief kinds are U. vulgaris, aquatic, yellow, a native of Europe, Asia and North America; and U. alpina (montana), terrestrial, white, a native of the West Indies.

UVA-URSI. Arctostaphyllos, which see.

UVULARIA—*Bellwort* (Uvula'ria). Hardy herbaceous perennial flowering plants of North America. They have a short, creeping, perennial

A native of the eastern United States, Uvularia sessilifolia is a shade-loving plant with greenish-yellow flowers.

rootstock and bear a number of slender stems, 18 in. in height. The light green leaves are ovate, with the stem often passing through the leaf (perfoliate). From their axils, near the tops of the stems, the flowers are produced; these are bell-shaped, pale yellow, 1½ in. long, and pendulous. Uvularia belongs to the Lily family, Liliaceae; the name is derived from *uvula,* a palate, and refers to the flowers, which hang and so suggest the uvula or palate.

Plants for Partial Shade. A semishaded location and a peaty soil are required. Planting is done in fall or spring. Mulching with peat moss or leaf mold should be done in summer to keep the roots cool, and water must be given in dry weather. The plants should not be disturbed until they show signs of deterioration, when they may be lifted, divided and replanted. Lifting and dividing the rhizomes is the principal method of propagation, although Uvularias can also be raised from seeds sown in a woodsy soil mixture.

The Chief Kinds. U. grandiflora, 18 in., lemon yellow, May; U. perfoliata, 12 in., yellow, May. The flowers of U. perfoliata are somewhat smaller than those of U. grandiflora. U. sessilifolia has greenish yellow flowers, which also appear during the month of May.

V

VACATIONS, CARE OF PLANTS DURING. Unless precautions are taken, plants in pots may suffer serious harm during the owner's absence if arrangements cannot be made to have them watered from time to time.

There are various ways of ensuring the safety of the plants. In summer if the pots containing the plants are plunged to the rims in the soil out of doors, or in a bed of ashes in a shady place, and the soil in the pots is watered thoroughly the day before the vacation begins, the plants are less likely to suffer for a few days. As a further precaution, the soil in the pots should be covered with peat or leaf mold which has been well moistened.

An alternative method is to spot porous bricks over the bottom of the bathtub, run in water almost to the tops of the bricks and then stand a plant on each. If the plant is well watered before the vacation begins, its porous pot will absorb enough water from the moist brick to prevent it from drying for quite an extended period.

Ferns and Palms, if well rooted, may be set in a vessel containing sufficient water to reach halfway up the flowerpots, and placed in a shady place out of doors. It is better to put them outside than to leave them indoors, for then they will have the benefit of any rain that may fall. If left indoors, they must be in a cool room, one facing north preferably.

House plants may also be set in saucers filled with water; if the soil is moistened thoroughly the water in the saucers will provide a reserve supply on which the roots can draw as the soil becomes dry. Merely covering the pots with moss is helpful, provided the plants are well watered.

Still another method is to place the plants in a large vessel, pack moss or burlap between them and siphon the water from a pail by means of wide strips of flannel. The plants may be set out of doors in a shady place or in a cool room.

Yet another helpful device is to encase the plant and its pot in a bag or other covering made of plastic polyethelene film (the kind used to contain food in deep freezers). Before doing this the soil in the pot should be soaked with water. It is advisable, too, to punch a few holes in the bag to permit the escape of excessive atmospheric humidity that may accumulate inside. The plant, in its bag, should be placed in a light location but where the sun will not shine directly on it at any time.

VACCINIUM — *Blueberry, Whortleberry, Cranberry, Cowberry, Bilberry* (Vaccin'ium). A large group of evergreen and leaf-losing shrubs or small trees, widely distributed over the cooler regions of the Northern Hemisphere, and also found in the mountains of South America. Many are hardy and some are found in very cold regions, extending well within the Arctic Circle. Some kinds form the chief vegetation over large areas of soils that are of a decidedly acid character and some members of the group occur both on well-drained soils and boggy land. The best results under cultivation are usually obtained where the ground is moist without being waterlogged, but some kinds, such as the American Cranberry, V. macrocarpon, must be grown in bogs.

Certain kinds are worth growing for their evergreen leaves, others for the color of their autumn foliage, while some are worth growing for the beauty of their flowers or fruits. The fruits of the various kinds are edible, and cultivated varieties of Cranberries and Blueberries are of much importance. See Blueberry and also Cranberry.

Vaccinium belongs in the Heath family, Ericaceae. The name is an ancient Latin one for certain Old World species.

Fruits of the Highbush Blueberry, Vaccinium corymbosum.

Flowers of the Highbush Blueberry, Vaccinium corymbosum.

Raising Seedlings. Propagation may be effected by means of seeds, cuttings, layers, or division. Seeds should be sown from January to March, using well-drained, sandy peat. The seeds are set an eighth of an inch deep, and the pots are covered by a sheet of glass and kept shaded until the seedlings appear. When the seedlings are large enough to handle, they are placed in pans or flats of similar soil and set an inch apart. When they begin to crowd each other in these, they are planted in nursery rows and kept there until large enough for planting in permanent places.

Taking Cuttings. Cuttings of the various kinds require rather different treatment; they may have to be tried in a close cold frame and a propagating greenhouse before the right conditions for a particular kind are found. Cuttings of many kinds, made from the current year's shoots, may be taken in July or August. They should be 1-3 in. long and have a slight heel of firm wood. The lower leaves are removed and the cuttings are placed in firm, sandy peat out of doors or in a frame; they are covered by a bell jar. They are shaded from bright sun and left undisturbed until the following spring. They should then be rooted and can be treated as seedling plants.

Layering. Branches may be layered in sandy peat in early spring. Some will be well enough rooted for removal the following autumn; others must be left for a second summer. The value of layering lies in the fact that the plants are

Vaccinium Nummularia, from the Himalayas, bears clusters of pink or rosy-red flowers, followed by black fruits.

often large enough for permanent planting when removed. The spreading kinds can be increased by division effected in spring. As a rule, the smaller and younger outer parts make the most satisfactory new plants.

Planting and Suitable Soil. Soils of sandy peaty character are particularly desirable for Vacciniums, but these shrubs also thrive in loam and clayey loam provided they are acid; they will not tolerate lime. Although they sometimes grow in wet land under natural conditions, anything approaching a state of water-logged sourness at the roots is usually fatal to cultivated plants.

For decorative purposes the shrubs should be planted in irregular-shaped groups and be associated with other acid-soil plants. Few are suitable for isolated beds on a lawn, though many are well adapted for planting in small groups in the rock garden.

American Cranberry or Large Cranberry, V. macrocarpon, is an evergreen plant with creeping stems which occurs as a native from Newfoundland to North Carolina and Minnesota. The leaves are about ¾ in. long and are whitish on their undersides. The fruits are red. This is the source of the commercial Cranberry crop in North America. For more detail, see Cranberry.

The Lowbush Blueberry is a variety of V. angustifolium. V. angustifolium is a leaf-losing kind about 1 ft. tall that grows from the Arctic to the mountains of New Hampshire and New York. It has greenish-white flowers and bluish-black fruits that are covered with a distinct bloom. V. angustifolium variety laevifolium (pensylvanicum), the Lowbush Blueberry, grows to a height of about 2 ft. and occurs wild from Newfoundland to Wisconsin and Virginia. The Lowbush Blueberry is cultivated for its fruits and improved garden varieties are available. Great quantities of fruit are also collected and marketed from wild plants. See Blueberry.

The Farkleberry. V. arboreum, the Farkleberry of the southern United States, is a shrub or small tree, 25-30 ft. high. The somewhat obovate leaves are 2-3 in. long; they may last throughout winter or fall in autumn, according to whether the parent plants came from the more southerly or northerly regions of its range. The white, bell-shaped flowers are borne singly from the leaf axils in July and August, and are followed by small black fruits. The Farkleberry, or Sparkleberry as it is sometimes called, is not hardy enough to plant in the North.

The Caucasian Whortleberry. V. Arctostaphylos, the Caucasian Whortleberry, is a shrub 8-10 ft. high, with larger leaves than most of the other kinds. They are broadly oblong, up to 4 in. long and 1-2 in. wide. The greenish-white, purple-tinged, bell-shaped flowers are borne in clusters in June and are followed by purple berries. The leaves often die off with a pleasing purplish tinge in autumn.

V. bracteatum is an evergreen shrub, 3-6 ft. high, native of Japan, Korea and China. The narrow, elliptic leaves are 1-3 in. long and ½-1 in. wide, thick in texture, and dark green above. The white flowers are borne in clusters 1-2 in. long, in early summer and are followed by red fruits. This kind is not hardy in the North.

The Dwarf Bilberry. V. caespitosum, the Dwarf Bilberry, is a North American leaf-losing shrub of dense, spreading habit, with small leaves often less than an inch long and ½ in. wide; the white or pale pink, pitcher-shaped flowers are borne in May, and produce sweet, black fruits covered by a glaucous bloom.

V. Oldhamii (ciliatum) is an erect bush, 10 or 12 ft. high, native of Japan. Its leaves, which fall in autumn, are ovate or oval, 1-3 in. long and half as wide. The bell-shaped reddish flowers are in clusters and are followed by black, edible fruits. This kind forms a shapely bush.

The Highbush Blueberry. V. corymbosum, the Highbush or Swamp Blueberry, is a leaf-losing shrub up to 12 ft. high, though often found as a much lower bush. It is a native of eastern North America and its white, pink-flushed, cylindrical flowers, in small clusters in May, are followed by black fruits. The leaves take on rich red shades in autumn.

Many Useful Kinds. V. crassifolium is a dwarf shrub of trailing or tufted habit with small evergreen leaves and rosy-red, but not very conspicuous, flowers, borne in May and June, which are followed by black fruits. It is native from North Carolina to Georgia. It is not hardy in the North.

V. deliciosum is a quite attractive dwarf shrub of western North America, resembling V. caespitosum, but with thicker leaves. The fruits are black and sweet.

V. erythrocarpum is a leaf-losing shrub 3-6 ft. high, native from Virginia to Georgia. The pale red flowers are borne several together in clusters from the axils of the leaves in June; the reddish fruits turn almost black when ripe.

V. glaucoalbum grows 2-4 ft. high and bears stiff, hard, evergreen leaves, 1½-2½ in. long and 1¼ in. wide, dark green above and whitish beneath. The pinkish-white flowers are borne in small clusters in July, and are followed by black fruits covered by a whitish bloom. It is a native of the Himalayas and is probably not hardy in the North.

V. floribundum (Mortinia), an evergreen bush, is native from Colombia to Peru, and grows 2-4 ft. high. The leaves are small, dark green, and thick in texture. The rose-pink flowers are borne in dense clusters from the leaf axils in June and the fruits are red. It is only suitable for planting in mild climates.

V. moupinense is one of the newer kinds from China. It was introduced into cultivation about 1909. It grows 1-2 ft. high, has small, leathery, evergreen leaves, dark red flowers in short, dense clusters in May and June, and purplish-black fruits. It is worth trying in the rock garden.

The Whortleberry. V. Myrtillus, the Whortleberry, is a leaf-losing shrub of Europe and northern Asia. It grows 3-18 in. high and in its native habitat covers large areas of ground, often intermixed with Heather. The pale pink flowers are produced singly in May and are followed by black fruits which ripen in July and August. These are collected for culinary purposes.

V. Nummularia, from the Himalayas, is a small, erect shrub with densely hairy shoots, small ovate or oval leaves and freely produced clusters of pink to rosy-red flowers followed by black fruits. It is probably not hardy in the North.

V. ovatum is an evergreen 10-12 ft. high with small dark, glossy green, leathery leaves, white, bell-shaped flowers produced in May and June, and round, black fruits about one third of an inch in diameter. It is a native of western North America. Its branches are cut and used extensively by florists as greens for decorative purposes.

The Small Cranberry. Vaccinium Oxycoccus, the Small Cranberry, is a trailing, evergreen shrub with long, slender branches, found wild in moist ground, often of a peaty and wet character, in the colder parts of the Northern Hemisphere, northern Europe, northern Asia, and North America. It produces very small leaves and attractive red fruits which are used for making into jelly and jam, for stewing, and in other ways.

The Madeira Whortleberry, V. padifolium, is a leaf-losing bush 8 ft. high. The leaves are up to 2¼ in. long and 1 in. wide, dark green above, pale beneath. The yellowish purple-tinged flowers appear in June and are followed by blue berries. It is a native of the mountains of Madeira.

The Bog Bilberry. V. uliginosum is the Bog Bilberry of North America, northern Europe and northern Asia. It grows 1-2 ft. high and has small dull green leaves which fall in autumn. The flowering time is May or June; the flowers may be red or white, but they are not very conspicuous. The fruits are black with a blue bloom, sweet, and used in some places for culinary purposes.

The Cowberry, V. Vitis-idaea, is a creeping evergreen kind, 4-9 in. high, that occurs as a native in Europe and northern Asia and has white or pink flowers.

The Mountain Cowberry, V. Vitis-idaea variety minus, forms dense mats 4-9 in. tall and has pink or red flowers. It is native from Labrador and Massachusetts to British Columbia and Alaska. Its fruits are made into jellies and preserves.

There are many more kinds of Vaccinium, but those mentioned include the most conspicuous and the most generally useful.

VALERIAN. Valeriana, which see.

VALERIANA — *Valerian* (Valeria'na). The Valerians are a group of mostly hardy perennials or shrubs, natives of the north temperate regions; a number of kinds occur as natives in North America. They belong to the Valerian family, Valerianaceae. The name is probably from *valere,* to be healthy, alluding to the healing properties of some kinds. Valerian has long been known for its medicinal value, especially as an antispasmodic. Among the true Valerians are several very attractive rock-garden alpine plants.

Valeriana arizonica grows about 6 in. high

A charming plant for a choice spot in the rock garden is the pink-flowered Valeriana supina. It is a native of Europe.

and bears heads of pink flowers in March. It is easy to grow in loamy soils, and is best increased by division of the roots in spring or early summer.

Marsh Valerian. V. dioica, the Marsh Valerian, is a pretty native plant of Europe, 6-9 in. high, with feathered leaves and heads of pale rose-pink flowers in summer. It is well worth cultivating in the moister parts of the rock garden, and is increased by division of the roots in spring.

V. celtica is common in the Alps, especially on nonlimy formations. It furnishes the valuable Nard, which is collected in great quantities and used in embalming, in incense, disinfecting, etc. The whole plant is fragrant. The yellowish-brown flower heads on 4-5 in. stems are insignificant.

V. globulariaefolia, from the Pyrenees, is perhaps the most attractive of all the rock-garden Valerians. The plant spreads freely, has fresh, glossy green foliage, and, in May and June, bears numerous erect 6-9-in. stems carrying heads of rose-pink flowers which are deliciously fragrant. Ordinary loamy soil suits this lovely and too-little-known rock plant, and it is easily increased by division of the roots in spring.

V. supina is a dwarf kind from the eastern European Alps, with rounded, dark green leaves, and heads of fragrant pink flowers in spring.

Effect on Cats and Rats. V. officinalis,

The common Valerian, Valeriana officinalis, is an interesting plant to grow in moist soil.

Common Valerian, which is also known by such names as Allheal and St.-George's-Herb, is a native of Europe and northern Asia and is naturalized in North America. It is found in damp woods and ditches, and grows 2-4 ft. tall, with handsome heads of pale pink flowers in summer. It is well worth planting by the pond or streamside or in the bog garden. The roots of the Common Valerian have an extraordinary effect on cats, sending them into hysterical ecstasies, and rats are affected in a similar way. It has even been suggested that the use of Valerian accounted for the success that the Pied Piper had with the rats of Hamelin.

VALERIANELLA—*Corn Salad* (Valerianel'la). Annual herbs which grow wild in Europe and two of which are cultivated in gardens for making salads. They belong to the Valerian family, Valerianaceae. The principal kind is V. olitoria, Lamb's Lettuce or Corn Salad, 12 in. in height, which bears small, bluish-white flowers in clusters. The other is V. eriocarpa, Italian Corn Salad, which is very similar. For cultivation, see Corn Salad.

VALERIAN, GREEK. Polemonium caeruleum, which see.

VALERIAN, RED. Centranthus ruber, which see.

VALLARIS (Vallar'is). A small group of plants belonging to the Dogbane family, Apocynaceae, that are natives of tropical Asia. The name is derived from *vallus,* a stake or palisade, and refers to the reported use of these plants for making fences in Java.

V. Heynei (dichotma) is grown in southern Florida as a vine to cover porches and arbors. It is a tall climber that bears creamy white or greenish-white, fragrant flowers in forked cymes (clusters). The leaves are 4-6 in. long by about 2 in. wide and are conspicuously pinnately veined. This kind is a native of India, Burma and Ceylon. It may be propagated by cuttings inserted in a mixture of peat moss and sand in a greenhouse propagating bench and by seeds.

VALLISNERIA—*Eel Grass, Tape Grass* (Vallisne'ria). A group of hardy and tender aquatic plants which are grown for their botanical interest and to decorate aquariums. They are submerged plants with tufts of narrow leaves, 6 in. or more in length, according to the depth of the water. The plants grow in the soil at the bottom of the water, and send up their flowers on long slender stalks to the surface. The stalks are in spiral formation, and in summer are terminated by small white female flowers. The male flowers are borne on very short stalks near the bottom of the water.

Fertilization is promoted by the stamens breaking away from the male flowers, which float to the surface of the water. As they drift about, they come into contact with the pistils of the

The Eel Grass, Vallisneria spiralis, growing in an aquarium.

female flowers, and pollination is effected. When fertilization is complete the female flower stalks contract and draw the ovaries to the bottom of the water, to ripen and deposit the seeds.

Vallisneria belongs to the Frog's-Bit family, Hydrocharitaceae, and the name commemorates Antonio Vallisneri, an Italian botanist who died in 1730.

Interesting Plants for Indoor Aquariums. These plants are easily grown in deep tubs or in an aquarium. Loamy soil to a depth of a few inches is placed at the bottom, and covered with a 2-in. layer of sand. The plants are then set in position, and the tub filled with rain water. A minimum winter temperature of 45 degrees is required.

To keep the water clean, a few water snails should be introduced. These feed on the green algae which collect on the sides of the tank. Very little attention is required except to replenish the water as it evaporates.

Propagation is by dividing the plant in spring, or seeds may be sown in the mud at the bottom of a tank of water.

Chief Kinds. V. americana occurs as a native from Maine to Florida and Mississippi and is hardy. V. spiralis, a native of Europe and western Asia, is hardy only in mild climates.

VALLOTA—*Scarborough Lily* (Vallot'a). A genus of only one species. Vallota speciosa (V. purpurea) is a tender bulbous plant that is suitable for growing in pots in greenhouses and window gardens and in the outdoor garden in frostfree and nearly frostfree climates. Vallota is a native of South Africa, belongs to the Amaryllis family, Amaryllidaceae, and is very closely allied to Amaryllis, the chief distinction being that the seeds of Vallota are winged at the base. The name Vallota commemorates Pierre Vallot, a French botanist.

This plant has a large brown scaly bulb from the apex of which are produced several strap-shaped dark green glossy leaves, 18 in. in length. In late summer it sends up a stout flower stalk, well above the foliage, and bears a cluster of attractive flowers; these are funnel-shaped and 2½ in. across. A large pot containing a number of bulbs, each bearing a large umbel of blooms, makes a very attractive display.

Soil and Potting. Vallotas succeed in fertile, well-drained soil. A potting compost consisting of 2 parts of loam, 1 part of peat moss or leaf mold and 1 part of sand is suitable for young bulbs; for potting mature bulbs the addition of 1 part of dried cow manure and a little bonemeal is beneficial.

Because these plants resent having their roots disturbed it is better not to repot them oftener than absolutely necessary. Young bulbs may be potted every year or two, but after they reach flowering size they will benefit from this attention only when the plants begin to deteriorate in vigor or when their roots become so crowded that there is danger of their breaking the pot; this normally means that they will need

The red-flowered Scarborough Lily, Vallota purpurea, is a good greenhouse or window-garden plant.

repotting only at intervals of several years.

When potting is necessary it should be done in June, the plants being transferred to well-drained pots, just large enough to hold them together with a little new soil that is packed around the ball of roots. The bulbs should be planted so that their lower halves only are below soil level, leaving their upper halves exposed.

Pots 6 in. in diameter are sufficiently large for a single, vigorous, mature bulb of Vallota, but as natural increase of the bulbs by offsets occurs, the original bulb, together with its progeny, may be transferred to a 7- or 8-in. container or even one 9 or 10 in. in diameter. Increase in pot size is accomplished gradually, by a series of repottings spaced 3-4 years apart. The diameter of the pot used in successive repottings is not more than 1-2 in. greater than that of the previous container.

Treatment after Potting. Place the potted bulbs in a sunny location in a window or greenhouse or in a cold frame and give very little water until growth becomes active. Then gradually increase the supply as the roots commence to penetrate the soil freely. During the period when little water is being given, spray the foliage lightly with water on all sunny days.

Established plants are kept growing vigorously by top-dressing them every July with rich potting compost, a little of the old surface soil being removed to make room for the new compost.

The plants may be set on a bed of ashes in a cold frame or be plunged to the rims of their pots in sand or ashes outdoors during the summer. They must be exposed to sun to ripen the bulbs and encourage flower production. During the winter they need a minimum night temperature of 40-50 degrees with a daytime rise of 5-10 degrees allowed.

Watering and Feeding. The bulbs of Vallota are not deciduous (leaf-losing), so that they must not be dried off completely in winter. During the winter months the soil is watered whenever it becomes nearly dry; from March to September it is kept decidedly moist at all times. During the summer months diluted liquid fertilizer may also be applied with advantage once a week.

In the cultivation of this plant many amateurs make the mistake of attempting to dry off the bulb in winter; it is most important that the soil be kept moist at that season. During the winter the plants must be kept in as sunny a position as possible; if they are crowded among other plants the leaves are liable to decay.

Outdoor Culture. For outdoor culture in mild climates Vallotas need a deep, fertile, porous soil that does not dry out completely at any time, and exposure to full sun.

Propagation is usually by offsets, which form near the bases of the bulbs. They are detached in spring or in June and buried to their tips in a well-drained pan of light soil. They are given the same treatment as the mature bulbs and grown until large enough to repot separately in small pots.

The chief kind is V. speciosa (purpurea), 18 in., scarlet, late summer. There are several varieties of V. speciosa, the principal of which are V. speciosa eximia, white and crimson; V. speciosa alba, which has white flowers; and V. speciosa minor, which has flowers of the same color as those of V. speciosa but smaller.

VANCOUVERIA (Vancouve'ria). A small group of hardy or nearly hardy perennial herbs, natives of western North America, named in honor of Captain George Vancouver. They belong to the Barberry family, Berberidaceae, and are closely allied to the Epimediums. They are plants of great charm, and are valuable for shady places in the rock garden, wild garden or open woodland garden; they delight in soil rich in leaf mold.

Vancouveria hexandra spreads by means of rather wiry running roots and sends up graceful airy sprays of thin-textured, bright green, six-sided leaves, and in June or July bears attractive panicles of quaint white flowers. A choice and interesting leaf-losing (deciduous) plant for shade, it is easy to grow and quite hardy. It is increased by division of the roots in spring.

V. chrysantha enjoys a rather more open and sunny location than V. hexandra and, whereas V. hexandra is deciduous, dying right down in autumn, V. chrysantha is almost evergreen, the leaves being thick and of leathery texture. The flowers are larger than those of V. hexandra, and soft yellow. The plant is increased by division of the roots in spring. This kind is less hardy than V. hexandra.

V. parviflora, the Inside-out Flower, is an evergreen kind that attains a height of about 20 in. and bears small white or lavender flowers. It is a native of Washington and Oregon and is probably not hardy in the north central and northeastern states.

VANDA (Van'da). A large and very varied group of Orchids which are natives of the Far East, from Ceylon to Java. All are epiphytal (grow on trees), without pseudobulbs, and have evergreen foliage. The roots, which are often thick and fleshy, arise on the stems in some kinds. Many have large handsome, long-lasting flowers produced in racemes from the axils of the leaves. The flowers of some Vandas are very fragrant. The name Vanda is a Sanskrit word and is applied to any plant of similar habit and also to parasitic plants.

Vanda caerulea is one of the loveliest of Orchids. The flowers are delightful tones of blue or lavender blue.

Easily Grown Orchids. A suitable compost consists of cut osmunda fiber, Tree Fern fiber, Fir bark or Redwood bark. One third of the pot should be filled with drainage (broken crocks) and the next third need only have a small proportion of compost and consists largely of crocks. The compost should be slightly raised in the center above the pot rim.

Many kinds are strong rooting, the roots clinging to the pots, and it is often difficult to repot without injury to them. The better plan is to remove as much of the old compost as possible in April and insert fresh compost.

Repotting when necessary should be done in

The white, purple-spotted Orchid named Vanda suavis.

Vandas develop stout aerial roots very high up on their stems.

spring, and if the plants are bare at the base the stem may be cut off beneath living roots, and potted.

Extra plants may be obtained by carefully taking off basal growths when they are sufficiently rooted. New roots may sometimes be induced to form by binding sphagnum moss around the bare stem and keeping it moist. Water should be given freely to all Vandas throughout the summer, but little is needed in winter. Shading is required in summer.

All Vandas require a tropical atmosphere during the summer, but the winter temperature must be governed by the natural habitat of the plants. A minimum temperature of 65 degrees suits V. Sanderiana, and one of 60 degrees suits V. tricolor, V. Amesiana, V. Kimballiana. V. teres should be wintered in a temperature of 55 degrees. The beautiful V. caerulea should be wintered in a temperature of 55 degrees and watered only occasionally, and the atmosphere should not be too moist or decayed areas will appear in the foliage.

The flowering season varies with the different kinds. V. caerulea usually blooms in September and October, V. luzonica in autumn, V. Parishii in May, V. Sanderiana in winter, and V. teres, V. tricolor and V. Dearei in spring and summer. V. Amesiana and V. Kimballiana usually bloom in early winter. V. Miss Agnes Joaquim produces a succession of blooms throughout the entire year.

The following are among the most popular kinds: V. Amesiana, fragrant, white and rose; V. Kimballiana, white sepals and petals and amethyst lip; V. Watsonii, white; V. caerulea, various shades of blue. V. tricolor and V. suavis are very similar; in V. tricolor the prevailing color is red-brown on a whitish ground with purplish lip: V. suavis is spotted with purple on a whitish ground. V. teres grows to a great length and has large flowers, three to seven on a spike; the color is rose-magneta. V. Hookeriana is whitish, beautifully spotted with purple. V. Sanderiana, possibly the finest of all Vandas, has flowers nearly 5 in. across, rose and yellow, veined with red. V. Sanderiana variety Terry is especially fine. A hybrid between V. Hookeriana and V. teres named Miss Agnes Joaquim has white, rose-pink and purple flowers, much used in leis in Hawaii.

VANDOPSIS (Vandop'sis). Orchids from Burma, New Guinea and the Philippines, which are often called Vanda. In Vandopsis the lip of the flower is not protracted into a "spur." All are evergreen Orchids without pseudobulbs and are epiphytal (grow on trees); the strap-shaped leaves are arranged in two opposite rows on a stem which eventually becomes somewhat woody. The flowers are on axillary spikes and are rather fleshy. These Orchids usually bloom in summer under cultivation. The name is derived from Vanda, another genus of Orchids, and *opsis,* resemblance.

Orchids for a Greenhouse. Vandopsis needs to be grown in a tropical greenhouse with a winter temperature of 60-65 degrees at night. A moist atmosphere is required throughout the year, and abundance of water in summer, but during the winter months the plants should be allowed to become comparatively dry between waterings.

All kinds attain considerable dimensions and need large pots; a suitable compost consists of **cut osmunda fiber, Tree Fern fiber, Fir bark or Redwood bark. Drainage must be free, because repotting should be avoided until absolutely necessary. Each year, in spring, much of the old compost should be removed and fresh substituted.**

If the plants become leggy (straggly) the stems are cut off, in March or April, below the aerial roots, and are replanted lower down in new pots. Shading is necessary in the summer.

The Chief Kinds. V. lissochiloides, most popularly known as Vanda Batemanii, has leaves 24 in. long; each spike bears 20 or more flowers, each about 3 in. across, crimson-purple behind; yellow and purple spotted in front. V. gigantea has shorter spikes and yellow flowers spotted with chestnut-brown.

VANILLA (Vanil'la). Climbing Orchids which are natives in both Eastern and Western hemispheres. They have fleshy stems which attain a considerable length. In some kinds the stems bear evergreen leaves; in others they are leafless; in some kinds the thick stems are mottled—almost snakelike—in their markings. The stems emit roots and the flowers are borne in clusters on short spikes. Though the flowers are of moderate size, they are dull in color; several are very fragrant.

From some kinds, particularly V. fragrans (planifolia), Vanilla is obtained from the prepared seed capsules which are 6 in. or more long and beanlike in shape. The name Vanilla is derived from a Spanish word, *Vaynilla,* the diminutive of *Vayna,* a knife or scissors' case, and alludes to the shape of the capsule. Vanilla was known to the Aztecs and the name was probably given by the Spanish adventurers.

To grow Vanilla in a greenhouse a tropical atmosphere is required; in winter a temperature of 60 degrees is suitable. The chief kind is V. fragrans (planifolia). A comparatively small **pot, with free drainage and a compost of cut osmunda fiber, Tree Fern fiber, Fir bark or Redwood bark suits this plant, which,** as it grows, is trained on wires near the glass. The greater part of its nourishment will be derived from the atmosphere. Repotting is not necessary, but new compost should be added occasionally. The long roots will attach themselves to the walls and benches of the greenhouse.

How to Obtain Fruits. To obtain fruits, the flowers, which appear in spring and summer, **must be pollinated by hand. The plant may be freely syringed on warm days, but should be** shaded from direct sunlight in spring and summer. The stems often branch and propagation is effected by cutting off pieces possessing roots, potting them and placing them in a propagating case.

There is a form of V. fragrans with variegated leaves. V. Phalaenopsis, from Madagascar, has leafless stems and rather showy rose-flushed flowers. V. Pompona, also known as V. grandiflora, has yellowish flowers and its seed pods also yield vanilla.

A good example of a variegated plant is this Hydrangea, which has its green leaves margined with areas of light creamy white.

This variegated-leaved variety of Corn is grown for ornament. Its green leaves are streaked with cream.

The variegation in this Agave consists of narrow bands of creamy white along the margins of the green leaves.

VARIEGATED. This term is used in the descriptions of the leaves of plants in which part of the normal green coloring is replaced by white, cream, yellow or, more rarely, other colors, which may be in the form of blotches or stripes.

Flowers and petals which show areas of different colors are also sometimes described as variegated.

VARIETY. Botanical usage and horticultural usage differ in the application of the term variety. To the botanist a variety is a group of wild plants which forms part of a species but which differs sufficiently from the other members of the species to warrant being given an identifying name, a technical varietal name. Most botanical varieties breed true from seeds.

As commonly used by gardeners, the term variety is applied to any distinct, uniform group of plants of less than specific rank that may be propagated and maintained true to character either by seeds or vegetative propagation. In this broad sense it includes botanical varieties, subspecies and forms, selected horticultural strains that breed true from seeds or may be maintained by vegetative (asexual) methods of propagation such as by cuttings, division and grafting. Varieties that are propagated by vegetative methods are known as clons. See Clon or Clone. See also Cultivar.

VARNISH TREE. Rhus verniciflua, which see. The name is also given to Aleurites moluccana and to Koelreuteria paniculata.

VEGETABLE GARDEN
Growing Vegetables at Home for Pleasure and Profit

The cultivation of vegetables in the home garden is a fascinating and useful activity. It is often pointed out that vegetables can be purchased so inexpensively that it is not profitable to grow them at home, particularly if one places any monetary value on the time expended. This in some cases may be true, but it is important to remember that the benefits derived from home vegetable gardening cannot be measured in terms of the market value of the produce alone.

To begin with, freshly gathered vegetables are very superior to those that are usually obtainable in the market. Secondly, the home gardener can grow varieties of the best quality and flavor that are not grown commercially because they do not ship well or for other reasons. Thirdly, the pleasure and satisfaction of cultivating vegetables at home is an intangible benefit upon which a money value cannot easily be placed.

Location and Soil. To have a satisfactory vegetable garden it is essential to locate it where it receives as much sunshine as possible; a minimum of six hours a day is necessary and more

Fresh vegetables picked directly from the home garden are both nutritious and appetizing.

A vegetable garden sufficient to fill the needs of a small family may be planted, as this one is, along the sunny side of the back yard. It can easily be made not only a useful but a decorative part of the garden. Here, Lettuce plants are used to take the place of edging plants.

Children can learn much and have fun cultivating a small vegetable plot of their own.

is very desirable. The soil should be deep and fertile or should be capable of being worked into that condition. It should be well drained because few vegetables will succeed if the subsurface drainage is inadequate. A level site or a gentle slope is best; steep slopes are to be avoided because of the trouble caused by erosion.

Trees should not be nearer to the garden than their own height; otherwise, their roots and shade are likely to cause trouble.

Planning the Garden. Before planting a vegetable garden it is important to plan it on paper. The plan need not be elaborate but the location of each crop should be shown and the sowing or planting date indicated. A piece of graph paper may be used for making the plan, the lines forming the little squares on the paper make it easy to indicate the location of each row of vegetables.

A Simple Plan Is Best. Elaborate path systems and other fancy features are out of place in the vegetable garden. Whenever possible the garden should be rectangular and the rows should run at right angles to the paths. There is some slight advantage in having the rows run north and south, because they then receive equal amounts of sun on both sides, but the benefit is so small that if other considerations, such as the slope or the shape of the plot, make it more convenient to run them in some other direction, there should be no hesitation in doing so. If the slope is at all steep the rows should run across it rather than up and down it.

Most vegetables are treated as annuals and are planted from seed each year but a few are perennials and occupy the ground for more than one year. Here belong Asparagus, Globe Artichoke and Rhubarb. Arrange to locate the perennial vegetables next to each other and, if small fruits such as Strawberries, Currants, Gooseberries and Raspberries are grown in the vegetable garden, these can usually also be located together with advantage. Tall crops such as Corn, Pole Beans and Tomatoes may be placed at the north side of the garden if the rows run east and west, so that they will not shade lower-growing crops. Melons, Cucumbers, Pumpkins, Squash and other spreading kinds of vegetables should be planted where they will not interfere with less rampant growers.

Crops that occupy the ground for the greater part of the season, such as Parsnips, Onions and New Zealand Spinach, may be grouped, and short-season crops may be placed together so that, as they are harvested, it will be easy to plant succession crops on the ground they occupied.

If hand cultivation is to be used, as is most often the case in home vegetable gardens, the rows should be spaced as close together as the production of good-quality crops will allow (the spacing differs, of course, for different vegetables). But if horse or mechanical cultivation is to be employed, the space needed by the implements used will determine the minimum distance between rows.

The Crops to Grow. Individual taste should, of course, largely determine what is grown in home vegetable gardens. It is usually wisest in a small garden to concentrate on kinds that need moderate space and give good returns for the effort expended. Most gardeners will want to include Tomatoes and String Beans, for these are easily grown and yield well. Carrots, Beets

Tomatoes are a favorite crop in the home vegetable garden.

Lettuce is a "must" for most home gardens.

Cabbages are easy to grow and mature early in the season.

and Broccoli are also prime favorites, and deservedly so, of the home vegetable gardener. Peas are a must in many sections and provide early crops that can be succeeded by Beets, Carrots or other vegetables that can be sown in June or early July. Asparagus is an excellent crop for early harvesting but should be attempted only where the soil is in fertile condition.

It should be the aim of every vegetable gardener to keep up a continuous supply of salad crops such as Lettuce, Scallions, Radishes, Cucumbers, and such leafy crops as Spinach, New Zealand Spinach, Cabbage and Celery should not be neglected. Onions, Parsnips, Turnips and Kohlrabi should be considered. Corn will be given a place in every garden except the very smallest, for although this plant takes considerable space the flavor of freshly gathered Corn is so superior to Corn from market sources that every effort to produce it is worth while.

Where climate and space permit, Potatoes, Lima Beans, Watermelons, Sweet Potatoes, Kale, Brussels Sprouts, Cauliflowers, Melons, Pumpkins, Eggplants, Peppers, Okra, Swiss Chard and other vegetables may be grown.

In small gardens all or most of the crops will be eaten fresh; on larger plots, produce may be grown for freezing, canning and storing in other ways.

Preparations for Planting. As soon as the plan is decided upon, it is possible to make out an order for the seeds that will be required. Approximate amounts of seed or plants required for each 50 ft. of row are given in the following table, either in terms of weight or, in the case of vegetables that are sown indoors in flats or outdoors in seedbeds and later transplanted, of number of plants that are needed for setting out.

Home-grown Corn is one of the most delicious of vegetables.

	Amount of Seed for 50-ft. Row	No. of Plants for 50-ft. Row
Bean, Bush Lima	½ lb.	
Bean, Pole	¼ lb.	
Bean, Pole Lima	¼ lb.	
Bean, Snap	½ lb.	
Beet	1 oz.	
Broccoli		25
Brussels Sprouts		25
Cabbage		26–33
Carrot	¼ oz.	
Celery		100
Corn	2 oz.	
Cucumber	¼ oz.	
Eggplant		33
Endive	½ oz.	
Kale		33
Kohlrabi	⅛ oz.	
Lettuce	¼ oz.	
Muskmelon	¼ oz.	
Onion	½ oz.	
Onion (sets)	1 lb.	
Parsnip	¼ oz.	
Pea	½ lb.	
Radish	½ oz.	
Rhubarb		25–36
Rutabaga	⅛ oz.	
Spinach	½ oz.	
Spinach, New Zealand	½ oz.	
Squash	¼ oz.	
Tomatoes (staked)		25
Tomatoes (not staked)		15–18
Turnip	⅛ oz.	
Watermelon	½ oz.	

Orders for seeds and plants should be placed with reputable dealers early enough to ensure the orders receive careful attention and are delivered in ample time for planting. At the time of making out the seed order the gardener should consider what fertilizers, sprays, tools and other supplies are needed, and place orders for these. If pots, seed flats, soil for indoor planting, etc., are to be used, they should be on hand well before they are actually needed.

The vegetable plot should be made ready for planting as early as practicable (see Digging). If possible, the heavier plowing or spading should be done in the fall and only the actual surface preparation of the seed and planting beds left until spring, but this is a counsel of perfection that not everyone can follow. If fall preparation is not possible an early start in spring is of the utmost importance. Besides

Beets are easily grown. They should be harvested before they become large and coarse.

Although it requires a little more skill to grow Celery well than some other vegetables, it is well worth cultivating in the home garden.

The soil of the vegetable garden should be spaded or forked over well in advance of planting time.

turning the soil to a minimum depth of 8 in. and loosening it with spade, plow or rotary tiller, it is also important to condition and improve it by mixing in manure, compost, fertilizer and possibly lime, according to the needs of the various crops.

Starting Plants Indoors. In many sections of Canada and the United States an advantage is gained by starting certain vegetables, such as Tomatoes, Celery, Eggplant, Pepper, Sweet Potato, early Cabbage, early Cauliflower and early Lettuce in a greenhouse or hotbed and setting the young plants outdoors after all danger of frost has passed and the weather is favorable to their growth.

Such plants should not be started too early; otherwise they will be so large at planting-out time that they will suffer a serious setback as a result of the operation of transplanting. The amount of time needed to raise plants indoors of a suitable size for setting out varies according to the crop. One very important point is to make sure that the young plants are properly hardened off by gradually accustoming them to outdoor conditions before they are actually transplanted into the garden.

If plants are purchased rather than raised at home, use every effort to secure sturdy, well-grown specimens that are not overlarge. Good plants are very much worth the slightly higher price you usually have to pay for them, because they will give infinitely better results than poorly produced stock.

Whenever possible, select dull, cloudy weather, when the atmosphere is moist, for planting;

Setting out in the garden young Cabbage plants that were started early indoors.

Succession cropping, the planting of a second crop in the same soil after the earlier crop has been harvested, makes maximum use of the vegetable garden.

but the soil must not be excessively wet, not so wet, for example, that it sticks unpleasantly to tools and hands and shoes. Immediately after planting, water each plant in either plain water or with a starter solution (a weak solution of a rapidly available nitrogenous fertilizer) and shade the plants temporarily if the weather is very sunny.

Seed Sowing. In the vegetable garden, seed sowing is one of the most frequent of tasks. Some crops, such as Peas, must be sown as early in spring as the ground is workable to ensure success; others, such as late Lettuce and late Turnips, are sown at as late a date as will ensure their attaining harvesting size before fall frost. With many kinds of vegetables, such as Carrots, Beans, Beets, and Lettuce, several sowings are made each season to provide succession crops that will provide harvests over as long a period as possible.

Never sow more at one time than can conveniently be used or stored at harvest time. The tendency of most beginners is to sow too much at once, particularly early in the season. Most vegetables are sown in drills or shallow trenches but some few are sown in hills.

Make sure that the soil is in a loose, crumbly condition at sowing time, neither so wet that it cakes to the tools and cannot be raked to a fine state, nor so dry that it is dusty. If the soil is excessively dry the bottoms of the drills should be soaked with water before the seeds are scattered along them; if the soil is too wet, sowing should be delayed until it has dried out sufficiently. Seeds should be sown at such a depth that they are covered with soil to a depth equal to 3-4 times their own average diameters.

Summer Care. Ensuring quick growth without any setbacks is a secret of producing good vegetables. From the beginning, weeds should

As vegetable plants have many fibrous feeding roots in the top 3 or 4 in. of soil, cultivation should be shallow and frequent. The wheel hoe being used here saves much time. Thinning is another important "must," as is diligent spraying or dusting to combat insects and pests.

be kept down and growth encouraged by frequent, shallow, surface cultivations of the soil, and these should be repeated often throughout the summer except where mulches are used to restrain weeds and conserve moisture. Weed growth is exceedingly harmful to all vegetables.

Ample supplies of moisture are necessary to produce good vegetables. In areas where natural rainfall is deficient, and during dry periods in regions where summer rains are usually more or less adequate, irrigation must be given to supplement natural supplies of moisture. The ground should never become so dry that growth is checked and the plants suffer.

Diseases and pests will take their toll of vegetables unless intelligent means are used to combat them. It is wise to ask your State Agricultural Experiment Station to send you bulletins on the control of pests and diseases of the vegetable garden in the region where you garden, and be guided accordingly. Many older methods of control have been superseded by newer ones and improved methods of controlling old enemies and of combatting new ones are constantly being discovered; it is well to keep up to date in these matters. See Pests and Diseases.

Staking vegetables that need this attention must not be neglected, and harvesting the crops will take a proportion of the gardener's time. It is a mistake to harvest crops so young that the returns are abnormally small from the land occupied, but it is equally foolish to allow vegetables to grow to such a size and maturity that they have passed their best eating quality when they are gathered; tough Peas, woody Beets, stringy Celery and Corn that has lost its early sweetness are poor returns for the effort of running a vegetable garden.

The vegetable gardener most certainly should keep a notebook in which are recorded sowing dates, transplanting dates, the names of varieties, comments on cropping and other pertinent information. Such a record is invaluable in planning the next year's garden.

VEGETABLE MARROW. A kind of Squash, which see.

VEGETABLE OYSTER. Salsify, which see.

VEGETABLE TALLOW. See Sapium sebiferum.

VELLA—*Cress Rocket* (Vel'la). Tender, evergreen shrubs which are found wild in Spain, and are of little horticultural value. They grow about 3 ft. in height, have oval, hairy leaves, and bear terminal racemes of yellow, four-petaled flowers in May. Vella belongs to the Mustard family, Cruciferae, and the name is derived from *velar,* the Celtic name for Cress.

A mild climate and a compost of loam and leaf mold are required. No pruning is necessary. Propagation is by inserting cuttings made from the tips of the shoots in summer. They are placed in sand, or sand and peat moss, in a close cold frame or propagating greenhouse and kept moist and shaded until well rooted. They are then hardened off and planted out in April.

The chief kind is V. Pseudocytisus, 3 ft., yellow, May.

VELTHEIMIA (Veltheim'ia). Tender bulb plants from South Africa, which belong to the Lily family, Liliaceae. They are very attractive both in flower and foliage and are suitable for a sunny window or greenhouse. They have large fleshy bulbs, shaped like inverted tops, measuring 4-5 in. in diameter. From their tips they produce large rosettes of somewhat pendulous leaves which are strap-shaped, wavy-edged, deep green and glossy, and measure 12 in. in length by 2-3 in. in width.

In winter or early spring the attractive flowers are produced; they are tubular, pendent, reddish with green tips (in the chief kind), 1 in. in length and in a compact raceme at the end of a stout stalk which is 12 in. in length, green mottled with reddish-purple. The name Veltheimia commemorates the Count of Veltheim, a German botanist of the early part of the nineteenth century.

When to Pot the Bulbs. A minimum winter temperature of 45 degrees, and a compost of two parts of sandy loam, one part of well-decayed leaf mold, and a little sand are required. Potting is done in September when the bulbs are potted firmly in well-drained pots, the tips above the surface of the soil. Very little water is required until growth becomes active in spring, when the supply should be increased; during the summer, liberal quantities are required. When the leaves commence to die off after flowering, the water supply is gradually lessened and the soil is kept nearly dry until early spring.

Repotting is not necessary oftener than once in 3 years. An annual top-dressing of rich soil in spring, and a weekly dose of liquid fertilizer during the summer, are sufficient to keep the plants in vigorous growth. After flowering, they benefit by being placed on a bed of ashes in a sunny cold frame for the remainder of the summer.

Offsets form freely around the old bulbs, and these are removed and potted separately when it is desired to increase the stock of plants.

The chief kind is V. viridifolia, 2 ft., green and deep pink, February and March. Other kinds are V. glauca, 18 in., pink, and V. intermedia, 18 in., pink, April.

VELVET BEAN. See Stizolobium.

VELVET GROUNDSEL. Senecio Petasitis, which see.

VELVET PLANT. See Gynura.

VENIDIUM (Venid'ium). A group of plants which are found wild in South Africa; they belong to the Daisy family, Compositae. Few of these plants are at present grown in North

Venidium fastuosum, an annual from South Africa. Its large flowers are vivid orange with a purple central zone.

Venidium decurrens.

America. The name is of uncertain derivation.

The chief kinds are two annuals, Venidium fastuosum and V. decurrens (calendulaceum); the former has not proved very satisfactory in the hands of amateurs, owing to the difficulty experienced in raising seedlings. Venidium fastuosum reaches a height of 2 ft. or more and bears large, marguerite-like flowers of the most brilliant orange coloring, each with a central zone of shining, black-purple formed by the bases of the ray florets.

Seedsmen have produced Venidium hybrids in shades of white, yellow, buff and orange. These are easier to grow than V. fastuosum.

When to Sow Seeds. The germination of the seeds is often disappointing. They should be sown in a flat filled with light, sandy soil in a greenhouse, temperature 50-55 degrees, in April; the flat is covered with a piece of glass and shaded from sunshine, and the soil is kept moderately moist. When the seedlings show through, the glass covering is removed and the seedlings are watered with great care, to prevent them from damping off (a diseased condition); they are hardened off in a cold frame and planted out of doors in May. Light or well-drained soil and a place exposed to full sunshine are necessary to their successful cultivation. Alternately the seeds may be sown out of doors in May. It is useless to attempt the cultivation of these plants in heavy soil or in any position except in full sunshine.

Venidium decurrens is more easily managed than V. fastuosum; it reaches a height of 12 in. and bears smaller flowers than V. fastuosum.

Greenhouse Culture. Venidiums are very handsome plants for growing in pots to bloom in the greenhouse in late winter and early spring. To secure large specimens in 7- or 8-in. pots, the seeds should be sown in September; smaller plants are obtained by sowing seeds from November to January.

The soil compost should be sandy and fertile and the pots well drained. When the seedlings are large enough to handle easily, they are transplanted individually into 2½-in. or 3-in. pots and are grown in the sunniest location possible in a greenhouse where the night temperature is 45-50 degrees and the daytime temperature slightly higher.

When the small pots are filled with roots the plants are transferred to 4-in. pots, and later, as growth makes necessary, to larger-sized pots. For these later pottings a rich, well-drained, coarse soil is preferred. At all times the plants are grown in a cool, airy, sunny environment. When they are well rooted in the pots in which they are to bloom, applications of weak liquid fertilizer are beneficial.

Watering must, at all times, be done with great care. The soil should quite decidedly approach a dry condition before watering, and then it should be thoroughly soaked. Overwatering brings disaster quickly in the form of rot. At no time should the plants be syringed, nor should water be allowed to accumulate on the foliage.

Because the flowers of Venidiums close at nightfall and in dull weather, the flowers have small value for cutting, but the plants are splendid for decorating a cool conservatory or greenhouse.

VENTILATION. In the management of greenhouses, hotbeds and cold frames, ventilation is a matter of great importance. Its purpose is not primarily to provide fresh air, because enough of this normally seeps through joints between panes of glass, through spaces around doors and other small apertures. The most important reasons for ventilating are to

Ventilating a cold frame by propping up the sash.

lower temperatures and reduce atmospheric humidity. Excessive humidity encourages the development of various fungous diseases.

The amount of moisture that is desirable in the atmosphere depends upon the kind of plants, the stage of growth they have attained and other circumstances. Quite usually, newly planted cuttings and freshly transplanted plants benefit from being kept in comparatively moist air (in what gardeners call a close atmosphere). To ensure such conditions minimum ventilation is given, taking into account the need to maintain temperatures within limits appropriate for the kinds of plants. Some plants, such as Chrysanthemums, Carnations, Cinerarias and other cool greenhouse kinds, benefit from being grown in freely ventilated greenhouses; others, such as hothouse Orchids, tropical foliage plants and other natives of the humid tropics, need less ventilation.

Greenhouses. In greenhouses the extent to which the ventilators are opened depends, of course, on the temperature it is necessary to maintain in the greenhouse and upon the outside temperature. However much ventilation may be needed, it is necessary to avoid strong drafts. If the greenhouse is fitted with ventilators on both sides, only those on the side away from the wind, the leeward side, should be opened in windy weather. In sunny weather, whenever the outdoor temperature permits, the top ventilators are opened a little, early in the morning, to prevent the temperature inside the greenhouse from rising too rapidly. As the temperature out of doors rises, the ventilation must be increased.

It is a mistake to allow the interior of the greenhouse to become very hot and then suddenly to open the ventilators for the purpose of lowering the temperature. As the warmth out of doors normally increases gradually as the day advances, so should the temperature inside the greenhouse rise gradually. A wide-fluctuating temperature is injurious to plants.

In spring, when cold winds prevail, careful ventilating is particularly necessary to avoid drafts and lowering the temperature suddenly. In the afternoon, ventilation should be reduced, and the greenhouse closed before the sun has ceased to shine on the roof. During the winter months, when the weather is mild, it is an advantage to open the ventilators slightly whenever possible without endangering the well-being of the plants. In hot summer weather it is beneficial to leave the top ventilators open, at whatever degree is appropriate for the crops being grown, throughout the night.

If the greenhouse is fitted with ventilators low down in the supporting walls, these can often be open slightly when it would be unwise to admit air through the top ventilators, for the air is warmed to some extent by passing over the heating pipes.

The ordinary small greenhouse, in which the temperature falls to 40 or 45 degrees in winter, should be ventilated as freely as possible in mild weather, for free air circulation is of great benefit to plants grown under those conditions. If insufficient ventilation is given, the air inside the greenhouse becomes very damp, the leaves of plants are liable to decay, and seedlings may perish from attacks of the damping-off fungus.

Cold Frames and Hotbeds. The ventilating of cold frames and hotbeds should follow the principles detailed above for greenhouses. Naturally, hotbeds are ventilated less freely than cold frames but in sunny weather the temperatures inside them are likely to rise quickly and, unless ventilation is provided promptly, may soon reach levels that injure or kill the plants they contain. A small amount of ventilation is likely to prevent damage, and this should always be given on the side of the hotbed away from the wind, the leeward side.

Cold frames that shelter plants that are tender and actively growing need ventilating in much the same manner as hotbeds; enough ventilation should be given to prevent the inside temperature from rising to excessive heights, but care must be taken not to allow strong drafts or cause undue lowering of the temperature inside the frame. This applies also to cold frames in which cuttings are being rooted.

Cold frames containing hardy or nearly hardy plants being held in a dormant or essentially dormant condition over winter need ventilating much more freely. Whenever the temperature inside the frame is above freezing (as indicated by the melting of the frost on the glass) some ventilation should be given and, as soon as the outside temperature is above freezing, the frames should be ventilated more generously. When the outside temperature approaches 40 degrees it is well to remove the glass sash entirely.

VENUS'S FLYTRAP. See Dionaea.

VENUS'S LOOKING-GLASS. See Specularia.

VENUS'S NAVELWORT. The botanical name is Omphalodes, which see.

VERATRUM—*False Hellebore* (Vera'trum). Hardy, herbaceous perennial flowering plants, of imposing appearance, but not very attractive in flower. They belong to the Lily family, Liliaceae, and are found wild in North America, Siberia and Europe. Veratrum is the ancient name for Hellebore.

These plants grow 3-9 ft. high from a fleshy rootstock; the stalkless leaves rise straight from the ground and overlap at their bases to form an elongated rosette. They are deep green in color, plicate (crinkled lengthwise), 12 in. or more in length and 5-6 in. wide. The flowers, which are not very striking, are small, greenish, or greenish-purple or white, borne in a loose spike, 18 in. to 2 ft. in length, in summer.

For the Woodland Garden. Veratrum is not a popular border plant, but is generally planted in irregular groups in woodlands. It likes moist soil in which peat or leaf mold is plentiful. A shaded or semishaded position is necessary, as the leaves are easily scorched by the sun.

When to Plant. Planting may be done in fall or spring. Established plants should not be moved unless they are not making good growth, when they may be lifted and set in fresh soil.

Propagation is by lifting and dividing the clumps at planting time, or new plants may be raised from seeds. The seeds are sown in a bed of peaty soil or in soil containing much leaf mold in a shaded position in April. When the seedlings are large enough to handle, they are lifted and set 6 in. apart in a similar soil and location, where they remain until large enough to plant in their permanent positions.

Veratrum album, which is wild in southern Europe and northern Asia, is grown in Germany and other European countries for its roots, which furnish Hellebore powder.

The principal kinds are V. album, European White Hellebore, 3-4 ft., white, July; V. californicum, 6 ft., white and green, summer; V. nigrum, 3 ft., purple, July; and V. viride, American White Hellebore, 4-8 ft., green, July.

VERBASCUM — *Mullein* (Verbas'cum). A group of hardy perennial and biennial plants, some of which have large woolly leaves; they bear tall spikes of flowers in summer. They are natives of southern Europe, northern Africa and

Perennial Verbascums, with their tall spires of yellow flowers, are handsome plants for naturalizing in wild gardens.

Many Verbascums have rosettes of large flannel-like leaves that are quite handsome.

western Asia; several kinds are naturalized in North America. They belong to the family Scrophulariaceae, the Figwort family. The name is an old Latin one.

These plants are of easy cultivation in ordinary garden soil in a sunny place. Some of them are suitable for the flower border; others are useful for wild and woodland gardens. They are easily raised from seeds sown out of doors in May; the seedlings are transplanted, 6 in. apart, in nursery rows, spaced 12-18 in. apart, to give them room for development, and are transplanted again in October or the following spring to where they are to bloom.

The biennial kinds have to be renewed from seeds every year, for they perish after the flowers have faded and seeds have formed. Several of the Mulleins are perennials, and these are of chief value in the garden.

Perennial Kinds. V. bombyciferum, 5-6 ft., has golden-yellow flowers among dense silvery woolly hairs. V. Chaixii reaches a height of 3-4 ft. and has yellow flowers; V. thapsiforme (densiflorum), which reaches a height of 4 ft., is one of the most attractive; it bears branched inflorescences of yellow and bronze-colored flowers; V. nigrum grows 2-3 ft. high and has yellow flowers; V. phoeniceum, the Purple Mullein, is 3 ft. high, with flowers of various colors.

There are several attractive named varieties of V. phoeniceum which are admirable plants for the hardy flower border, where they are in full bloom in summer. They reach a height of about 2 ft. The colors range through violet, purple, salmon and rose.

Other perennial Mulleins are V. simplex (giganteum), which is very vigorous, reaching a height of 8 ft., and bears yellow flowers; V. longifolium variety pannosum, 5-6 ft., with gray leaves and light yellow flowers; V. pyramidale, 4-5 ft., yellow; and V. Wiedemannianum, 3 ft., purplish-violet. The plant known as V. Broussa is V. bombyciferum.

Biennial Kinds. Of the biennial kinds, the most imposing is V. olympicum, which reaches a height of 6 ft., has gray-white leaves and bears yellow flowers. V. Thapsus, the Common Mullein, is 4-5 ft. high and has gray leaves and yellow flowers; it is naturalized in North America but is too weedy a plant to be worth cultivating, except, perhaps, in wild gardens.

Several named hybrid Verbascums have been developed which are usually biennials but sometimes live longer than two seasons. These kinds do not always come true to type from seeds but may be propagated by root cuttings. One of the finest is named Harkness Hybrid; it grows 5 or 6 ft. high and bears yellow flowers. Bridal Bouquet, 5 ft., has white flowers. Silver Spire, 6 ft.,

The yellow flowers of Verbascum bombyciferum are borne on white woolly stems.

has gray-white leaves and yellow flowers. Others are Cotswold Beauty, 4 ft., bronze; Cotswold Gem, 4 ft., soft terra-cotta; Cotswold Queen, 4 ft., salmon-bronze; Gainsborough, 3½ ft., soft yellow; and Pink Domino, 3½ ft., mauve-pink.

VERBENA—*Verbena, Vervain* (Verbe′na). A group of some eighty hardy and tender annual or perennial herbs or shrubs, mostly native to the Americas. Verbena belongs to the Vervain family, Verbenaceae. It is an ancient Latin name.

Comparatively few of the wild kinds are in cultivation at the present time, but the garden varieties are brilliant for summer beds and flower borders. Strains which come true to color from seed have been raised in recent years, and it is now usual to raise seedlings annually instead of keeping old plants of named varieties in greenhouses during winter and propagating by means of cuttings in spring, as was once the common practice.

Garden Verbenas. The garden Verbena, V. hortensis, which is of hybrid origin, is among the most beautiful and satisfactory of all flowers for massing in flower beds and borders for summer display. Varieties may be raised from seeds sown in a greenhouse, temperature 55 degrees, in spring, and planted out in the garden in May. They flower profusely until killed by frost in autumn.

The common garden Verbena hortensis may be had in a variety of colors. It is a fine annual for summer flower beds.

Because these Verbenas grow rather slowly in their early stages it is well to sow the seeds in February or early March. As soon as the young plants are big enough to handle with ease, they should be transplanted to flats at a spacing of 2-3 in. between the plants. The soil should be decidedly sandy and the flats well drained. Grow the plants in a sunny location at all times.

These Verbenas are of spreading, prostrate habit and the flowers are in flattish heads, several inches across.

The colors range from white through pale pink to deep rose, cerise and scarlet to crimson and pale lavender to deep violet, with endless intermediate shades of mauve, purple, and wine red, some self-colored, others with a white eye. An excellent effect is obtained by raising a good strain of mixed colors and planting them in masses.

A Brilliant Scarlet Verbena. Verbena peruviana (chamaedrifolia) is a creeping, tender herbaceous plant with heads of intensely brilliant scarlet flowers. It has become popular during recent years, largely as a rock-garden plant.

In effect this kind is like a smaller edition of the regular garden Verbenas. It may be rooted from cuttings and should be wintered in a greenhouse or cold frame that is protected from severe frost where winters are harsh. It may be used in drifts in flower borders and as a permanent ground cover in places where winters are decidedly mild.

A Verbena with Fragrant Flowers. Verbena corymbosa is a herbaceous plant of running habit, forming clumps of dark-green, rough foliage; in June and July it throws up numerous erect branched stems carrying heads of flowers of purple or red-violet color with the delicious fragrance of Heliotrope. The plant is hardy in milder parts of North America and thrives in moist, loamy soil. It has value in the flower border and as a cut flower. It was introduced into cultivation from southern Chile in 1928.

V. corymbosa is easily propagated by division of the roots, by cuttings taken in spring and rooted in sand in a cold frame, or from seeds sown in a mixture of loam, leaf mold or peat moss and sand in a cold frame.

For Beds and Flower Borders. Verbena rigida

One of the most brilliant of all garden flowers is the scarlet Verbena peruviana. It is winter hardy in mild climates and is very suitable for growing in rock gardens.

(venosa), from southern Brazil, is an extremely handsome, tender herbaceous plant, growing 18-24 in. tall, with spikes of bright reddish-violet flowers produced during a long summer season. It is effective for massing in beds and flower borders and also for cutting. In mild regions it lives over winter outdoors. It is easily raised from seed sown in a pan of loam, leaf mold or peat moss and sand in a greenhouse in spring, or even from seeds sown directly outdoors in spring (plants raised from outdoor sowings bloom later, of course, than those started early indoors). Alternatively, plants may be lifted and wintered in a well-protected cold frame or root cellar, to be planted out again in the open in spring. They have thick rhizomes.

A Shrub Type. V. tridens is an interesting and attractive shrub, with erect or sometimes ascending branches, clothed with short, stiff, heathlike leaves. It grows 2-3 ft. tall and in June–July produces small, intensely fragrant lilac flowers in tufts all up the wiry stems. It is suitable for warm climates.

Verbena tenera. Whether or not the plant grown by this name in gardens is correctly identified appears uncertain. The garden plant is a low trailer that spreads rapidly and is a favorite for planting in rock gardens. Its flowers are pink. A variety called V. tenera Maonettii, sometimes called the Italian Verbena, has flowers in which the pink petals are clearly edged with white. The variety occasionally produces branches bearing flowers of the same color as the ordinary type.

Verbena tenera and its variety are not generally hardy in the north, although they may survive in sheltered locations perhaps as far north as Philadelphia. The plant referred to here is

Verbena tenera and its variety Maonettii are charming plants for growing in rock gardens.

The Clump Verbena is the hardiest of garden kinds. Its botanical name is Verbena canadensis.

sometimes misnamed V. pulchella and sometimes is grown as V. alpina.

The Moss Verbena, V. tenuisecta (often known in gardens as V. erinoides), is a tender perennial with decumbent (reclining) stems and lilac, violet or purple flowers. It is easily grown as an annual, either from seeds sown early indoors to give plants for setting outdoors later, or from seeds sown directly outdoors. In parts of the South it is naturalized.

A Good Hardy Verbena. The Clump Verbena, V. canadensis, is hardy at least as far north as New York City in its more usual bright, reddish-purple-flowered form, but its choicer, clear pink, rich crimson and white-flowered varieties are seemingly more tender, for they do not usually withstand winters as far north. It is native from Virginia southward and westward.

The Clump Verbena is a vigorous grower and attains a height of 12-18 in. It bears fine heads of handsome flowers and is very worth while cultivating as a garden plant. It is readily raised from seeds and propagated by division in spring and by cuttings.

Other Verbenas. There are a number of other Verbenas that are sometimes cultivated. V. bipinnatifida is a prostrate kind with showy lilac-purple flowers, a native of the southeastern United States and Mexico.

V. bonariensis, from South America, is naturalized in the South. It attains a height of 3-4 ft. and is sometimes grown as an annual or perennial. Its flowers are lilac to violet; it is easily raised from seeds.

V. radicans is a vigorous grower that forms a perfectly flat carpet of greenery studded with heads of lilac flowers. It is hardy, in sheltered places, as far north as Washington, D.C. This kind is a native of the Andes of South America.

VERBENA, LEMON. See Lippia.

VERBENA, SAND. See Abronia.

VERBESINA (Verbesin'a). A group of American annuals, herbaceous perennials and shrubs that are of minor importance in gardens. The shrubby kinds are natives of subtropical and tropical regions. Verbesina belongs to the Daisy family, the Compositae. Its name is reported to be based on a printer's error for Forbesina.

The Verbesinas that are occasionally cultivated are suitable for wild gardens; they are easy to grow in any ordinary garden soil. V. encelioides, sometimes called Ximinesia encelioides, is an annual that grows to a height of about 3 ft. and has golden-yellow flowers. It occurs as a native from Kansas to Montana and southwards to Texas, Arizona and Mexico. It is raised from seeds sown in spring. V. virginica is a coarse perennial, a native of light woodlands from Virginia to Missouri and Kansas and southwards to Florida and Texas. Its flower heads have white ray florets and it attains a height of about 6 ft. It may be propagated by seeds and by division.

Verbesina encelioides.

Variegated Foliage

[13—12a]
Caladium bicolor variety

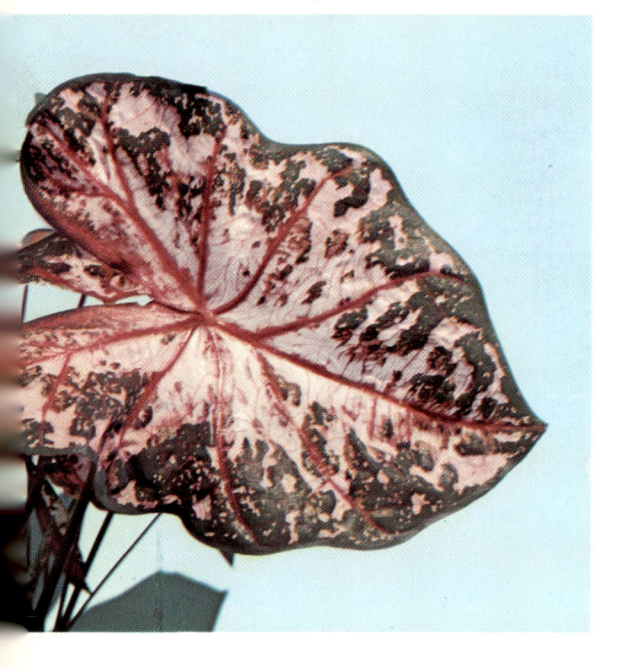

[13—12]
Liriope

[13—12c]
Sansevieria trifasciata Laurentii

[13—12b]
*Joseph's-Coat
(Amaranthus tricolor)*

Vines

[13—13a]
Allamanda cathartica

[13—13]
Campsis radicans

[13—13c]
Euonymus radicans

[13—13b]
Clematis

VERMICULITE. A product made from micaceous ore, now used extensively in hydroponic cultivations and as a propagating medium (material in which to root cuttings and sow seeds).

VERMONT, GARDENING IN. See Regional Gardening.

VERNAL GRASS, SWEET. See Anthoxanthum odoratum.

VERNONIA—*Ironweed.* (Vernon'ia). Hardy, herbaceous flowering plants which are occasionally cultivated in wild gardens. They are not very ornamental. They form dense clumps of slender stems, up to 5 ft. in height, which are clothed with lanceolate green leaves, 4-12 in. in length. The flowers are small, purple or rose and are in dense cymes (spreading clusters) on the ends of the stems. Vernonia belongs to the Daisy family, Compositae; the name commemorates William Vernon, an English botanist.

These plants are most suitable for planting at the edge of a woodland in a sunny position. Rich, sandy loam is the most suitable soil but they grow well in ordinary ground. Planting may be done in fall or spring. When it is desired to increase the plants, they are lifted and divided into small, rooted pieces which are planted in their permanent positions. They may also be raised from seeds.

The chief kinds are V. altissima, 5 ft., purple and violet, autumn; V. crinita (arkansana), 4 ft., purple, autumn; and V. noveboracensis, 5 ft., purple, autumn. All these kinds are natives of North America. In the tropics some Vernonias are trees and shrubs.

VERONICA or SPEEDWELL
Beautiful Rock-Garden and Border Plants

Veronica (Veron'ica). A group of mostly hardy herbaceous and somewhat subshrubby plants belongs to the Figwort family, Scrophulariaceae, and is widely distributed over the temperate and frigid regions of the globe. The name Veronica is of doubtful origin, but is possibly in honor of St. Veronica.

Easy to Grow. The Veronicas are nearly all easy to grow. As a group they are sun lovers, and they prosper in almost any reasonably good garden soil. They are easily propagated by seeds and by division of the roots in spring or early fall and by cuttings in spring. Selected varieties of the natural species (kinds as they exist

A favorite blue-flowered perennial, Veronica maritima variety subsessilis.

Veronica spicata growing well in a rock-garden crevice.

in their native habitats) must be increased either by division or cuttings, because they usually do not reproduce themselves true to type from seeds.

Among the Veronicas there are both low-growing kinds and others of taller habit. The former are extremely useful for planting in rock gardens and the latter are good flower-border plants. Some of the taller kinds, such as V. maritima and its variety subsessilis and such named varieties as Royal Blue, Blue Spires and Blue Peter, provide useful cut flowers.

There is, of course, no sharp line of division between the kinds suitable for rock gardens and those adaptable for planting in borders. Many of the ones listed here as suitable for the former purpose are quite suitable for setting at the fronts of flower borders, and some of those

Veronica repens is a low creeper that covers itself with pale blue flowers in spring.

classified here as flower-border plants may be used with good effect in rock gardens, particularly those which are of fairly large extent. It is chiefly a matter of selecting kinds whose heights are appropriate to the particular locations in which they are to be planted.

Veronicas for Rock Gardens

V. armena grows as a rather tufted plant and has a somewhat woody rootstock. Its stems are prostrate and are furnished with pinnately divided leaves. The flowers, which are lavender-blue or blue, are produced in such profusion in May that the foliage is practically hidden. This plant sometimes has a tendency to die out unless it is propagated every year; it is a good plan to divide and replant it every year in early September. V. armena is a native of Armenia.

V. Bonarota is a very pretty plant found in the eastern Alps of Europe, where it dwells in crevices of limestone cliffs, hanging out its 4-5-in. stems, clothed with dark green, glossy leaves and bearing, in summer, terminal blunt spikes of pretty blue flowers. It is best grown in limestone scree or a crevice in the rock garden. It is increased by careful division; or nonflowering shoots may be rooted as cuttings in spring in sand in the cold frame.

V. caespitosa comes from the mountains of the Levant and from Lebanon. It is a densely tufted dwarf plant, with silvery-white, woolly-haired leaves and rather large pink flowers. There is a variety of this named leiophylla, which is without the white, woolly hairs except on the inflorescence. Both require light, well-drained loam in a sheltered location in the rock garden or scree.

One of the Smallest Flowering Plants. V. canescens, from New Zealand, is perhaps the smallest of all flowering garden plants. It creeps over the ground with the finest threadlike stems, and has pinhead-sized leaves of brownish-green, clothed with fine hairs. The plant is inconspicuous and almost invisible, until it flowers in July, when it covers itself with a multitude of lovely pale blue flowers. It is easy to grow where the winter climate is not too cold and summers are not excessively hot and humid, and is suitable for carpeting the rock garden, or for the crevices in a flagstone path. It is increased by division in early summer.

V. cinerea, a native of Greece, is a mat-forming plant with silvery white leaves and spikes of rose-pink flowers, 3-4 in. high. It thrives in any open sunny place in the rock garden, or in the front of a flower border. It is easily increased by division of the roots at almost any time in spring or summer.

V. filifolia, from the Caucasus, is a very pretty plant, forming clumps of erect, wiry stems clothed with leaves which are divided into threadlike segments, and has large flowers that are white with blue veins. It grows 6-12 in. high, and is easily increased by division in spring.

V. filiformis is a perennial or sometimes an annual kind which is so very amenable to cultivation that it sometimes becomes a weed in lawns. If it is to be set in rock gardens, its tendency to prosper and take over territory allotted to neighboring plants should be remembered at planting time and a location given it where its invasive character can do no harm. V. filiformis forms slender, prostrate, rooting stems and carries its pretty blue flowers on fine, threadlike stems. It blooms from April or May onward. It is a native of the Caucasus.

V. fruticans (saxatilis) is an extremely pretty dwarf alpine, found all over the European Alps and occasionally in Scotland and other parts of northern Europe. It is semiprostrate, with subshrubby stems, 3-4 in. tall, clothed with small, dark green leaves, and bears spikes of vivid blue flowers, each with a central ring of red. It is a delightful rock-garden plant, easy to grow, and easy to propagate by seeds sown in a pan of loam and sand in a cold frame in spring, or by division of the roots in spring. There is a particularly brilliant form, first grown in the famous rock garden at St. John's College, Oxford, England, which has been distributed under the name of St. John's.

V. incana is a splendid low plant, with silvery-white leaves and spikes of violet-purple flowers, 6-8 in. high. It is a native of Siberia and the Caucasus. There is a rare form with clear rose-pink flowers which is named variety rosea. V. incana is a first-rate plant in well-drained loam in a sunny position in the rock garden or the front edging of the flower border. It is increased by division in spring or autumn.

A Splendid Plant. V. latifolia (V. Teucrium) is a variable plant, widely distributed in Europe and Asia Minor, and giving us several varieties of rock-garden and flower-border plants of first-class importance. Of those suitable for rock gardens the most valuable is perhaps V. latifolia variety dubia, one of the finest of all rock-garden plants. It is of prostrate growth, with evergreen foliage, and in early summer bears innumerable spikes, 3-4 in. tall, of blue flowers. It will flourish in almost any soil and position, and is a glorious sight when in flower; being a strong grower, it must be placed with due regard to less-rampant neighbors. It should be in every rock garden, and is very fine in the alpine lawn. In the wall garden, too, it is superb, and also in the very front of the flower border. Propagation is by simple division at almost any time of year. V. latifolia variety dubia is also known in gardens as V. rupestris and as V. prostrata.

There are variations of V. latifolia variety dubia which have white, pink and blue flowers.

V. orientalis has prostrate stems and linear leaves, toothed at their edges. The spikes of pale blue or pink flowers are produced in May. This is a very charming rock-garden plant from Asia Minor. The plant named in gardens V. taurica (V. orientalis tenuifolia) is very similar.

V. pectinata is like a downy edition of V. rupestris with deep-blue flowers, each with a white center. It is of prostrate habit and a good rock-garden plant, flowering in May–June. It is easily increased by division in spring; loamy soil and a sunny place suit it.

V. peduncularis, from the Caucasus, forms dense clumps of bronze-colored leaves, with wiry 3-6-in. stems carrying loose heads of rather large white flowers in May or June. There is a variety with pale blue flowers which is especially desirable. It is increased by division in spring.

V. prostrata is a name sometimes given to V. latifolia variety dubia, which see.

A Valuable Carpeting Plant. V. repens, from Corsica, is a valuable dwarf carpeter, spreading rapidly and, in early summer, becoming covered with a dense mass of rather large, almost stemless flowers of pale, delicate lavender (almost white). It is an admirable ground cover for bulbs in the rock garden and for covering the soil under tiny shrubs, as well as for planting in the crevices of flagstone paths. It may be raised from seeds sown in a pan of loam and sand in a cold frame in spring, or by division of the roots at almost any time of year.

V. rupestris is V. latifolia variety dubia, which see. See also V. prostrata.

V. saturejoides, from Dalmatia, is nearly allied to V. fruticans (saxatilis). It is a mat-forming rock plant and one of the earliest of all Veronicas to flower, opening its blooms in early spring. The dark blue flowers are borne on dense short spikes 2 in. high. This useful rock plant is easily increased by division in spring or autumn.

V. saxatilis is V. fruticans, which see.

V. spicata variety nana forms a tight, carpeting mass of foliage and in summer sends up spikes of rich purple-blue flowers to a height of 4-6 in. Another distinct variety of V. spicata which is excellent for rock gardens is the one named corymbosa. The flowers are spikes but a few inches tall and they branch freely. The flowers are indigo-purple in color.

V. telephifolia is a charming dwarf rock plant from Ararat, with gray-blue foliage, and sprays of blue flowers on 2-3-in. stems in early summer. It is worthy of a choice place in well-drained light loam in the rock garden, and may be increased by careful division of the roots in spring.

Veronicas for Flower Borders

V. austriaca, a native of southeastern Europe and Asia Minor, grows to a height of about 2 ft. and in June bears racemes of large blue flowers. The leaves of this kind are deeply lobed.

V. Chamaedrys, the Germander Speedwell, is a native of Europe and Asia that is naturalized in North America. It grows to a height of 12-18 in. and bears bright blue flowers in May and June.

V. euxina, from Bulgaria, grows 12-18 in. tall, and has long spikes of fine violet-blue flowers. It is an attractive plant in the flower border, and is best propagated by division of the roots in spring or autumn. It is closely related to V. spicata.

V. gentianoides is a fine border plant, forming clumps of glossy-green, oblong-lanceolate leaves, and throwing up 12-18-in.-high spikes of large pale blue flowers in early summer. It is a native of the Caucasus. There is a variegated variety of which the leaves are silver-edged. V. gentianoides may also find a place in the outskirts of the rock garden, and especially in the alpine lawn. It is increased by division in spring or early summer.

V. maritima (longifolia) grows some 18-24 in. tall and bears handsome spikes of lilac-purple flowers in summer. It is a fine plant for the flower border, and is easily increased by division of the roots in spring or autumn; it thrives in ordinary soil. There are white-, pink-, and violet-flowered varieties. This plant is native of Europe and northern Asia and is naturalized in North America.

A Favorite Kind. V. maritima variety subsessilis is a superb plant from Japan, flowering in late summer. It is frequently cultivated under the name V. longifolia subsessilis. It is 2 ft. tall, with long, handsome spikes, somewhat arched, and the flowers of violet-blue color. It is suitable for the flower border, and well repays a liberal allowance of fertilizer. It is increased by cuttings of young shoots, taken with a "heel" in spring, and rooted in sand in a cold frame, or by division in spring or autumn.

With Golden Foliage. V. maritima variety Trehanii is of tufted, rather erect habit, and the spikes of azure flowers contrast remarkably with the golden-yellow leaves. A brilliant border plant which some people like to have in the rock garden, it grows 6 in. high and is easily increased by division at almost any time.

Garden Varieties. A number of fine flower garden varieties, all or most probably derived from V. latifolia, are grown. They attain heights of 12-18 in. and bloom freely in sunny places in ordinary garden soil. They are easily propagated by division in spring or fall and by cuttings. Among the best of these are Royal Blue, Blue Champion and Blue Peter all of blue-purple flowers, Crater Lake Blue, with blue flowers, Icicle with white flowers, and the pink-flowered variety Pavane. V. Minuet has silver-gray foliage and dusty-pink colored flowers.

V. spicata is a valuable plant, widely distributed in the Alps and some other parts of Europe. It bears erect spikes, varying from 3-4 in. to 12-18 in. in height, of flowers ranging in color from bright-blue to pink and white. It is easily grown in ordinary soil in full sun and the dwarfer forms are especially valuable in rock gardens. The taller-growing varieties of this species are suitable for the flower border.

The variety rosea of V. spicata has not-too-attractive, bluish-pink flowers; the variety alba, white flowers; and the variety rubra, purplish-red flowers. V. spicata variety Erica has pink flowers in spikes.

The variety alpina is dwarf and compact, with brilliant blue spikes only 3-4 in. high, and is well adapted for planting in rock gardens. Veronica spicata and its varieties are easily propagated by division in spring and fall.

Hebes. From New Zealand come a number of tender shrubs, with broad, leathery leaves and spikes of white, lavender, violet and pink flowers that were once included in Veronica and are often known by that name in gardens. Their botanical name is Hebe, which see.

Another group of New Zealand shrubby plants are sometimes known as Whipcord Veronicas. These are curious plants with stems which are clothed with small scalelike leaves so that they look somewhat like Club Mosses. Their flowers are small and insignificant, but many of them are decidedly ornamental. They, also, now belong in Hebe, which see.

VERSCHAFFELTIA SPLENDIDA (Verschaffel'tia). A Palm from the Seychelles Islands, where it grows to 80 ft. in height. It has a tall, slender, ringed trunk and a terminal cluster of deeply divided leaves, 5-8 ft. long. Verschaffeltia belongs to the family Palmaceae, and the name commemorates Ambroise Verschaffelt, a Belgian botanist of the early nineteenth century. This Palm is not commonly grown. It is probably suitable for outdoor cultivation in the far South.

A Palm for a Shady Greenhouse. A moist, shady greenhouse in which the temperature does not fall below 55 degrees in winter is required for this Palm's indoor culture. The atmosphere is kept moist by damping the floor and the benches, and the foliage is syringed daily in summer, but only on mild or sunny days in winter. The soil is kept moist throughout the year, but less frequent watering is required in winter.

When small, the plants are repotted annually in March but, later on, they are set in large pots or tubs and are kept growing vigorously by top-dressing them annually with fresh soil. The best compost for potting and top-dressing consists of two parts of fibrous peat and one part of equal portions of loam and sand with some dried cow manure added.

Propagation by Sowing Seeds. Seeds must be fresh because they lose their powers of germination quickly. They are soaked in tepid water for several days to soften the seed coats. Then they are sown in sandy soil. To hasten germination the seed pan may be plunged in a propagating case with a bottom heat of 70-75 degrees. The seedlings are potted separately in 3-in. pots and replaced in the propagating case until well rooted; afterwards they are set on the greenhouse bench and are subsequently potted in larger pots.

VERVAIN. See Verbena.

VESICARIA—*Bladderpod* (Vesica'ria). Dwarf, hardy perennials or annuals, suitable for a sunny rock garden. They belong to the Mustard family, Cruciferae, and are found wild in central and southern Europe. The name Vesicaria is derived from *vesica,* a bladder, and refers to the inflated seed pods. The plants are closely allied to Alyssum, in which group some kinds of Vesicaria are included by botanists.

The principal kind, V. grandiflora, grows 12 in. in height, has linear leaves and bears terminal racemes of yellow flowers, which give rise to small, bladder-like seed pods. It is treated as an annual by sowing the seeds in April where the plants are to flower in summer. Ordinary garden soil is suitable and a sunny position is necessary. When the seedlings are 2 in. high, they are thinned out to 4 in. apart, and allowed to flower without being given any further attention.

VETCH. See Vicia.
VETCH, CROWN. See Coronilla.
VETCH, KIDNEY. See Anthyllis.
VETCH, MILK. See Astragalus.

VIBURNUM: MANY USEFUL KINDS
A Selection of the Best, Both Leaf-losing and Evergreen

Viburnum (Vibur'num). Widely distributed leaf-losing and evergreen shrubs, or occasionally small trees, many of which are hardy and of considerable decorative value because of their foliage, flowers or fruit. They have a long flowering period, for in mild climates some bloom outdoors in midwinter, while other kinds bloom some six months later. Some kinds produce a mixture of fertile and sterile flowers in the same cluster or cyme, the sterile flowers being more attractive than the others; in some kinds the fertile blossoms give place entirely to sterile ones, large, attractive, ball-like heads of flowers being produced. A familiar example is the Snowball or Guelder Rose, V. Opulus roseum.

The Viburnums are found wild through a great part of Europe, in northern Africa, Asia, Java and in North and Central America. Viburnum belongs to the Honeysuckle family, Capri-foliaceae, and the name is the ancient Latin name for V. Lantana. See also Berried Trees and Shrubs.

The Japanese Snowball, Viburnum tomentosum sterile.

Viburnum prunifolium is esteemed for its superb habit of growth, its effective foliage and its blue-black fruits.

Seeds Germinate Slowly. Propagation of many kinds can be effected by means of seeds, but the seeds often take 1-2 years to germinate. They should be sown as soon as possible after they are ripe, in pots or flats of sandy soil buried to their rims in sand or ashes out of doors for the winter; they are placed in a warm greenhouse at the end of February. Some seeds may germinate the first spring. Any that do not should be placed out of doors again for the following winter. The alternation of cool and warm conditions hastens germination. If a greenhouse is not available the containers of seeds may be left in the frames until germination does take place, usually in the second spring.

Cuttings of young shoots, 4 in. long, may be taken in July or August and set in a propagating bench in a greenhouse or in a cold frame. Those in a greenhouse root in a few weeks and may then be potted; those in a cold frame must remain undisturbed throughout winter. It is possible to increase many kinds by layers, although this means of propagation is rarely followed. In some instances rare kinds and varieties have been grafted, but this means of propagation is not recommended because the understocks are likely to produce troublesome suckers. Hard wood cuttings made in fall just after the leaves have dropped afford an easy means of propagating the deciduous (non-evergreen) Viburnums.

Planting and Pruning. Young plants should be planted in nursery beds for 2-3 years before being transferred to their permanent places. Viburnums thrive in a variety of soils. Some are well adapted for limestone soils, particularly V. Lantana and V. Opulus. Others appear to thrive equally well in soils containing lime and on soils that are lime-free and acid, and there are some, such as V. Carlesii, that appreciate somewhat acid conditions and respond well when peat moss is mixed with the soil.

No regular pruning is required. When the

Rooted cuttings of Viburnum tomentosum.

bushes are young, a little may be necessary to ensure sturdy and shapely growth, but afterwards all that is needed is a little thinning or cutting back after flowering, if they are outgrowing their allotted space.

Viburnums in Pots. Sterile-flowered forms of V. Opulus and V. tomentosum are worth growing in pots for forcing for greenhouse decoration in spring, and plants of V. Tinus (Laurestinus), V. Carlesii and V. fragrans are worth a place in the cool greenhouse for flowering in winter.

The following selection of kinds includes those most useful for general planting in gardens.

The Dockmackie, V. acerifolium, grows natively from New Brunswick to North Carolina and Minnesota. It is a shrub of moist or dry woods and attains a height of 5-6 ft. It has value for planting in shaded and partly shaded locations and succeeds under drier conditions than do most Viburnums. In fall its foliage assumes deep rose-pink to rich, vinous-purple hues. Its fruits, which at first are red but become nearly black when ripe, succeed creamy white flowers of no particular beauty that are borne in May or early June.

V. alnifolium, the Hobblebush or American Wayfaring Tree of the eastern United States, bears a resemblance to V. Lantana, the Wayfaring Tree of Europe, but it often has larger leaves. This kind grows natively from New Brunswick to North Carolina and Michigan. It has been known as V. lantanoides. Growing 9-10 ft. high, it is recognized by its broadly rounded leaves, 4-8 in. long, green above and covered by gray felty hairs beneath. The white flowers are in flat heads, 4-5 in. across, and are followed by fruits which are red when partly ripe and black when fully ripe.

V. betulifolium is a vigorous shrub from China, introduced into cultivation in 1901. It is chiefly remarkable for its flat heads of white flowers, which are followed by bright-red, fleshy fruits.

V. bitchiuense is regarded by some botanists to be a distinct species, closely related to V. Carlesii, and by others to be a variety of V. Carlesii distinguished by being of slenderer, more straggling growth and having smaller leaves and flower clusters. Be that as it may, the plants grown and sold in America under this name seem to be not distinct from seedling plants of V. Carlesii. These seedlings develop into splendid shrubs, 10 ft. or more tall, of rounded form and less stiff habit than the clonal form (see Clone) of V. Carlesii that is usually cultivated under that name. See V. Carlesii, below.

Viburnum betulifolium.

Viburnum Carlesii bears its white, pink-tinted, fragrant flowers in April-May. They are densely clustered and have a waxy texture.

V. buddleifolium is closely allied to V. Veitchii and V. Lantana. It is a native of central China and was introduced into western gardens in 1900. It bears white flowers and red fruits and grows to a height of about 6 ft.

Hybrids of Merit. V. Burkwoodii is a hybrid between V. Carlesii and V. utile. When left unpruned it becomes a broad shrub some 6 ft. in height and usually wider than tall. It is of rather loose growth but, if pruned judiciously as soon as the flowers are past, it may be maintained in a more compact and generally more acceptable form. Its foliage is dark-green, glossy and partially evergreen where winters are not exceptionally severe; elsewhere it persists until late into the fall.

In bloom V. Burkwoodii is very similar to V. Carlesii and is as pleasantly fragrant although its scent differs from that of its parent. This kind is hardy at least into southern New England.

Another good hybrid is V. Carlcephalum, the parents of which are V. Carlesii and V. macrocephalum. This kind resembles V. Carlesii in habit of growth and foliage, but its flower heads are much larger and may measure 5 in. or even 6 in. across. The flowers are delightfully fragrant; except for a reddish tinge on the outsides of the buds they are white. The foliage of this Viburnum colors attractively in fall. V. Carlcephalum is hardy in New England.

Fragrant Flowers in Spring. V. Carlesii is a very attractive leaf-losing kind, native to Korea. It grows 4-8 ft. high, has rounded or heart-shaped, gray-green leaves and very attractive waxy white, pink-tinged, deliciously fragrant flowers produced in dense heads, 2-3 in. across, in April and May.

Most of the plants grown and sold as V. Carlesii represent a single clone that is propagated vegetatively (by cuttings and by grafting on V. Lantana). Plants of this clone form roundish bushes of rather stiff appearance and usually are somewhat broader than high. Specimens grafted on V. Lantana are not to be recommended, because the understock sends up sucker shoots that crowd out and are likely eventually to kill the plant of V. Carlesii.

When V. Carlesii is raised from seeds, the resulting plants are of freer and more open growth and seem to be identical with the plant known in North America as V. bitchiuense, which see, above. The very excellent Viburnum named V. Juddii appears to be a selected one of these seedlings that has been named and propagated vegetatively. A better name for it would be Viburnum Carlesii variety Juddii.

The Withe Rod, V. cassinoides, occurs as a native from Newfoundland to North Carolina and Minnesota. It attains a height of 6-12 ft. It is a good hardy shrub for garden purposes but, because its foliage tends to be ill-scented in fall, it is well not to plant it near doors and windows. V. cassinoides has clusters of yellowish-white flowers in June or July, and these are followed by fruits which are first pink but become dark blue when ripe.

V. coriaceum is a large evergreen bush, or, in its native habitat, the Himalayas and China, a tree of moderate size. The oval or oblong leaves are 3-8 in. long and 4 in. wide, dull green and waxy above, paler beneath. The white flowers are produced in spreading heads several inches across in summer. The fruits are black. This kind is adapted for mild climates only.

For Mild Climates. V. Davidii is an evergreen, spreading shrub of low stature, taking many years to attain a height of 2-3 ft. The leathery leaves are narrowly oval, 2-6 in. long and 1-2½ in. wide, with three very definite veins. The white flowers are borne during late spring and early summer and are followed by blue fruits. This is a good shrub for rock gardens and

One of the most fragrant of flowering shrubs, Viburnum Carlesii blooms in spring.

foundation plantings. It is not hardy in the North.

The Arrowwood, V. dentatum, is native from New Brunswick to Georgia and Minnesota. It is a plant for moist soils and is useful for naturalistic plantings. It stands shade well. Of upright habit of growth, the Arrowwood attains a height of about 15 ft. In May or June it bears attractive clusters of white flowers on long stalks, the clusters measuring 2-3 in. in diameter. The fruits, which are blue-black, ripen in fall.

V. dilatatum is a Japanese native. It is a splendid kind that grows to a height of 8-10 ft. and is best adapted for soils that are not too dry. The leaves of this Viburnum are roundish and coarsely toothed. The flower clusters, which are 4-5 in. wide, are borne in May or June; the flowers are white and rather ill-scented and are succeeded by red fruits produced in great abundance. The fruits remain on the bush for a long time. In fall the foliage is colored orange and red. V. dilatatum variety xanthocarpum is distinguished by having yellow fruits.

The large flower clusters of Viburnum dilatatum are followed by red fruit. The foliage colors beautifully in the fall.

Blooms in Winter. V. fragrans, a leaf-losing kind, forms an erect bush up to 12 ft. high. Its chief value lies in its heads of attractive white or pink fragrant flowers which, in mild climates, open in winter, in other places in early spring, before the development of its leaves. The fruits, which are red, are not very attractive. It is a native of northern China.

V. grandiflorum is a large shrub. It is a native of the Himalayas, is leaf-losing, and bears heads of fragrant rose-colored or white flowers in early spring. It requires a mild climate.

V. Harryanum is an evergreen shrub, 6-8 ft. high, with small rounded or ovate leaves. The flowers are white, the fruits black. It is a native of western China and is not hardy in the North.

V. Henryi forms a rather loose evergreen bush, 8-10 ft. high, with narrow leaves; small white flowers are borne in rather rigid panicles in July, and they are followed by small fruits which are first red, then black. It is a native of central China. It is not hardy in the North.

V. ichangense is a leaf-losing shrub, 5-10 ft. high, that has white, fragrant flowers and clusters of bright red fruits. It is hardy as far north as Philadelphia.

V. japonicum (macrophyllum) is an evergreen bush, 4-6 ft. high, with thick, glossy evergreen leaves. The white summer flowers are in clusters 4 in. across, and are followed by red fruits. It is a native of Japan. It is not hardy in the North.

The Wayfaring Tree. V. Lantana, the Wayfaring Tree of Europe, grows 12-15 ft. high and has stiff branches, clothed with gray-green leaves which assume dark purplish coloring in fall and remain until late in the season. It bears flat heads of fertile white flowers in May and June; the flowers are followed by red fruits which turn black as they ripen.

V. Lentago, the Sheepberry or Nannyberry, is a large shrub or small tree that may attain a height of 30 ft. It occurs as a native from Hudson Bay to Georgia and Mississippi. Of rather erect growth and not very spreading, this is a good shrub for naturalistic plantings in partial shade or sun; it requires a moderately moist soil.

The Sheepberry has creamy white flowers in clusters measuring 4-5 in. across in May or early June. These are succeeded by fruits which at first are red but which become blue-black at maturity and remain throughout the winter.

V. lobophyllum, a western Chinese bush, has as its most attractive feature a profusion of bright red fleshy fruits in autumn. Growing at least 10 ft. high, it bears broad-ovate or obovate leaves and heads of white flowers. It is at fruiting time that it commands attention.

V. macrocephalum, or as it is perhaps more correctly named, V. macrocephalum variety Keteleeri, is a natural species that is a native of China. It was introduced to western gardens in 1844. It grows to a height of about 12 feet and is hardy in New England. It is partially evergreen and bears clusters of white flowers, the marginal ones of which are showy and sterile, the interior ones small and fertile.

V. macrocephalum variety sterile, the Chinese Snowball, is most ornamental, for its large, sterile white flowers are borne in globular clusters 6-8 in. across. The flower clusters are larger than those of the Japanese Snowball, V. tomentosum variety sterile.

V. nudum, the Smooth Withe Rod, is native from southern New York to Florida and Louisiana and is not reliably hardy north of that range. It attains a height of 15 ft. and has yellowish-white flowers succeeded by fruits which are first pink but change to dark blue upon ripening. It blooms in June and July.

V. odoratissimum is a handsome evergreen shrub or small tree with large glossy green, leathery leaves up to 8 in. long and 4 in. wide. The pure white fragrant flowers appear in spring and are followed by fruits which are first red and later black. This kind is hardy in mild climates only. It is useful for growing in tubs or pots in cool greenhouses for late winter bloom. It is a native of Japan, China and the Himalayas.

The European Cranberry Bush, V. Opulus, is a large leaf-losing shrub, wild in Europe, northern Africa and northern Asia. It may exceed 12 ft. in height and bears heads of white flowers in which fertile flowers are surrounded by sterile blooms. The variety roseum (sterile) is the Snowball Tree or Guelder Rose. In this, only sterile flowers are produced and they are in large round heads. It is an easily grown shrub, flowering in June, the fertile flowers being followed by bright red fruits. As a garden shrub V. Opulus is inferior to the native American Cranberry Bush, V. trilobum, which it closely resembles. V. Opulus roseum (sterile) is less satisfactory for garden purposes than the Japanese Snowball, V. tomentosum variety sterile.

A dwarf, nonflowering variety of V. Opulus that is grown in gardens has limited use as a subject to plant to form low hedges. This is V. Opulus variety nanum. It attains a maximum height of 2-3 ft.; mature specimens, when planted singly, tend to open at their centers and become unsightly. Viburnum Opulus variety xanthocarpum has yellow fruits.

The Black Haw, V. prunifolium, is a North American kind of considerable value for naturalistic plantings. It occurs naturally from Connecticut to Florida and Texas and will thrive in much drier soils than the majority of Viburnums. It forms a more or less spreading shrub,

The red fruits of the European Cranberry Bush, Viburnum Opulus.

Viburnum prunifolium is a native American kind that is handsome in flower, foliage and fruit.

This fine specimen of the evergreen Viburnum rhytidophyllum is growing in a sheltered location at The New York Botanical Garden.

12-15 ft. tall, of good appearance in foliage and bearing clusters of white flowers in April or May. Its blue-black fruits are carried on red stalks. In fall its leaves assume handsome shades of wine-red.

V. rhytidophyllum is one of the most remarkable of the Chinese shrubs introduced during the present century. It is an evergreen bush, 10-12 ft. high, the young shoots being covered with gray or buff-colored feltlike hairs. The leaves are oblong or strap-shaped, up to 8 in. long and 2½ in. wide, the upper surface glossy green and curiously wrinkled, the underside covered by gray or buff felty hairs. The flower heads are formed in autumn and persist throughout winter, the cream-white flowers opening from April to June. The fruits are red at first, later black. This kind will live outdoors in sheltered locations as far north as New York City.

V. rufidulum, the Southern Black Haw, is native from Virginia to Florida and Texas. It is a handsome kind that attains a maximum height of about 30 ft. It has dark green, glossy foliage and pure white or creamy white flowers which are borne in May or June. The fruits are blue-black.

The Southern Black Haw has spreading, stiffish branches. It is a shrub or small tree for moist soils. It is hardy as far north as Massachusetts.

V. Sargentii is a native of northeastern Asia

Viburnum Burkwoodii bears densely clustered, waxy-textured, white fragrant flowers in April and May.

Viburnum Sargentii.

that grows to a height of about 12 ft. and has clusters of flowers the marginal ones of which are sterile and showy and the inner ones small and fertile. Its fruits are red except in the variety named xanthocarpum, which has yellow fruits.

V. setigerum (theiferum) is a broad, rounded shrub 10-12 ft. tall at maturity and of rather coarse appearance. It is undistinguished in flower but is probably the most splendid of all Viburnums in fruit. The fruits are bright red or, in the variety auranticum, orange-red, and are borne in great hanging clusters. The foliage becomes bronzy-purple in fall. This species is a native of China.

A Large Shrub or Small Tree. V. Sieboldii is one of the finest of all leaf-losing (deciduous) Viburnums. It forms a large shrub or small tree 12-20 ft. tall, and bears handsome rich green foliage. Its flowers are borne in large clusters in June and are creamy-white. The fruits change from green to pink to bluish-black and are exceedingly attractive. As with many Viburnums the foliage, in fall, has a rather objectionable odor. This is a splendid kind to use as a specimen plant on a lawn.

V. suspensum, a native of the Ryukyu Islands, is an evergreen shrub of handsome appearance that is not hardy in the North but is useful in southern gardens. It may also be grown as a potted or tubbed specimen in cool greenhouses. This Viburnum attains a height of 4-6 ft. and in early spring (in winter in greenhouses) bears small, drooping, roundish clusters of pinkish cream-colored flowers. Its fruits are red.

Laurestinus. In mild climates V. Tinus, the Laurestinus, is a well-known evergreen. It is a native of the Mediterranean region and forms a bush 6-12 ft. high, clothed with dark green, oblong leaves. The flower heads are first noticeable by reason of the reddish buds during late summer. The waxy white flowers begin to open in autumn and continue in mild weather throughout winter, the best show of flowers being in early spring. It can be grown as an informal hedge as well as in bush form. Of its several varieties, lucidum, with large, glossy green leaves and larger heads of flowers than the type, is the best. The variety purpureum has purple-tinged leaves, and variety variegatum has variegated foliage. The Laurestinus is a good shrub for growing in pots or tubs in a cool

Viburnum suspensum, a tender evergreen kind, has drooping clusters of pinkish-cream flowers.

The Laurestinus, botanically Viburnum Tinus, is a favorite evergreen in mild climates.

greenhouse. This shrub is not hardy in the North.

A Handsome Shrub. V. tomentosum is a very popular shrub from China and Japan. It forms a dense bush, 6-10 ft. high, with ovate, prominently veined leaves. The inflorescence is flat, 3-4 in. across, and composed of fertile and sterile flowers. An improvement on the type is the variety Mariesii, but the form with all sterile flowers called variety sterile (plicatum) is more commonly grown than either. This variety is the Japanese Snowball Bush. Its large white, sterile flowers are borne in ball-like clusters several inches across and appear with exceptional freedom in May. This handsome shrub is perfectly hardy and rarely fails to flower well. It should be planted in rich, loamy soil. V. tomentosum and its varieties thrive in partial shade as well as in full sun. They prefer a moderately moist soil.

V. tomentosum variety Lanarth is a dwarf, spreading kind of much merit. Its flower clusters include both fertile and sterile flowers.

The Cranberry Bush or High-bush Cranberry, V. trilobum (americanum), is very closely related to the European Cranberry Bush, V. Opulus, and is to be preferred for garden purposes. V. trilobum is native from New Brunswick to British Columbia and southwards to New Jersey and Oregon. It is a rather coarse shrub of spreading habit that attains a height of 10-12 ft. It is a native of moist woods but in cultivation it is adaptable and grows in sun or partial shade and in a variety of soils provided they are not too dry.

The Cranberry Bush has clusters of creamy white flowers in May or June, the outer ones of each cluster being showy and sterile, ringing the smaller fertile ones that form the centers of the clusters. The fruits ripen very early, assuming their bright red color by the end of July and remaining plump and attractive until well into the winter and sometimes all winter long. The fruits are not eaten by birds. In fall the foliage assumes brilliant orange and crimson hues.

V. utile is an evergreen shrub with slender branchlets covered with downy hairs; the leaves are 1-3 in. long, and up to an inch wide. The white flowers are borne in dense heads, 2-3 in. across, in May. This kind, a native of China, is not hardy in the North.

V. Wilsonii is a leaf-losing shrub, up to 10 ft. high, a native of China. It bears white flowers in June which are followed by bright red fruits.

V. Wrightii is a leaf-losing kind that is a native of Japan. It grows 6-10 ft. high and in May or June bears white flowers in heads that measure 2-4 in. in diameter. The flowers are succeeded by red fruits. V. Wrightii variety Hessei is dwarfer and has smaller flower heads than the type. Both V. Wrightii and its variety are hardy in southern New England.

VICIA—*Vetch* (Vic'ia). A large group of hardy perennial and annual plants, none of which is ornamental enough to be grown in gardens. V. Faba is the Broad Bean (see Bean). The majority of Vicias have slender stems clothed with pinnate leaves terminated by a pair of tendrils. In the axils of the leaves are produced clusters of small, pea-shaped flowers. One kind, V. argentea, has silvery leaves.

Vicia belongs to the Pea family, Leguminosae, and the name is an ancient Latin one for Vetch.

VICTORIA—*Queen Victoria's Water Lily, Royal Water Lily, Santa Cruz Water Lily* (Victor'ia). Victoria regia is a remarkable Water Lily which was introduced into gardens from tropical America at about the middle of the

The Cranberry Bush, Viburnum trilobum, is an American kind that grows well in sun or partial shade. Its bright red fruits remain attractive over a long period.

Victoria Cruziana, cultivated in a large conservatory. Here we see the large floating leaves, a flower and flower buds.

nineteenth century. It was first discovered in 1801, and several previous attempts were made to get it to grow in European greenhouses, but all were unsuccessful until seeds were sent in bottles of fresh water. These seeds were collected and dispatched by two English physicians and arrived in England in February, 1849; the first flower, which opened in the conservatory at Chatsworth House in Derbyshire, England, was sent to Queen Victoria. The plant was named in honor of Queen Victoria. It belongs to the Water Lily family, Nymphaceae.

The large leaves floating on this outdoor pool at The New York Botanical Garden are those of Victoria Cruziana. The flowers in the foreground are those of a tropical Nymphaea.

Leaves 6 ft. in Diameter. This giant aquatic can only be grown outdoors where tropical summers prevail; elsewhere it must be accommodated in a large greenhouse or conservatory such as is maintained in botanic gardens. It forms a number of round, floating leaves, averaging 6 ft. in diameter, the margins of which are turned up at right angles to a height of 2 or 3 in.

The lower surfaces of the leaves are furnished with large prickles, and they are also perforated with minute holes, which prevent water from collecting on the leaves. The leaves are remarkably buoyant and capable of sustaining great weight if it is evenly distributed. The leafstalks which radiate from the central crown are several feet in length, 2 in. or more in diameter and armed with prickles.

Fragrant Flowers Which Last for Two Days. The large fragrant flowers are 12-18 in. in diameter and open on two successive days. On the first day they are creamy white and the next day they change to reddish-pink. The flowers have a delicious pineapple-like fragrance and are surrounded by large prickly sepals. After fertilization, they produce enormous prickly berries containing hard black seeds resembling Peas.

In addition to V. regia another species of this remarkable genus is cultivated. This is V. Cruziana, the Santa Cruz Water Lily, which is hardier and is better suited for outdoor cultivation. The leaves of V. Cruziana are smaller, rarely exceeding 4 ft. in diameter, and have deeper (6-8 in.) upturned rims than those of V. regia. Otherwise the plants are similar.

Raising Plants from Seeds. The seeds of V. regia are sown in January in a pan of loamy soil, which is plunged with its surface 2-3 in. under water heated to 80 degrees. When the seedlings are large enough to handle, they are potted separately and submerged in a tank, so that the soil surface is 4-6 in. below the surface. In the meantime the planting bed is made ready in the main tank or indoor pool. The soil mixture for this consists of three parts of loam and one part of well-decayed cow manure, mixed and placed in a large bin (built of brick or other suitable material) in the center of the tank. The bin or container should be large enough to hold 8-9 cubic yards of soil.

Early in April the plants are set firmly in the center of the container with the crowns 2 ft. below the surface. No shading is required on the greenhouse glass but the temperature must not fall below 60 degrees at night until midsummer, when more ventilation may be given. If too many leaves form, a few may be moved to prevent overcrowding.

Victoria Cruziana, which may be grown out of doors in the North, should be started from seeds sown as advised above for V. regia, in February or March. The young seedlings are successively transplanted to 3-in. pots and 8- or 9-in. pans and are planted outdoors after the weather is settled and warm and the water in the pool is not likely to drop below 75 degrees. This means sometime during the first two weeks in June in climates similar to that of New York City. V. Cruziana attains its most impressive dimensions only if it has very ample root room (several cubic yards of rich earth in which the roots may ramify) but smaller specimens may be grown in as little as one or two cubic yards of good earth. The top of the soil should be 18-24 in. beneath the surface of the water.

Saving Seed. When the seed pods are swelling, they should be enclosed in cheesecloth bags so that the seed is not lost when it ripens and falls from the pods. The ripe seeds are kept in a jar of water in a temperature of 65 degrees until required for sowing in spring. It is necessary to pollinate the flowers to induce them to form seeds.

Kinds. V. regia, white and rose, is called by some botanists V. amazonica. It is a native of the Amazon. V. Cruziana has white and pink flowers, is sometimes known as V. Trickeri and is a native of Paraguay.

VINCA—*Periwinkle* (Vin'ca). A group of some ten kinds of tender and hardy herbaceous plants and subshrubs, widely distributed, and belonging to the family Apocynaceae, the Dogbane family. The name Vinca or Pervinca is the Latin name used by Pliny.

Vinca major, a native of Europe, is a useful evergreen plant of trailing habit, excellent for using in mild climates on banks and other rough places; it quickly clothes these with its glossy green foliage and long, green shoots, which root themselves as they go. The large, round flowers are of clear lavender-blue, and

[13—14]
Confederate Violet
(Viola Priceana)

[13—14a]
Johnny-jump-ups
(Viola tricolor)

[13–15]
Vinca minor variegata

[13–15a]
Madagascar Periwinkle
(Vinca rosea)

[13–15b]
Watering
With hose

[13–15c]
Watering
With rotating sprinkler

Vinca rosea, a tender plant from Madagascar, may be grown as an annual for summer bloom.

open in spring. There is a variegated variety called V. major variety variegata, of which the leaves are boldly edged and blotched with cream-white. This is much used as a pot plant and a subject for planting in window boxes, porch boxes and hanging baskets. Neither V. major nor its variety variegata is hardy in the North.

Vinca minor is a neat, miniature edition of V. major, smaller in all its parts, and bearing its lovely blue flowers very early in spring. It is hardy in the North and is very easy to grow, flourishing in almost any soil, and forms good ground cover in shady places and partially shaded places. There are double-flowered and variegated-leaved varieties as well as one with white flowers. Vinca minor variety Bowlesii (Bowles' variety) has dark blue flowers and blooms more freely than the ordinary kind. This native of Europe has naturalized itself and run wild in the eastern United States.

V. herbacea, from eastern Europe, is a very pretty Periwinkle, perhaps the best of all. The habit of growth is neat, the leaves are narrow, and the flowers, which are produced in great quantity over a long period, are blue. It thrives best in a sunny location and is easily increased by division of the roots in spring or autumn.

V. difformis, sometimes called V. acutiflora, is a charming plant from southern Europe, with large flowers of pale lavender-blue, which it produces in mild climates all through the winter. It is a good plant, too, for the cool greenhouse. Clumps may be lifted in autumn, potted and placed in the greenhouse, where the slight protection afforded enables the flowers to open more freely and in perfection. This kind is not hardy in the North.

Propagation of the evergreen, trailing Vincas is easily accomplished by means of cuttings in late summer and fall. These root readily in a cool greenhouse propagating bench or in a close cold frame. Division of the plants in early fall or spring is also a very simple and sure means of securing increase.

A Tender Kind. Quite different from the evergreen trailing kinds of Vinca is the Madagascar Periwinkle, V. rosea. This is technically a tender perennial but is most often grown in gardens as an annual and is especially useful for filling summer flower beds and porch and window boxes. It also is a satsifactory plant to grow in pots in greenhouses.

Vinca rosea grows 1-2 ft. tall, is branched and has attractive glossy foliage; the leaves are oblong. In its typical form the flowers are rosy-purple in color, but a white-flowered variety, V. rosea variety alba, is grown, and also one, V. rosea variety oculata, which has flowers that are white with a red eye. Each flower measures about 1½ in. in diameter and the plants are practically everblooming.

The most common method of raising the Madagascar Periwinkle is from seeds, which are sown in a warm (temperature 60-65 degrees) greenhouse in February or March. The young plants, when they have developed their second pair of leaves, are transplanted individually to small pots; then grown in a warm greenhouse, hardened off and planted out of doors after the weather is really warm and settled.

This plant is also easily propagated from cuttings taken in late winter from stock plants carried over in a greenhouse. The cuttings root readily in a bed of sand or vermiculite in a warm propagating case and, after rooting, are potted and treated like seedlings.

VINE, GRAPE. See Grape and also Vitis.

VINES. The word vines, as employed by gardeners, is used to include all plants the stems of which are too frail to support themselves in a

These hardy vines climb in various ways: English Ivy by aerial rootlets, Honeysuckle by twining, the Virginia Creeper by tendrils.

more or less erect position; or plants that have horizontal stems that are not stiff enough to support themselves without trailing on the ground. It is not a precise term, for all manner of gradations occur between obvious vines and ordinary shrubs. There are annual vines and perennial vines, woody vines and herbaceous (nonwoody) vines, evergreen vines and deciduous (leaf-losing) vines, flowering vines and vines grown primarily for their foliage. Some kinds bear handsome fruits; others develop beautiful autumn coloring.

Vines Are Invaluable in the Garden. Vines are useful for covering walls and fences, for decorating pillars and posts, for use as screens, for covering arbors, pergolas and trellises; and some may be permitted to trail over the ground without support, to form ground covers.

Vines attach themselves to their supports in various ways. Some, such as English Ivy, Trumpet Vine and Philodendron, do so by means of stem roots or by rootlike protuberances with clinging, sucker-like discs at their tips. Many vines, including Wisteria, Pole Beans and Akebia, climb by twining their stems around their support, and others, including Peas, Sweet Peas, Grapes and Passion Flowers, attach themselves by means of slender, twining organs called tendrils.

Vines that cling by means of stem roots or similar devices are not suitable for planting against wooden houses or other surfaces that must be painted from time to time; they are best adapted for use against masonry, to which they cling firmly. Twining vines such as Wisteria and Actinidia, which have stout, perennial stems, should be given strong wires or iron pipes to twine around; those of a frailer character may be supported by wires or, in the case of annual kinds, by strings stretched taut. When

An interesting tropical vine, Cissus discolor, trained over a wire pyramid.

training twining vines it is important to remember that some twine naturally in a clockwise direction and others counterclockwise. The stems should always be twined in the direction natural to the particular kind of vine, a fact which can be ascertained by observation.

Some plants that the gardener classes as vines do not attach themselves to their supports but instead naturally scramble over them. When grown in gardens, these scramblers are usually held erect by tying their stems to the supports. Good examples of this group of plants are Climbing and Rambler Roses.

The following are selections of useful vines. For further information about them, refer to each under its respective name elsewhere in this Encyclopedia.

Vines That Cling by Rootlets or Sucker Discs: Campsis (Trumpet Creeper), Doxantha, Euonymus Fortunei, Ficus pumila, Hedera (Ivy), Hydrangea petiolaris, Parthenocissus quinquefolia (Virginia Creeper), Parthenocissus tricuspidata (Boston Ivy), Phaedranthus buccinatorius, Pileostegia viburnoides.

Vines That Cling by Means of Tendrils: Ampelopsis, Bignonia capreolata (Trumpet Flower), Boussingaultia basselloides (Madeira Vine, Mignonette Vine), Cardiospermum, Cissus, Clematis, Cobaea scandens, Lathyrus, Passiflora (Passion Flower), Vitis.

Vines That Climb by Twining Stems: Actinidia, Akebia, Aristolochia, Celastrus (Bittersweet), Decumaria barbara, Dolichos, Eccremocarpus scaber, Gloriosa, Gourds, Humulus, Ipomoea, Lonicera, Menispermum, Momordica, Periploca graeca, Phaseolus, Polygonum Aubertii (China Fleece Vine, Silver Lace Vine), Pueraria Thunbergiana (Kudzu Vine), Quamoclit, Thunbergia, Trachelospermum, Tripterygium Regelii, Tropaeolum (Nasturtium), Wisteria.

VIOLA: VIOLETS AND PANSIES
Beautiful Flowers for Rock Gardens, Wild Gardens and Flower Beds

Viola (Vi′ola). This large group consists chiefly of hardy perennials, though some are annuals, and a few are subshrubby plants. They are natives of the North Temperate regions, South America, South Africa and eastern Africa, Australia and New Zealand. Viola is the old Latin name used by Virgil. These plants belong to the Violet family, Violaceae.

Viola embraces a wide range of beautiful rock-garden and woodland plants, as well as the more horticulturally developed Pansies, Bedding Violas and Sweet Violets. Pansies are descended or, perhaps more correctly, have ascended largely from the native European wild Violas, V. tricolor and V. lutea. Bedding Violas originated as hybrids between Pansies and Viola cornuta. They are sometimes called Tufted Pansies. Where climatic conditions are favorable, these are longer-lived perennials than Pansies, which are usually regarded as biennials. The Sweet Violets have been derived from the European wild Sweet Violet, V. odorata.

Two Types of Flower. A curious feature of many species or wild kinds of Viola is that they produce two distinct types of flower, and this trait is well shown by the sweet Violet itself. The fine showy flowers, for the sake of which the plant is grown, are usually sterile and produce no seeds. In addition to these, the

Bedding Viola, Purple Walmark.

Bedding Violas have pansylike flowers and are available in a wide variety of colors.

plants produce what are called cleistogamous flowers, which come later than the showy scented ones. They are inconspicuous, having no showy petals, and are usually produced on short stems close to the ground; they are fertile and produce seeds. Pansies and Bedding Violas and some other kinds produce seeds from the normal showy flowers, but there are many species of Viola which produce these two distinct types of flowers.

Bedding Violas, Pansies and Sweet Violets

Bedding Violas, Pansies and Sweet Violets are horticulturally developed kinds of Violas that are generally adapted for planting in more formal places than are the horticulturally unimproved wild species. Pansies and Sweet Violets are also grown in greenhouses.

Bedding Violas. In climates where summers are relatively cool and moist, Bedding Violas are invaluable plants for providing broad masses of color throughout the summer; and are useful in formal bedding, in mixed flower borders, as ground covers under Roses and for other purposes. They are less rich in color, perhaps, than Pansies and less handsomely marked, but, where weather conditions are agreeable, they have a far longer flowering season. They are not well adapted for regions of hot, dry summers. Whereas Pansies may start the season with very large flowers, they become smaller as the season advances, but Violas maintain the size, quality and abundance of their flowers from spring until autumn in a truly remarkable manner.

Among the Bedding Violas there is a wide range of colors, from white through pale yellow to deep gold, pale lavender, violet, mauve-purple and rose-lilac, as well as many fancy bicolors.

Pansies are deservedly popular for their large flowers of rich and varied coloring and handsome marking. A few varieties of special merit, such as Arkwright's Ruby, which has blood-red flowers, are sometimes propagated from cuttings, but the usual way with Pansies is to raise them annually from seeds. An interesting curiosity is the black Pansy, which comes fairly true from seed and in its best forms is probably the blackest flower there is, a beautiful velvety black sometimes shading to a deep violet-black center. See also Pansy.

Sweet Violets represent another section of the great genus Viola and are universal favorites. They are grown chiefly to produce flowers for picking and bunching and are cultivated both in greenhouses and outdoors. Their cultivation is somewhat exacting. See Violet.

Pansies and Bedding Violas from Seeds. This is the most common means of propagation employed in the case of Pansies although, like Bedding Violas, they can be increased by cuttings. Bedding Violas, in climates where summers are cool enough to be adapted to their culture, are usually propagated by cuttings but are easily raised from seeds. Named varieties come true to type only when propagated by cuttings.

For the best results with Bedding Violas and Pansies from seeds it is important to have fresh seeds and to select suitable dates for sowing. In many sections late July or early August is the best time to sow. The seeds may be planted either outdoors or in well-ventilated cold frames. In either case the soil should be made agreeable by forking it to a fine condition and mixing with it liberal amounts of compost, leaf mold, peat moss or humus and, if it is clayey, some coarse sand. Sow in drills and keep the seedbed shaded and evenly moist, but not constantly saturated.

Gradually reduce the shade as the seedlings develop and, when they are big enough to handle conveniently, transplant them to nursery beds outdoors or in cold frames. If outdoors, let the rows be 1 ft. apart and the plants 6 in. apart in the rows; if the young plants are set in cold frames, space them 6 in. apart each way. The soil into which the young plants are transplanted should be fertile and well supplied with organic matter. The addition to it of liberal amounts of well-rotted manure, compost, leaf mold, humus or peat moss is very beneficial. It is also helpful to mix a generous dressing of bone meal with the upper few inches.

The beds of young plants must be kept free from weeds and watered if the weather is dry. By October they should be sturdy and quite

The white-flowered Canada Violet, Viola canadensis.

sizable specimens, probably bearing a few flowers. Where winters do not bring temperatures materially lower than 20 degrees F., the plants may be transferred to their flowering locations in October, but in severer climates it is generally wisest to wait until spring before doing this.

Where winter temperatures are likely to go lower than 10 degrees F., it is wisest to give the plants some special protection. If they are in the open, a light covering of evergreen branches or of salt-marsh hay will do; if they are in frames the sash should be kept on during periods of really low temperatures. It is important, however, not to make the plants tender by excessive protection. Covering should not be put on until the ground has frozen to a depth of 1-2 in., and, whenever the temperature inside the frames rises above 32 degrees F., ventilation should be given.

Plants wintered in nursery beds or cold frames should be transplanted to their flowering quarters in early spring.

Alternative methods of raising Pansies and Bedding Violas from seeds, but usually less satisfactory than the one detailed above, are: (1) to make sowings of seed in cold frames in September or early October, leave the young plants undisturbed until spring and then transplant them early to where they are to bloom; and (2) to sow in a greenhouse in January or early February, transplant to flats and, later, when planting-out time approaches, gradually harden off the plants prior to transplanting them to the open garden.

Propagation by Cuttings. Cuttings of Bedding Violas and, more rarely, of Pansies are obtained by cutting back plants in late summer, taking the young, vigorous shoots that spring from the bases of the cut-back plants and rooting them as cuttings in cold frames in a bed of sandy soil over which a half-inch layer of coarse sand has been spread.

The cuttings are planted about 4 in. apart; the frame is kept close, humid and shaded until rooting has taken place, after which the plants are gradually accustomed to more light and ventilation. Their subsequent treatment through the winter is the same as that recommended above for plants raised from seeds. The young plants are set in their flowering quarters in early spring.

Garden Care. After planting in the garden, Pansies and Bedding Violas need little in the way of care. They should not be permitted to suffer from lack of moisture; but watering at too frequent intervals, so that the soil remains constantly wet and muddy, is to be avoided. One of the most important chores is to keep all faded blooms picked off; if this is not done the plants will expend their energies producing seeds, and flower production will be seriously impaired or may cease. An occasional application of weak liquid fertilizer during the growing season stimulates growth. See also Pansy.

Violas for Rock and Woodland Gardens

The genus Viola gives us a splendid range of beautiful and interesting plants suitable for the rock garden as well as some for woodland gardens. A few are difficult to manage and so will appeal to the rock-garden specialist who enjoys mastering a temperamental plant, but the majority respond to ordinary good treatment, and repay with a lavish display of really lovely flowers. The following list includes the best of such Violas.

V. alpina is a very beautiful mountain Pansy which might be classed as the V. calcarata of the limestones of the eastern Alps. It is of neat tufted habit, with rather large violet-colored flowers on stems some 3 in. tall. It is local in distribution but abundant where found, and it is rare in gardens.

Seed sown in a pan of light loam and sand in a cold frame in spring is the readiest means of propagation, but cuttings may be taken after flowering, and rooted in sand in a cold frame.

In the rock garden, V. alpina requires light loam, with sand, leaf mold and limestone chips added, and an open, sunny, well-drained position.

V. altaica, from the Mountains of Asia Minor and the Altai, is said to be one of the early parents of our race of hybrid garden Pansies. It is related to V. calcarata, and its flowers vary in color through mauve, lilac, yellow and purple. The blossoms are large and handsome. It is increased by seeds or cuttings.

V. arborescens is a rare and extremely pretty tree Violet, found only in sandy places by the Mediterranean. It has little woody trunks, surmounted by dark-green narrow leaves, and violet-like flowers of a beautiful mauve color.

V. arenaria is a pretty little compact Violet with lilac-blue flowers. It is common in many parts of the Alps. There is a variety, rosea, with flowers of a reddish-violet color. Both type and variety are pretty in the rock garden and seed freely.

A Beautiful Alpine Viola. V. biflora is an extremely pretty little alpine, common in woods and shady places in many parts of the Alps. It grows about 6 in. high and has fresh green leaves and little flowers, borne in pairs; they are of brilliant golden color. It comes readily from seeds sown in a pan of loam, sand and leaf mold in a cold frame in spring, and may also be increased by division of the roots. Any well-drained loamy soil suits it, and it should always have a shady, cool position in the rock garden or the wood.

V. blanda is a charming rock-garden Violet of dwarf compact habit, and extremely free flowering. It has pure white flowers, which are scented. This kind self-sows freely. It is known as the Sweet White Violet.

V. calcarata is a beautiful mountain Viola which grows with amazing freedom in many parts of the Alps, on nonlimy formations at an elevation of 5,000 to 6,000 ft. or more. It fills the short alpine turf by the million, and by the acre, making one of the most superb flower pictures to be seen in the Alps. The flowers are large, and the color varies endlessly through every shade of mauve, lavender and yellow, pale and dark, with occasional whites, and sometimes a pale pink.

A yellow-flowered form has been distinguished as Zoysii, but where the plant abounds it is possible to find yellows of every shade, from pale sulphur to rich gold. It is classed as a distinct species by some authorities.

V. calcarata may be increased from seeds sown in a pot of sandy loam in a cold frame in spring, or by cuttings rooted in sand in the frame, after flowering. The plant likes light, well-drained loam with leaf mold added.

The Canada Violet, V. canadensis, has stems 1 ft. or slightly taller and it bears white flowers, each of which is purple-tinged on the outside and has a noticeable yellow central blotch or eye. It occurs as a native from New Brunswick to Saskatchewan and southwards to Alabama and Arizona and is a worth-while plant for the woodland garden.

V. cenisia is a high alpine Violet, found at 7,000-8,000 ft. in the Alps of Europe, in nonlimy formations, and always in pure scree. Its stems ramble through the loose stones, forming tufts of leaves of a gray-green color, bearing small but beautifully formed pansy-like flowers of clear lilac-purple with darker lines radiating from the centers. In the rock garden it is not easy to keep for long. It should be given granite, slate or schist scree, and watered freely in the early part of the year when in growth and flower. It is very local in the wild state, but locally abundant; it is a great treasure, well worth much trouble to grow.

The Horned Violet, V. cornuta, is a native of hay fields in the Pyrenees, and is one of the easiest, showiest and altogether most satisfactory of all the Violas. It forms strong clumps bearing quantities of long-stemmed lavender-blue flowers, but there are several color forms, such as alba, with white flowers, and George Wermig, deep violet-purple. It has given numerous hybrids by crossing with other kinds. One of the best of these hybrids is V. florariensis, which bears fine pansy-like flowers practically all the year round. V. cornuta is invaluable in the rock garden and especially in the alpine lawn. It is useful, too, in the flower border, and in spring bedding. It is easily propagated from seed sown in sandy loam in a cold frame in spring; named varieties are rooted from cuttings in August-September, or may be divided in spring or autumn. V. cornuta is possibly one of the parents of the variety of Viola named Jersey Gem. See V. gracilis, below.

V. corsica (Bertolonii) is a very attractive mountain Viola that is a native of Corsica and Sardinia. It forms sturdy, free-flowering clumps, and bears great quantities of fine pansy-like flowers of a clear mauve color, and of rounded outline. It is best increased by cuttings of non-flowering shoots taken in summer after flowering, and rooted in sand in a cold frame, or by simple division of the flower's roots in spring.

V. cucullata is an eastern North American woodland plant, with big, heart-shaped leaves and long-stalked, mauve-blue flowers, scentless but beautiful. It is easy to grow in loamy soil and a cool location, and may be increased by seeds sown in loam, leaf mold and sand in a cold frame in spring. Or the roots may be divided in spring or autumn. There is a variety alba, with lovely pure white flowers.

V. delphinantha, from Mounts Athos and Olympus, is an extremely rare and beautiful Viola, of cliff-haunting habit, with trailing mats of wiry stems, narrow leaves and beautiful little flowers in astonishing profusion.

V. elatior is a curious plant of erect habit, with stems 9-12 in. tall, clothed on the upper half with many leaves, and large flowers of pale lavender-blue. It is easily increased by division of the roots in spring, or from seeds sown in a pan of sandy loam and leaf mold in a cold frame in spring.

Very Free-blooming. V. elegantula (bosniaca) is a most useful and free-flowering mountain Viola of a quite unusual color. The flowers are of bold shape and curious reddish lilac shade. The plant seldom lives more than a couple of years, but it seeds freely, and so is easily perpetuated by this means. It also crosses freely with other Violas, giving many interesting and beautiful hybrid seedlings.

V. eizanense is a Japanese native that has leaves divided into lanceolate segments which are again lobed or cleft, and fragrant flowers that are normally pale-rose or violet in color with darker veinings on the petals. This kind is suitable for rock gardens.

A Beautiful Purple Viola. V. gracilis might safely be classed among the dozen or so best rock-garden plants. It is a native of Asia Minor, southern Italy and Greece, and is reliably hardy. It forms a dense, close mat of rich glossy-green foliage, and from early spring until well into summer it produces an almost endless succession of flowers on 4-5-in. stems, graceful and dainty in outline, and of an intense violet-purple, with small white eye. No Viola seems to start flowering so early and continues so long with such a solid mass of lovely flowers.

All the plant demands is an open position and reasonably good loam. It is increased with the greatest ease by cuttings in spring, set in sand in a cold frame. Seeds may be sown in a pan of sandy loam and leaf mold in the cold frame in spring, but seedlings cannot be relied upon to come true to type.

Many very beautiful hybrids of V. gracilis have been raised, some of them of great value. Among the best are Swallow-tail, pale yellow; Golden Wave, rich gold; Grandeur, violet-blue; Mrs. Samuel Pepys, dwarf, free-flowering, lavender-blue; and Lady Crisp, light clear lavender-blue. The popular Viola Jersey Gem is probably a V. gracilis seedling, though V. cornuta was possibly one of the parents.

Australian Violet. V. hederacea is better known as Erpetion reniforme, a pretty little plant from Australia. It has a running habit of growth, kidney-shaped small leaves, and numerous violet-like flowers on 2-3-in. stems, half white and half lilac-blue. The plant is not always hardy, but may be kept safely in a cold frame during winter, or it is a fine plant for a pan in the cold alpine house. It is easily increased by simple division of the roots in spring or autumn, or by seeds sown in a pan of loam, sand and leaf mold in a cold frame in spring.

V. Jooi is a native of Hungary. It has pinkish-violet colored flowers and is an interesting plant for cultivation in rock gardens.

V. lutea is a delightful European native. It is an extremely variable plant, in general aspect like a small Pansy, the flowers ranging through endless tones and combinations of violet, lavender and yellow. Special varieties make charming and free-flowering rock-garden plants, but they hybridize with other Violas, giving rise to endless pretty sorts. The best place perhaps for V. lutea is the alpine lawn, where it may seed about profusely and spangle the turf with promiscuous flowers of many shades.

V. odorata is the European wild Sweet Violet, parent or ancestor of all the sweet Violets, single and double, of gardens (see Violet). The common wild type is well worth establishing in odd, out-of-the-way, half-wild parts of the garden where it can ramble and spread at will. With it may be grown its white variety, the curious lilac-colored form, and a wine-red variety. There is a curious and very pretty variety called

V. sulfurea, an exact counterpart of the common wild Sweet Violet with flowers of soft buff-yellow. V. odorata flowers in early spring.

The Meadow Violet, V. papilionacea, is native from Maine to Georgia and Oklahoma. It inhabits moist fields and low wet woods and is frequent near habitations. Its flowers vary in color from light to deep violet. Viola Priceana is, by some authorities, considered a variety of V. papilionacea.

The Bird's-Foot Violet, V. pedata, is a native of eastern North America, from Massachusetts to Minnesota and southwards to Florida. This species has interestingly divided leaves and very attractive flowers which have the two upper petals of a dark violet color and the three lower pale lilac (this is a plant often, but incorrectly, known in gardens as V. pedata variety bicolor). Commoner than V. pedata is V. pedata variety lineariloba, in which all of the petals are of the same dark violet hue. A white-flowered variety named alba is also known.

All of these are plants of dryish open places and acid, sandy soils. They are not easy to grow. They usually succeed best in a sunny rock garden, in a well-drained location in gritty loam and peat moss or leaf mold. Propagation is best effected by seeds sown in a pan of loam and leaf mold and sand in a cold frame in spring.

The Confederate Violet, V. Priceana, is native from Kentucky to Georgia and Arkansas. It is perfectly hardy in the North. Its flowers are pale grayish-white or bluish-white, strongly veined with dark blue. This kind is easy to grow and is well suited for partially shaded places. By some authorities it is considered to be a variety of V. papilionacea.

The Downy Yellow Violet, V. pubescens, has one erect stem or occasionally more, and rather pale green foliage. Its flowers are clear yellow with brownish or purplish veinings near their centers. This kind is a native of rich, dryish woodlands from Nova Scotia to South Dakota and southwards to North Carolina, Georgia, Mississippi and Oklahoma. It is suitable for shady wild gardens.

The Rouen Violet, V. rothomagensis (hispida), is a neat, tufted plant with pretty little lilac-colored flowers produced with great freedom all summer. It is a form of V. tricolor and is best propagated by seeds sown in a pan of sand, loam and leaf mold in spring in a cold frame.

V. septentrionalis is a handsome North American Violet with heart-shaped leaves on 3-in. stems, and flowers like big Sweet Violets, white, veined with blue, and carried on 6-9-in. stems in early summer. It is easily grown, but is too leafy to be really effective in gardens. The flowers, though scentless, are useful for picking.

This plant enjoys loam and leaf mold and a cool location, and is worth growing in a suitable but unimportant corner of the garden. It is easily increased by simple division of the roots in spring, or by seeds sown in a pan of loam, leaf mold and sand in a cold frame in spring. A white-flowered variety called alba is pleasing.

V. tricolor, the Johnny-jump-up, Heartsease or Wild Pansy, is a charming kind that comes in many color variations and has flowers that resemble miniature Pansies. It grows 6-12 in. tall and thrives in partly shaded and sunny locations. It is an annual or short-lived perennial but, as it sows itself freely from seeds, there is usually no difficulty in maintaining a stock. The colors most common in the flowers of this kind are blue, creamy white and yellow.

A native of Europe, V. tricolor has escaped from gardens and has become somewhat established in waste places in parts of North America. This is one of the parents of the large-flowered garden Pansies. See also V. rothomagensis, above.

V. valderia is very closely related to V. cenisia. It is found in granite screes at great elevations in the European Maritime Alps. It is rather less difficult to grow than V. cenisia, and should be grown in the scree or moraine (which see). It can be increased from seeds sown in very sandy, gritty soil in a cold frame in spring. It is a very rare plant, extremely local in its distribution. It is abundant in its chosen habitat.

VIOLET. See Viola.

VIOLET, SWEET. The Sweet Violet, Viola odorata, has been a favorite for very many years and is represented by numerous beautiful varieties having a fair range of color. It is possible to have Violets in bloom out of doors from early spring until May, and winter Violets by growing the plants in cold frames or cool greenhouses. If a few plants are set at the foot of a sheltered wall they will come into bloom considerably earlier than others in the open garden, and where winters are mild it will be possible to pick flowers from them even in winter.

Where to Plant Violets. The Violet can be grown in a partly shady location in the garden; a border facing west or northwest is considered to be ideal. It needs deeply dug soil enriched with decayed manure; cool, moist conditions are essential to success. If the plants are in soil that dries out quickly in hot weather, or if they are in a hot, dry location, they are almost certain to suffer seriously from the attacks of red spider mites. It is most necessary to plant in soil that will remain moist.

Propagation. Many amateurs often fail to grow Violets well because they leave the plants undisturbed too long; as a result they become overgrown and weak, and produce small, short-stemmed flowers which are very disappointing. The way to grow the finest blooms is to make a fresh Violet bed every year. When flowering is over, in May, the old plants are lifted, separated into rooted pieces, and the strongest and youngest of the latter are replanted; they should be set about 10 in. apart in rows not less than 12 in. from each other.

If it is not wished to disturb the Violet bed, runners pegged down in the soil will soon form roots; when rooted, they are detached and replanted in a nursery bed for the summer.

During the summer months care must be taken to cut off all runners which form and to cultivate frequently between the plants to keep down weeds. If prolonged dry weather sets in, a mulch of peat moss, leaf mold or decayed manure, will be of great benefit.

In October it is worth while lifting a few plants and setting them in a warm sheltered border at the foot of a sunny wall for the sake of the earlier flowers they will yield.

The Best Varieties. These are some of the best varieties of Violet:

Single: Admiral Avelian, rose; Askania, deep violet; Coeur d'Alsace, rose; La France, violet-blue; Princess of Wales, large violet-blue flowers on long stalks; Royal Robe, violet-blue; Rosina, pink; and White Czar, white.

Double: Comte de Brazza, white; de Parme, lavender-blue; Farquhar, similar to Marie Louise (mentioned below) but with larger flowers and blooming more freely; Lady Hume Campbell, lavender; Double Russian, violet-purple; and Marie Louise, mauve-blue.

Greenhouse Culture. For the most satisfactory culture of Violets a low greenhouse, which assures that the plants will be fairly near the glass, is best. Violets thrive better in solid (ground) beds than in raised benches and it is better that the structure be heated with hot-water pipes than by steam because the intense local heat of the latter encourages red spider mites and its intermittent character is less satisfactory than the more steady warmth provided by hot water.

To produce good Violets indoors it is important to have a suitable soil. A loamy mixture consisting of choice topsoil or well-rotted grass sod and thoroughly decayed manure (one part of manure to four or five parts of soil) is ideal. If the soil is acid the addition of lime is advantageous, and bone meal should be added at the rate of half a pound to each bushel of soil. Artificial fertilizers should be used not at all, or with caution, in cultivating of Violets.

Violets must have cool growing conditions. A temperature between 40 and 45 degrees at night is ample, with the daytime temperature averaging ten degrees higher. Free ventilation should be given on all favorable occasions.

Shade from really strong sunshine is essential. The glass should be sprayed or painted with a mixture of lime and gasoline or shaded in some other effective manner (see Greenhouses for Amateurs) from the time of planting until the end of October, when the plants may be given full sunlight. For three or four weeks before removing the shade entirely it should gradually be reduced.

Hygiene, the picking off of dead and drying leaves, keeping paths cleaned, keeping weeds pulled, shallow cultivation of the surface soil, etc., is of great importance. It is also important to keep all runners that develop cut off.

A mulch of well-rotted manure applied to the beds of Violets in November encourages good growth.

Propagation of Violets for greenhouse culture is by "cuttings" (really single stem divisions, for they usually have some roots). These are made by digging up the mother plant, freeing it of soil and pulling it apart. Only strong shoots are used. The older leaves are trimmed from these and they are planted in a flat or propagating bench filled with well-packed sand and kept in a shaded greenhouse until rooted.

The cuttings are made in early May and the rooted plants are ready for planting in newly prepared beds in the greenhouse (shaded, of course) during June or early July. Double-flowered Violets are spaced 9 in. apart each way, single-flowered varieties 12 in. each way.

Cold-Frame Culture. Early Violets may be secured from plants grown in cold frames. The general culture detailed above for growing Violets in greenhouses may be followed, with the exception that when this crop is grown in frames it is usual to propagate by dividing the old plants in April, selecting strong, rooted side crowns for replanting and discarding weak and old woody parts of the mother plants.

Cold frames for Violets should be located in a sheltered location where they are not exposed to sweeping winds. It is better that they be above ground rather than sunk into the soil, because this assures good drainage. On cold winter nights they may be protected from excessively low temperatures by covering with heavy mats or other insulating material.

VIOLET, AFRICAN. Saintpaulia, which see.
VIOLET, BOG. See Pinguicula.
VIOLET CRESS. See Ionopsidium.
VIOLET, DAME'S. Hesperis, which see.
VIOLET, DOG'S-TOOTH. See Erythronium.
VIOLET, USAMBARA. Saintpaulia ionantha, which see.
VIOLET, WATER. See Hottonia.
VIPER'S BUGLOSS. See Echium.
VIRGINIA COWSLIP. See Mertensia.
VIRGINIA CREEPER. See Parthenocissus.
VIRGINIA, GARDENING IN. See Regional Gardening.
VIRGINIAN STOCK. See Malcomia.
VIRGINIA SPIDERWORT. See Tradescantia.
VIRGINIA WILLOW. Itea virginica, which see.
VIRGINIA WITCH HAZEL. See Hamamelis virginiana.
VIRGIN'S BOWER. See Clematis.
VIRUS. See Pests and Diseases.
VISCARIA. Lychnis, which see.
VITEX—*Chaste Tree, Hemp Tree* (Vi'tex). Evergreen or leaf-losing trees and shrubs, widely distributed in tropical and subtropical countries in both hemispheres. Some grow to a large size and produce useful timber. Two species only are represented in gardens and both are deciduous (leaf-losing) kinds. Of the kinds cultivated V. Negundo variety incisa is the hardiest. It survives in southern New England.

The Chaste Tree, Vitex Agnus-castus, bears spikes of lilac flowers late in the summer.

A bush of the Chaste Tree, Vitex Agnus-castus, pruned back hard in spring.

Vitex belongs to the Vervain family, Verbenaceae, and the name is the old Latin name for V. Agnus-castus.

The Chaste Tree, Hemp Tree, or Monk's Pepper Tree, Vitex Agnus-castus, a native of southern Europe and western Asia, grows 10 or 12 ft. high, has four-angled branchlets, leaves rather like those of Hemp, with five to seven leaflets, dark green above, gray beneath, and attractive terminal heads of small lilac or violet-colored flowers in September. The variety alba has white flowers, and is more attractive. The variety latifolia (macrophylla) is hardier and more vigorous. It survives outdoors in New Jersey and southern New York.

The other kind that can be grown out of doors in the North is V. Negundo variety incisa. This variety is much hardier than the straight species V. Negundo, which is a native of China and India, grows 15-18 ft. high, and bears slender terminal heads of lilac or lavender-colored flowers. The variety incisa has narrower leaflets than the type. It needs light, well-drained, loamy soil and a location exposed to full sun.

For Shrubberies and Borders. Members of the Vitex group are attractive plants for shrubberies and for the rear of perennial borders. They bear their flowers on current season's shoots and hence, if killed back in winter or pruned hard back in spring, they will bloom the following summer. In the North they are often killed back to the ground in the winter but, provided the roots survive, this does not prevent them from flowering. V. Negundo variety incisa is a good bee plant.

Culture. Vitex thrives in any ordinary garden soil provided it is well drained; the plants even succeed in sandy soils of comparatively poor fertility. They need an open, sunny location.

Because they have rather few and coarse roots, the plants suffer rather easily at transplanting time if they are not handled properly. It is important to dig them in such a manner that as many as possible of the roots are preserved, and these must not be exposed to sun and wind so that they become dry while they are out of the ground. Spring is the best time to transplant.

Even in regions where the tops are not killed back in winter it is often desirable to prune these shrubs to the ground each spring and thus keep them to a moderate size.

Propagation is effected by means of seeds sown in a cool greenhouse in spring, by cuttings of leafy shoots taken in August and rooted in a greenhouse propagating case or in a cold frame, and by layering.

VITIS—*Grape Vine* (Vi′tis). Leaf-losing woody plants of climbing or trailing habit. Many are hardy; they are found wild in many parts of the Northern Hemisphere, but particularly in China, Japan and North America.

Vitis belongs to the Grape family, Vitaceae. The name is the old Latin name for the Wine Grape (V. vinifera).

Propagation. All the kinds can be increased

Young plants of Vitis rooted from hardwood cuttings.

A variety of the Fox Grape, Vitis Labrusca, trained as an espalier against a fence. The vine has just been pruned.

by means of seeds, cuttings and layers. Seeds should be sown in light soil in a warm greenhouse, as soon as separated from the fruits; germination will follow in the course of a few weeks. Cuttings may be made of soft shoots in summer, and inserted in sand in a greenhouse propagating bench or in a cold frame; or of ripened wood (hardwood cuttings), 9 in. long, made in autumn. The vigorous kinds can be increased by means of single eyes or buds with 1-1½ in. of wood on each side, inserted in a warm greenhouse early in the year. Layering may be done in spring.

For Covering Walls, Pergolas, and Trees. The plants thrive in ordinary soil and may be used for covering walls or pergolas, or for planting near bushes or trees over which they can ramble. Some kinds, such as V. Coignetiae, may be expected to grow 30-40 ft. or more high, and festoon the branches of large trees. They are very effective throughout summer and particularly so in autumn, when the leaves have changed to brilliant shades of red and bronze previous to falling.

When trees are used as supports the vines should not be planted against the trunks of trees, but in the ground under the ends of the tree branches with poles or other suitable supports provided for the vines to cling to until they reach the branches. When planted in this

The same Grape vine in full foliage a few weeks later.

way, the vines thrive much better than if they are required to fight their way from the center of the tree. Vines should not be planted to climb over valuable trees because they harm the trees to a certain extent by shutting out light, impeding air circulation and competing with the trees for moisture and nutrients.

Pruning. Those vines that are grown against walls or pergolas have to be pruned rather drastically to keep them within bounds. This pruning must be done in summer and early winter. If it is carried out in spring, a month or two before the leaves appear, there will be a good deal of "bleeding" or loss of sap.

The various kinds of Vitis have no value as flowering plants, the flowers usually being small and greenish. Some, however, bear attractive fruits, and in certain instances the fruits have a very great economic value.

As most kinds cling by tendrils, they need little tying to their supports and require very little care once they are established.

V. aestivalis, the Summer Grape, is a handsome and vigorous climber bearing leaves 4-12 in. across, and rather small, black, sweet fruits. Several cultivated American Grapes have originated from it. It is native from New York and New England to Florida and Kansas.

V. amurensis, the Amur Grape, is a very vigorous kind, suitable for planting to grow over a tree. Its leaves are up to 10 in. long and wide, and they color well in autumn. It is a native of Manchuria, Korea and North China.

V. Bourquinia, the Southern Summer Grape, is a name given to a group of cultivated varieties that are derivatives, perhaps hybrids, of V. aestivalis, the Summer Grape.

The Best Ornamental Grape. V. Coignetiae, also called V. Kaempferi by some, is undoubtedly the most beautiful of the vigorous decorative Grape Vines. It is a native of Japan and may be expected to reach a height of at least 40 ft. and spread its branches over a very considerable area.

The leaves on different plants vary a good deal in size but they may be 12 in. long and 10 in. wide on the most vigorous forms. They are attractive during summer and, in autumn, color brilliantly before they fall. The fruits are black with a black or purple bloom. They are scarcely edible. Seeds are the best means of propagation. This Grape should be planted in deep, loamy soil.

V. Davidii is a very decorative and vigorous kind from central China. The shoots are covered with gland-tipped spines or bristles, and the more or less heart-shaped leaves are prominently lobed, 4-10 in. long and $2\frac{1}{2}$-8 in. wide, dark green above, paler beneath, coloring well in autumn.

V. flexuosa is a slender-branched kind, but of graceful appearance, and well suited for planting against a trellis or the posts of a pergola. The leaves are very variable in shape and 2-$3\frac{1}{2}$ in. wide, stiff in texture with a smooth, glossy surface. The fruits are very small and black. It is a native of Japan, Korea and China.

The Fox Grape. V. Labrusca, the Fox Grape, is a vigorous, large-leaved native American kind that is a parent of an important group of varieties of Grape that are cultivated for their fruits throughout most of North America east of the Rocky Mountains. (See Grape.) It is of considerable decorative importance and is useful for covering a large bush or tree and for planting to cover arbors and other supports. The fruits are dark purple or reddish, with a sweet, musky taste. This kind is native from New England and New York to Georgia and Tennessee.

V. Piasezkii is a vine with slender stems and three-lobed leaves, a native of central China. Its branches grow very long, and it is handsome because of its wealth of leaves, which turn red in autumn. The variety Pagnuccii, sometimes called V. Pagnuccii, is an equally desirable plant.

V. Romanetii is a Chinese kind of vigorous growth, with bristle-clothed stems and large, handsome leaves that color brilliantly in autumn. The fruit is black.

V. rotundifolia, the Muscadine or Bullace Grape, is the parent of one group of varieties of Grape cultivated for their fruits in North America. The varieties are referred to as Muscadine Grapes. (See Grape.) V. rotundifolia is a very vigorous kind and its branches may grow to a length of 100 ft. The rounded or ovate leaves are up to $4\frac{1}{2}$ in. long and wide, the fruits large, round and usually purple with a musky flavor.

V. Thunbergii, a Japanese plant, is much weaker than most kinds of Vitis, with slender stems and three- or five-lobed leaves 2½-4 in. across. It may be grown on a pergola. It should not be confused with V. Coignetiae.

The Wine Grape. V. vinifera, the Wine Grape, is one of the most important kinds in the Vitis group. It has been cultivated for the sake of its fruits and the wine prepared from them, from very ancient times; no one knows when this Grape was first cultivated and improved varieties raised. It is regarded as being a native of southern Europe and adjacent Asia, but many of the wild plants of the present day are probably escapes from cultivation.

The management of the Wine Grape is dealt with under Grape (which see), but reference must be made here to the vineyards of France, Spain, Italy, Australia, South Africa, California and other regions which extend to a vast acreage and provide not only most of the wine used throughout the world, but vast quantities of fresh fruits and the dried fruits—raisins, currants, sultanas and muscatels.

These so-called dried fruits are the sun-dried berries of various kinds of Grapes. Muscatels are dried bunches of Grapes. Several varieties are used for the purpose, Muscat of Alexandria and a variety called Rosaki being very popular. Muscat of Alexandria is also one of the kinds dried for raisins. Sultanas are small seedless Grapes, and the pale color is brought about by bleaching in sulphur vapor. Currants are a small seedless form of Red Muscatel Grape, sometimes called V. vinifera corinthiaca, the name being taken from Corinth, an important region of production.

In addition to the dried fruits and the wine prepared from fresh berries, tartaric acid and cream of tartar are prepared from Grape juice, and a fatty oil is expressed from the seeds.

The Parsley-leaved Grape. V. vinifera is not often grown as a purely decorative climber, but there are two or three varieties showing leaf variations from the type that are sometimes used. In V. vinifera variety apiifolia the margins of the leaves are divided into many fine segments; it is commonly called the Parsley-leaved Vine. V. vinifera variety purpurea has purple leaves and bears small, purple, sweetish fruits freely. This is the Teinturier Grape.

V. Voinieriana, a native of eastern Asia, is a tender kind that is planted for ornament in southern Florida and southern California. It is a strong grower with a treelike trunk. It bears large, acid fruits.

V. vulpina (cordifolia), the Frost Grape, Chicken Grape, or Raccoon Grape, is a North American kind of very vigorous growth, suitable for planting to cover a large bush or tree. The leaves are 3-5 in. across, the fruits black. The fruits are unpalatable until they have been touched by frost. This Grape is native from Pennsylvania to Florida, Kansas and Texas.

VITTADINIA TRILOBA. The plant usually grown under this name is Erigeron Karvinskianus, which see.

VOODOO LILY. A name sometimes given to Sauromatum guttatum, which see.

VRIESIA (Vries′ia). Tender, evergreen flowering plants which are found wild in tropical America. They belong to the Bromelia or Pineapple family, Bromeliaceae, and differ little from Tillandsia, except for technical differences in the flower. They require the same culture as Tillandsia, which see. Vriesia was named in honor of the Dutch botanist W. H. de Vriese.

Kinds. In addition to the wild species a number of very fine hybrid Vriesias are grown by fanciers of these interesting plants. Of the species, the following may be found in cultivation:

Vriesia carinata, a decorative tropical American relative of the Pineapple.

V. Barilletii, with broad, dark green leaves faintly striped with red, flowers yellow, bracts purple, edged with yellow; V. carinata, a dwarf plant with pale green leaves, bracts crimson and yellow, flowers yellow; V. Duvaliana, leaves tinged red beneath, flowers yellow, tipped with green, bracts scarlet and green; V. fenestralis, leaves broad, green, to 2 ft. long, flowers pale greenish-yellow, bracts green spotted brown; V. hieroglyphica, leaves light green banded irregularly with dark green above and brownish-purple beneath, flowers yellowish; V. incurvata, leaves green, flowers yellow spotted with green at their tips, bracts red or orange-red with green ends; V. Philippo-Coburgii, leaves light-green, purplish at their bases and with reddish-brown tips, flowers yellowish-green, bracts red; V. speciosa (splendens), foliage blue-green banded crosswise with dark brown, flowers yellowish, bracts bright red. V. speciosa major is an especially vigorous variety. Its handsome flowers are red suffused with copper.

W

WACHENDORFIA (Wachendorf'ia). Tender, uncommon, tuberous-rooted plants from South Africa, which belong to the family Haemodoraceae. They grow about 30 in. in height and have narrow, elliptic leaves, sheathing at the base. The flower spikes are terminated by small clusters of purple, red or yellow flowers in April and May. The name Wachendorfia commemorates E. J. Wachendorf, a Dutch botanist.

Cultivation as Pot Plants. Potting is done in November, when three roots are placed 1 in. deep in a 5-in. pot. A sandy soil is used. After potting, they are placed in a cold frame or cool greenhouse (where frost will not reach them) and covered with sphagnum or peat moss until shoots appear above the soil. They are then taken into a greenhouse with a minimum temperature of 45 degrees. Very little watering is required until they are growing vigorously; after that the soil is kept moist.

After flowering, the water supply is gradually withheld and the soil is kept dry until potting time.

Planting Out of Doors. These plants can be grown out of doors only in mild localities. Light, rich soil and a sunny, well-drained location are necessary. The tuberous roots are planted in autumn, 4 in. deep and 2 in. apart. They should be lifted and replanted annually in autumn, when the smaller roots are removed for purposes of propagation, if an increased stock is required. Before replanting, a little well-decayed manure or some rich compost is dug into the soil and the largest roots are replanted.

The best results are obtained by planting in a bed of soil in a cold frame, where the plants can be protected from frost in winter and from excessive rain.

The chief kinds are W. paniculata, April, golden-yellow, and W. thyrsiflora, May, yellow.

WAFER ASH. Ptelea trifoliata, which see.

WAHLENBERGIA (Wahlenberg'ia). A group of tender perennial herbaceous and annual plants, many of them of great beauty and suitable for the rock garden. They are natives of the Southern Hemisphere, of China and Japan and of the tropics of America and the Old World, the Mediterranean region and western Europe. Wahlenbergia was named in honor of George Wahlenberg of Upsala, Sweden, 1780-1851, who was the author of the book, *Flora Lapponica*.

These plants belong to the Bellflower family, Campanulaceae. Some kinds have from time to time been classed as Campanula and Edraianthus. They are best suited when grown in the rock garden in light or well-drained loam in an open, sunny position.

Rock-Garden Plants. Wahlenbergia albomarginata is a pretty, dwarf plant, which spreads by means of underground runners, rather in the manner of some of the Campanulas. It forms tufts or rosettes of narrow, spoon-shaped leaves, an inch or so high, and in early summer produces white flowers tinged with gray-blue, borne singly on 3-4-in. stems. It is a native of New Zealand and is an extremely choice and ornamental rock-garden plant. There is a dwarf alpine form, only an inch or two tall, with lavender-blue flowers, which is known as variety pygmaea.

W. cartilaginea, from New Zealand, grows 3-4 in. tall, has rosettes of spoon-shaped leaves, and bears white, fragrant, bell-shaped flowers singly on erect stems. It is rare in cultivation, and should be set in light, gritty, well-drained loam, or scree, in an open, sunny location.

W. Matthewsii is a very beautiful New Zealand plant, 9-12 in. high, with slender, wiry stems and large, white, bell-shaped flowers in early summer. It enjoys light loam, and is best increased by seeds sown in a pan of loam, leaf mold and sand in a cold frame in spring. This is one of the best of the taller Wahlenbergias.

W. vincaeflora, from New Zealand, is similar to W. Matthewsii in habit and requirements and is perennial. The flowers are a lovely periwinkle-blue, borne in profusion in early summer, on graceful 12-18-in. wiry stems. It is increased by seeds, which are produced freely; they should be sown in a pan of loam, leaf mold and sand in a cold frame in spring. This is a really beautiful rock-garden plant.

W. hederacea is one of the prettiest European wild flowers. It is found growing naturally always in damp or marshy places, where it trails over the ground; it has slender prostrate stems, small ivy-shaped leaves, and lavender-blue, bell-shaped flowers on slender stems about half an inch high. It does well in a cool, moist corner of the rock garden. The best method of propagating these flowers is by careful division in spring.

A Charming Alpine Plant. W. (Edraianthus) Pumilio is one of the best of all alpine plants. It is a perennial, forming close turflike mats of narrow, grassy, somewhat silvery leaves, which, in May and June, are thickly studded with bell-like flowers of a vivid violet color on short stems. A well-grown plant is 4-6 in. across, and when in flower is a solid mass of color. It is best grown in a sunny, open place in the rock garden in light, gritty, well-drained loam, or scree. It is easily increased from seeds, which are freely produced, sown in a pan of loam, leaf mold and sand in a cold frame in spring. W. Pumilio is native of limestone mountains in Dalmatia.

W. (Edraianthus) dinarica, which is more commonly known in gardens, though less correctly, as W. pumiliorum, is like a large, loose-growing W. Pumilio, with larger, darker flowers on rather taller stems in early summer. It needs the same treatment as W. Pumilio.

WAHOO. See Euonymus.

WAHOO ELM. Ulmus alata, which see.

WALDSTEINIA (Waldstein'ia). A small genus of hardy perennials, of strawberry-like habit and belonging to the Rose family, Rosaceae. The name honors an Austrian botanist, Count Franz A. Waldstein-Wartenburg.

The Waldsteinias thrive in any ordinary soil, are suitable for the rock garden and are easily increased by division in autumn or spring. They are widely distributed throughout the temperate regions of the Northern Hemisphere. All have strawberry-like foliage and yellow flowers. The principal kinds are W. sibirica (trifoliata) and W. fragarioides. They bloom in April–May. They may be propagated by division and seeds.

WALKING FERN. See Camptosorus.

WALL CRESS. See Arabis.

WALLFLOWER. Cheiranthus, which see.

WALL GARDEN. A wall garden is a dry wall built of stone in which plants are grown for decorative effects. A dry wall is constructed without cement or mortar, but when such a wall is built for the cultivation of plants a layer of gritty soil about 1 in. thick is used between the stones in place of mortar, and the back of the wall is packed with 6-12 in. of

A wall garden planted chiefly with Alyssum saxatile and Cerastium tomentosum.

fertile, porous soil in which the roots of the plants can ramify. In some wall gardens the stones are cemented together but holes extending through the wall to the soil behind it are left and these are filled with soil and planted.

Wall gardens can be charming and give opportunities to grow a wide variety of the more vigorous rock-garden plants and exhibit them effectively in limited spaces. Often a wall garden can be installed as an adjunct to a rock garden or even as part of a rock garden; or it may serve as a border to a sunken garden or as a retaining wall for a bank or terrace.

Wall gardens should be built in sunny or partly shaded locations and the kinds of plants set in them should be selected with proper consideration of the amount of sun or shade they will receive.

Types of Wall Gardens. Wall gardens may be free-standing or built against banks as retaining walls. Free-standing walls can be planted on both sides. In effect a free-standing wall consists of two walls, back to back, with their faces leaning slightly backwards from bottom to top and with a core of soil 12-24 inches wide between them. Because free-standing wall gardens dry out more quickly than those set against banks of soil, special attention must be given to watering during dry weather. To facilitate this it is a good plan to install along the top of the wall a water pipe, pierced every few inches along its underside with tiny holes and fitted with a conveniently placed valve which, when open, permits water to fill the pipe and pass through the holes to moisten the soil that forms the center of the wall.

Building a Wall Garden. When building a

Cross section of dry retaining wall showing backward sloping face of wall and soil used in place of mortar between the stones.

A free-standing wall garden in course of construction.

dry wall it is important to have a firm, well-drained foundation. This is accomplished by digging a ditch or trench to a depth of at least 18 in.—certainly below the level of frost penetration in winter (frost level)—and filling it with coarse cinders, crushed stone, gravel or similar material, well packed down, to within about 1 ft. of the soil surface. Upon this base the stones that form the wall are laid, care being taken to set them so that every stone is stable and in such a pattern that the joints between the ends of adjacent stones do not come one above the other but are staggered like the joints in a brick wall.

So that water that falls on the face of the wall will soak backwards through the soil between the stones and become available to the roots, the top of each stone should slope slightly downwards from front to back and the face of the wall should slope slightly backwards from base to top. A few stones should be placed at right angles to the others so that one end of the stone is flush with the face of the wall and the other end extends backwards from the back of the wall and ties the stonework more securely into the soil that backs it. The soil is placed and is packed firmly between and behind the stones at the same time as the wall is being constructed.

Sowing Seeds and Planting in a Wall. The least expensive way to furnish the wall with plants is to purchase seeds of suitable kinds and, late in August or early September, or in March–April, mix them with a little sifted soil and place the mixture in the crevices between the stones. In favorable climates the seedlings will soon make progress and become established; they will naturally take longer to provide a show of bloom than if young plants are put in; but, for most amateurs, the latter plan is best.

If plants are used, care must be taken that they are fairly small, and that their roots are thoroughly moist at the time of planting; the roots should be disentangled, as far as is possible without damaging them, and spread out in the soil.

The most convenient way of planting is to set the plants in position as the wall is being built. The best time to plant is in September, but the work may be done in spring.

The wall garden should be watered thoroughly in dry weather.

Flowers to Grow in a Wall. These are some of the most suitable of plants for the wall garden: Aethionema; Alyssum saxatile; Androsace

This wall garden is built of stones cemented together, with holes for planting which run through to the soil behind the wall.

lanuginosa; Androsace sarmentosa and its fine variety Chumbyi; Arabis; Aubrieta in variety; Campanula cochlearifolia, C. Elatines variety garganica, C. Portenschlagiana and others; Cheiranthus or Wallflower; Cytisus Ardoinii and C. kewensis; Dianthus gratianopolitanus (caesius), D. plumarius and other Pinks; Edelweiss; Erinus alpinus; Erodium; Foxglove; Geranium sanguineum variety prostratum; Gypsophila cerastioides and G. repens; Helianthemum in variety; Hypericum Coris and H. reptans; Lavender; Leontopodium; Linaria alpina; Linum alpinum, L. narbonnense; L. perenne; Nepeta Mussinii; Oenothera missouriensis; Ononis fruticosa; Oxalis rosea; Phlox amoena, P. nivalis, P. subulata and other low-growing Phloxes; Ramonda pyrenaica; Santolina; Saponaria ocymoides; Saxifrages in variety; Sedums; Sempervivums; Thymus Serpyllum and its varieties; Tunica Saxifraga.

WALLICHIA (Wallich′ia). Tender Palms, from the Indo-Malayan region. They are suitable for growing outdoors in sheltered locations in southern Florida and in greenhouses. W. disticha attains about 15 ft. in height, and has a cylindrical stem bearing pinnate leaves 6-10 ft. in length. W. caryotoides is similar, but has a much shorter stem. They belong to the Palm family, Palmaceae, and their name commemorates Nathaniel Wallich, a Dutch botanist.

Palms for a Warm Greenhouse. Wallichias may be grown in a greenhouse with a minimum winter temperature of 55 degrees and need a moist atmosphere and a semishaded location. In their young stages they are repotted annually in March in slightly larger pots, but eventually they are set in large tubs, and kept growing vigorously by top-dressing them in spring with fresh soil.

From April to October the plants require an abundance of water, but during the winter the soil is moistened only when it becomes moderately dry. The atmosphere is kept moist by damping the floor and benches, and the foliage is syringed daily in summer, but occasionally only in winter.

Young plants may be obtained by removing basal suckers in spring or summer, and potting them separately in small pots. These are kept in a propagating case until established; afterwards they are set in the open benches and repotted as required. They may also be raised from seeds that are sown in a warm greenhouse.

The chief kinds are W. disticha, 15 ft., and W. caryotoides, 10 ft.

WALL PEPPER. Sedum acre, which see.

WALNUT. Various species of the botanical genus Juglans are known by the common name of Walnut. They produce edible nuts. Some of the Walnuts are grown as orchard trees and are represented by distinct horticultural varieties.

The Walnuts are monoecious—the male and female blossoms are separate on the same tree. The pollen-bearing male flowers are borne in long catkins; the female flowers are less conspicuous, small-stalked bunches of greenish, curved stigmas, borne on the ends of young growths. The flowers are wind-pollinated. Many seedling trees are persistently unfruitful because male and female flowers are not open at the same time. To overcome this, provision for cross-pollination must be made by growing two or three trees reasonably near each other.

The two principal Walnuts in cultivation in North America are J. nigra, the Black Walnut, and J. regia, the English or Persian Walnut. Other kinds of some importance are J. cinerea, the Butternut, and J. Sieboldiana, which is of use for hybridizing with the English Walnut because it is hardier. J. Sieboldiana variety cordiformis, the Heartnut, bears nuts of superior quality. See also Juglans.

The English Walnut may be grown over a wide area in the United States, even as far north as New York, but for nut production its cultivation is confined almost entirely to California and parts of Washington and Oregon. It is exacting in its requirements when grown as an orchard tree. It needs a deep fertile soil, preferably of a light (sandy) character and entirely free from alkali, and must have an adequate supply of moisture at all times. Little pruning is required other than the removal of sucker shoots. Trees are spaced 60-70 ft. apart; crowding is detrimental to Walnuts.

Propagation is effected by budding and grafting either on seedlings of English Walnut or of the native Californian Juglans Hindsii.

Varieties of English Walnut of importance include Blackmer, Chase, Concord, Ehrhardt, Eureka, Franquette, Mayette and Placentia.

The Black Walnut is much hardier than the English Walnut. It is an ornamental tree of great value for lumber and its nuts are collected from native stands of the tree. Selected varieties that produce superior nuts with comparatively thin shells have been named, propagated and planted. Noteworthy among these are Huber, Kettler, Ohio, Snyder, Stabler, Stambaugh, Ten Eyck and Thomas.

WANDERING JEW. A common name applied to several creeping plants, but chiefly to Zebrina pendula (Tradescantia zebrina). See also Tradescantia fluminensis and Setcreasea.

WANDFLOWER. Sparaxis, which see.

WARATAH. Telopea speciosissima, which see.

WARDIAN CASE. A glass case invented by N. B. Ward, author of *Plant Growing in Closely Glazed Cases* (published in London in 1842). Wardian cases are made in various sizes and are like miniature greenhouses. They were, at one time, and occasionally still are, used for transporting delicate plants on long journeys. As the cases are almost airtight, the plants are kept in a moist atmosphere and are protected from fumes and injurious external conditions during transport by sea and rail. By the aid of these cases many delicate tropical plants have been transported from one part of the world to another. The modern terrarium is a modification of the Wardian case. See Terrarium.

WARREA (Warr'ea). A small group of Orchids found wild in Central America and northern South America. All are terrestrial and have rather small cylindrical pseudobulbs and long leaves; they are similar in habit to Phaius. The flowers are on tall, erect stems; they are somewhat globose, with fleshy segments, the petals narrower than the sepals. They usually bloom in summer. The name commemorates Mr. Frederick Warre, who discovered the first Warrea.

Warreas require a warm greenhouse with a winter temperature of 60 degrees to 65 degrees and a tropical temperature in summer. Shading is necessary in bright weather. A suitable compost consists of two parts of osmunda fiber, two parts of fibrous loam and two parts of sphagnum moss; good drainage is needed.

The pseudobulbs and leaves are very susceptible to decay during winter. The plants should be carefully examined in spring and if the pseudobulb is decayed the damaged parts should be cut off, the pseudobulb being rubbed with a mixture of powdered charcoal and lime; repotting should then be done.

Water must be given during winter but with care; the compost must not become sodden, nor should moisture be allowed to remain on the foliage.

The principal kinds are W. grandiflora, white and rose, with red lip; and W. tricolor, yellowish with purple suffusion on the lip.

WASHINGTON, GARDENING IN. See Regional Gardening.

WASHINGTONIA (Washington'ia). Two species of tender Palms, which grow wild in Sonora and Lower California in Mexico, and in southern California and southwestern Arizona. They belong to the family Palmaceae, and were named in honor of George Washington. In their native habitats they grow 80-100 ft. in height. They have massive cylindrical trunks, covered with the dead, pendent leafstalks, and surmounted by immense, long-stalked, roundish leaves, which are deeply divided, almost to the petioles (leafstalks). They bear trusses of white flowers which produce black, fleshy fruits. The leafstalks are edged with prickles.

Outdoor Culture. Washingtonias are handsome Palms for outdoor culture and succeed in central and southern California, in Florida and along the Gulf Coast. They are especially valuable for use as avenue plantings. They are relatively hardy and succeed in any reasonably good soil. They are easily raised from seeds.

Greenhouse Culture. Although these plants grow to a great height, they are slow-growing, and small plants in pots are very ornamental. When grown in greenhouses, they require a minimum winter temperature of 50 degrees and a moist atmosphere, and should be shaded from strong sunlight.

Repotting is done in February or March, or as soon as growth commences in the spring. A potting soil composed of equal parts of peat and loam, with sand added freely, is used for potting. The plants are taken out of their pots, all loose soil is removed from their roots, and they are set in slightly larger pots. The soil is made moderately firm.

After repotting, the soil is not watered until it is moderately dry, and then it is thoroughly moistened. This system of watering is continued until the pots are filled with roots, when abundance of water is required throughout the summer. On the approach of autumn the supply is gradually lessened, and during the winter the soil is only watered when it is moderately dry.

Propagation by Seeds. The seeds, which must be fresh, because they quickly lose their powers of germination, are chipped on one side and soaked in tepid water for a day or two. They are then sown 2 in. deep in sandy soil. The soil is moistened and the seed pan is plunged in a propagating case with a bottom heat of 75-80 degrees, and the soil is kept moist. The seedlings are potted separately in small pots and replaced in the case. When the pots are filled with roots, the plants are placed on the open greenhouse benches and repotted as becomes necessary.

Kinds. W. filifera, 80 ft., and W. robusta, 100 ft. W. robusta is a more slender tree than W. filifera and is better suited for cultivation near the coast.

WASHINGTON PLANT. Cabomba caroliniana, which see.

WASP. See Pests and Diseases.

WATER ARUM. Calla palustris, which see.

WATER CHESTNUT. See Trapa.

WATER CHESTNUT, CHINESE. Eleocharis dulcis, which see.

WATERCRESS. See Nasturtium.

WATER ELM. Planera aquatica and Ulmus americana, which see.

WATER FEATHER. Myriophyllum proserpinacoides, which see.

WATER FERN. Ceratopteris, which see.

WATER GARDEN. A water garden consists of a lake, pond or pool, or a series of such bodies of water, planted with aquatic plants arranged pleasingly. Often marginal plantings of waterside plants are considered to be part of the water garden (see Waterside Plants). A water garden may be of large size and elaborate or as simple as a tub or half barrel sunk to its rim in the ground and planted with a miniature Water Lily, two or three other aquatics and, perhaps, some Japanese Irises beside it.

Water gardens are simple to maintain. Little or no weeding, fertilizing, staking, spraying, pruning, watering and other chores associated

This pool is being developed as a water garden in connection with a large rock garden.

with growing land plants need attention; once planted, the garden more or less maintains itself for a season or longer. It is necessary to give periodic attention to picking off yellowing or dead leaves and sometimes to restrain overvigorous growers. One absolute requisite of a water garden is exposure to full sun or nearly full sun; aquatic plants of garden worth will not thrive in shade.

Natural ponds and lakes are sometimes suitable or can be adapted for use as water gardens, or streams may be dammed, and they are particularly useful for the cultivation of Water Lilies, Lotus (Nelumbium) and other strong-growing aquatics, but more often the amateur gardener is concerned with an artificial pool made of concrete. Such a pool may be strictly formal or it may be naturalistic in outline and appearance. In either case it must be well constructed if it is to serve its purpose satisfactorily.

A sunny, sheltered place should be chosen for a garden pool; the shape is marked out roughly, and the soil is removed to a depth of 2½-3 ft. The soil may be removed to another part of the garden or thrown up in the form of a bank at one end, to form a rock-garden background.

Constructing a Pool. Provision must be made for draining the pool before any concrete is laid. Very small pools may be emptied by siphoning the water out with a hose, but a drain in the bottom is almost a must for a pool of moderate or large size. It should empty into a sewer, ditch, stream, dry well or an outlet lower than the bottom of the pool. Small pools may be filled with a hose; for larger pools a supply of water should be piped in, the necessary pipes being installed before any concrete is poured.

Suitable forms of wood or metal are built, in which to pour the concrete to make the sides, and the bottom is covered with a layer of stones, cinders or gravel, at least 6 in. thick, rammed firmly to prevent cracks by subsequent sinkage of the ground. This base also provides an excellent "key" for the concrete.

A delightful water garden planted with Water Lilies and other aquatic plants.

Stone steps lead to this small water garden. Blue-flowered Pontederia and Water Lilies are the chief plants used here.

Formal pools can be used effectively as water gardens.

The side walls should be at least 6 in. thick. Wire mesh or metal rod reinforcement should be placed in position in the bottom of the pool before any concrete is poured, and in the walls a little ahead of the pouring of the concrete.

Mixing and Pouring Concrete. A good mixture for the major portion of the work consists of one part cement, two parts sand, and three parts broken stone or gravel of half-inch size. The materials are turned over two or three times while dry, then the heap is moistened by using a hose fitted with a sprinkler. The materials are again mixed until the whole assumes the consistency of thick mortar. The materials may be mixed in a wooden or metal trough of a kind made for the purpose.

It is important that concrete for the bottom and walls be poured in one operation so that no leaky joints develop where wall joins bottom or elsewhere.

At the end of forty-eight hours, remove the forms and rub the concrete surfaces with a suitable brick, carborundum stone or piece of hard sandstone to make them smooth. Or, if you prefer, apply a thin coat of cement with a trowel and finish perfectly smoothly. Keep the new concrete protected from sun and wind by covering it with straw, earth, burlap or some similar material. Keep this moist for ten days or so, or fill the pool with water and allow it to remain for 3-4 weeks before planting.

In any case the pool should be filled and emptied three or four times before planting is done or fish are put in, allowing the water to remain in the pool at least 2-3 days between each filling and emptying. The water absorbs free alkali from the concrete and this must be gotten rid of before either plants or fish are put in.

Care of Pool. Where winters are severe it is usually advisable to empty pools in fall and protect concrete from cracking by covering it with a thick layer of leaves, straw, salt-marsh hay or some similar material and roof it over with boards or tar paper. The plants are carried over in pools or tanks in greenhouses, or in a dormant state in sheds, cellars, garages or other frostproof places, according to their kinds and

(Top) A cement pool, showing construction. The nine stone structures are designed to hold soil in which the roots are planted. The square holes are for deeper-water plants. The overflow pipe controls water level and may be removed for drainage. *(Bottom)* The planted pool.

according to the convenience of the gardener.

Hardy aquatics may be left outdoors, provided their roots are below the freezing level. Wooden barrels or light logs floated on the surface of a pool in fall take up some of the pressure caused by expansion as ice forms, and will do much to prevent the concrete from cracking.

Planting and Summer Care. Aquatics are normally planted in spring. The hardy kinds are planted just as their new growth begins. The tender, tropical kinds are not planted until the weather is really warm and settled and the water temperature is established at a steady warm level that suits the particular plants being set out.

All aquatics thrive best in rich, fertile soil. It is usual to spread an inch or two of clean sand over its surface so that, when the soil is covered with water, small pieces of leaves and other debris will not float to the surface or muddy the water. Aquatics may be planted in tubs, pots, or other containers, or in soil spread directly over the bottom of the pool; the former plan is generally to be preferred.

The best depth of the soil surface beneath the water varies for different kinds and is given in the cultural directions for the various plants under their respective names in this Encyclopedia.

It is a great mistake to allow large amounts of fresh water to run into a pool containing water plants; a tiny, continuous flow is all right because it has time to warm and does not noticeably reduce the water temperature, but heavy flows lower water temperatures and are harmful. Still water is best for ornamental aquatics.

Dead leaves and other debris should be removed from the pool once or twice a week. If the water is stocked with fish and other aquatic animal life a good biological balance may be established and the water will remain clean. Goldfish and other kinds feed on the larvae of mosquitoes, and these will not multiply in garden pools stocked with such fish.

Kinds of Plants. The more important aquatic plants for water gardens are Water Lilies, Lotus, Euryale and Victoria, all of which root in soil beneath water and have large rounded leaves. Those of Water Lilies, Euryale and Victoria float; those of Lotus stand well above the water surface.

Other kinds suitable for planting in soil in shallow water are Arrowhead (Sagittaria), Sweet Flag (Acorus), Floating Heart (Nymphoides), Flowering Rush (Butomus), Pickerel Rush (Pontederia), Wild Calla (Arum), Water Snowflake (Nymphoides indicum), Parrot's Feather (Myriophyllum proserpinacoides), Water Poppy (Hydrocleys), Water Clover (Marsilea), Cyperus and Thalia.

Floating aquatics include Azolla, Water Fern (Ceratopteris), Water Lettuce (Pistia) and Water Hyacinth (Eichhornia).

Among submerged aquatics suitable for water gardens are Anacharis, Cabomba, Ceratophyllum, Myriophyllum and Eel Grass (Vallisneria).

WATER HAWTHORN. See Aponogeton.
WATER HEMLOCK. Cicuta, which see.
WATER HYACINTH. See Eichhornia.
WATER IN. This is a gardener's term for the first watering that is given to a newly planted or potted plant or to cuttings that have just been inserted. Usually the water is applied in

Watering newly potted Coleus.

the form of a spray so as not to disturb the soil or rooting medium, but enough is given to saturate it. Watering in settles the soil or other rooting medium about the plants.

WATERING. This is one of the most important details in the successful management of plants, and particularly of those grown in flowerpots or tubs. Amateurs find great difficulty in deciding when plants in pots need watering. They often make the great mistake of giving a little water to the soil every day. With few exceptions, plants should not be watered until the soil is moderately dry; the pots should then be filled to the rim with water so that the entire soil mass is saturated, and no more should be

A fine spray is used for watering young seedlings.

Leaves of this specimen of Allophyton mexicanum are drooping because the soil is deficient in moisture.

Within one hour of being well watered the foliage ceases to wilt and the plant is revived.

added to them until the soil is moderately dry.

Several ways are adopted by professional gardeners to ascertain whether or not a plant needs water. They rap the flowerpot with the knuckles or with a small wooden mallet; if the pot sounds "hollow," if a ringing sound results, the soil is dry; if, on the other hand, the sound is what may be described as dull or heavy, the soil is moist. Another way is to lift the pot; if it feels heavy, no water is needed; if it is light, watering should be done.

In spring and summer, plants usually need a great deal more water than in winter, for at those seasons most kinds are growing freely. In hot weather they may need watering every day, or possibly twice a day, yet in winter watering once a week may be enough.

Newly potted plants need to be watered carefully; if the soil is too moist before it has become full of roots it is apt to become sour and the plants are likely to fail. Plants should be thoroughly watered before being potted or repotted; it is usual to water them a few hours before, so that the soil is not too wet to be handled conveniently. But no routine schedule for watering can be established. Good judgment must be exercised at all times. Even in winter plants that are located near radiators or other sources of dry heat and specimens growing in rooms where the atmospheric humidity is low are likely to dry out comparatively quickly and require watering fairly frequently.

Plants in sunny locations and in fairly high

To avoid wetting the foliage, the leaves of African Violets may be pushed aside when the plants are watered.

temperatures usually need watering more often than those that receive little direct sun and those grown under cooler conditions. When plants lose some or all of their foliage, as may happen when they are pruned, as a result of pests or disease or from some other cause, they do not absorb as much water as previously and consequently less frequent wetting of the soil is necessary to maintain it in a suitably moist condition.

The question as to whether it is better to water the soil from the top or from beneath by immersing the pot in a container of water is one that frequently causes amateur gardeners concern. Except in very special instances professional gardeners and greenhouse operators water from above and by doing so achieve entirely satisfactory results.

Watering by immersion. The pot is allowed to stand in a container of water until the whole body of soil is soaked through.

Watering from above. It is important to give enough to saturate the entire ball of soil thoroughly.

The truth is, it does not matter which plan is followed so long as the entire body of soil is saturated each time the plant is watered. With plants that have filled their pots tightly with roots and when the surface soil is high so that it is difficult to soak the earth by top watering the immersion method offers advantages. This is true too when a well rooted ball of soil has become really dry. Then it may be difficult to wet it through by watering from above because the moisture tends to run down between the sides of the pot and the root ball rather than to soak into the soil. With some hairy-leaved plants, such as African Violets, it is generally advisable not to wet the foliage. To avoid doing this it may prove easier to immerse the pot when watering is needed than to lift the foliage aside and water the surface soil beneath it.

A hose, with the flow of water carefully controlled so that the soil is not washed out of the pot, is used for most greenhouse watering.

Outdoor Gardens. Flower beds, vegetable gardens and lawns should not be watered unnecessarily, for water applied by means of a garden hose is not so beneficial as rain. During prolonged hot, dry weather, however, it becomes necessary to attend to the watering of the garden or the plants will suffer. This applies to all the trees and shrubs as well as other plants.

Many devices for watering outdoor gardens are available. These include permanently installed overhead irrigation systems, (which are of especial value in vegetable gardens and cut flower gardens), permanently installed underground irrigation systems (which are particularly adaptable for lawns and rock gardens) and a great variety of movable sprinklers that can be used to good advantage in most garden areas.

A fairly recent innovation is the use of plastic pipes for underground irrigation. These are easily installed and do not need to be laid with the necessity for draining the pipes in winter as do metal pipes. Another advantage is that it need not be buried so deeply as metal pipes.

It is far better to soak the soil deeply every 5-7 days than to sprinkle it every day. It does good to spray the plants lightly with the garden hose in the evening of a hot day, but it is a mistake to moisten the soil a little and frequently. One thorough soaking about once a week is usually sufficient, except perhaps on very light soil. The soil between plants should be cultivated the day following watering. Plants

Outdoor watering with an oscillating sprinkler.

Watering a lawn with a rotary sprinkler.

that have been recently transplanted outdoors are likely to need watering more frequently than well-established specimens that have had time to send their roots deep into the soil.

WATERLEAF. Hydrophyllum, which see.

WATER LETTUCE. Pistia Stratiotes, which see.

WATER LILY. See Nymphaea and Victoria.

WATERMELON. The Watermelon, Citrullus vulgaris, is a member of the Gourd family, the Cucurbitaceae. It is a native of Africa but grows wild as a naturalized plant in various parts of the Western Hemisphere. It is a tendril-producing vine that has long rambling stems, large-lobed or dissected leaves, light yellow flowers and red-fleshed, watery fruits that have a hard outer rind, usually attain large size and are much valued for eating. A variety of C. vulgaris named citroides has small fruits with hard flesh. This kind, known as the Citron or Preserving Melon, is used only for preserving.

Watermelons are easy to grow. They need fertile, well-drained soil, preferably enriched with a liberal application of rotted manure or rich compost which should be worked into the planting hills. A long growing season, with hot summers and humid atmospheric conditions, suits this crop; for these reasons Watermelons are particularly adapted for growing in the South. Early-maturing varieties can be grown as far north as New York and will mature their fruits. The early-maturing varieties are usually less rampant than later kinds and because of this are often better suited for garden cultivation. They may be spaced about 8 ft. apart each way. The later maturing varieties are usually spaced 10 ft. apart each way.

The cultivation of Watermelons is essentially the same as for Cantaloupe Melons (see Mellon). The seeds are sown, after the weather is

Water flowing slowly from a hose, the end of which rests on a plank, soaks the soil effectively.

warm and settled, several to each hill and the seedlings are thinned so that only two or three remain. Popular belief to the contrary, proximity to Pumpkins or Squash cannot affect flavor or quality of Watermelons; neither are the Squash or Pumpkins affected by the Watermelons.

Varieties. Congo, Florida Giant, Dixie Queen, Stone Mountain or Dixie Belle, Klondyke, Striped Klondyke, Coles Early, Kleckley's Sweet, New Hampshire, Midget. The variety Citron is grown for making into preserves.

WATERMELON PILEA. Pilea Cadieri, which see.

WATER MILFOIL. See Myriophyllum.

WATER PLANTAIN. Alisma, which see.

WATER POPPY. Hydrocleys nymphoides, which see.

WATER SHIELD. Brasenia and Cabomba, which see.

WATERSIDE PLANTS. The margins of ponds and other bodies of water can be made exceedingly attractive by planting them appropriately with plants that thrive in moist soil. Such plantings need not be continuous but may be broken by low grassy areas or paths that permit the water to be seen easily and approached.

Waterside plants, as the term is used here, refers to land plants that succeed in soil that is above water level, but not so far above that the roots cannot reach a continuous supply of moisture. Not included are purely bog plants or true aquatics, although both types may be grown and used effectively at the fringes of bodies of water. Waterside plantings are mostly at their best during late spring, summer and fall.

The Marsh Marigold, Caltha palustris, is an exception and is, perhaps, the earliest of good waterside plants. Its gay, golden-yellow flowers appear in April or early May. Other good early bloomers are the Globe Flowers or Trollius. The Globe Flowers flourish either in full sun or partial shade, but they must have ample moisture at their roots.

Other interesting plants for growing beside water are the Cardinal Flower, Lobelia cardinalis, which has brilliant red flowers in late summer, and its handsome blue-flowered relative, Lobelia siphilitica. The Willow Gentian, Gentiana asclepiadea, is a pretty and graceful plant to use. Helonias bullata, the Swamp Pink, produces erect spikes of small pink flowers in spring or early summer. Good ground covers are the Forget-me-nots, Myosotis scorpioides (palustris) and M. scorpioides variety semperflorens. The latter flowers continuously all summer.

The double-flowered varieties of Ranunculus aconitifolius, which blooms in May, have flowers which are produced in succession for a very long time. The variety called flore-pleno has yellow blooms; variety luteo-plenus has yellow flowers. The double-flowered variety of R. acris produces small double yellow flowers, and is attractive.

Astrantia is a moisture-loving plant which thrives by the waterside. A. carniolica has pinkish flowers on 2-ft. stems. A. major has greenish flowers on 2-ft. stems and the diminutive A. gracilis bears greenish flowers on 6-in. stems.

The Flowering Rush, Butomus umbellatus, is also excellent for waterside planting.

Irises, Primroses and other waterside plants add charm to this small lake.